Dad

Merry 1991

Christmas,

I love you

Jennifer
Lucille

D0396487

60 YEARS OF USC-UCLA FOOTBALL

60 YEARS

O F

USC-UCLA FOOTBALL

Steve Springer
Michael Arkush

Longmeadow Press

Jacket design by Dorothy Wachtenheim

Interior design by Richard Oriolo

Library of Congress Cataloging-in-Publication Data

ISBN: 0-681-41168-6

Printed in the USA

First Edition

0 9 8 7 6 5 4 3 2 1

To Dina,
who serves as a constant source
of inspiration to me and everyone
else fortunate enough to know her by turning
obstacles into stepping stones and sadness into joy

To Stephen Berk,
who taught me how to learn,
and to Pauletta,
who taught me how to love.

Contents

Foreword by O.J. Simpson   ix

Foreword by Gary Beban   xi

Acknowledgments   xii

1   The Biggest Game: 1967   1

2   The First Games: pre–1929   21

3   The Worst Games: 1929–1938   40

4   The War Games: 1939–1948   59

5   Red's Games: 1949–1957   81

6   The Political Games: 1958–1966   105

7   Playing McKay's Game: 1968–1975   129

8   Games of Sudden Death: 1976–1982   155

9   Games of Measles and Mediocrity: 1983–1989   179

10   The Game that Would Not Die: 1990   198

Appendix A: Where Are They Now?   206

Appendix B: Line Scores   208

Foreword

I always wanted to beat Texas and Stanford and Notre Dame, but, for me, UCLA was the game.

With UCLA, we were buddies from the same neighborhoods, so basically, I played against friends.

I didn't have to live with Terry Hanratty or other Notre Dame players if we lost. But if we lost to the Bruins, I would have to see those guys at a party, maybe the very same night. I'd have to spend the whole year with them and deal with it on a daily basis. It's a little bit different from a 3–0 loss to Oregon State.

To this day, the 1967 USC-UCLA game remains the highlight of my athletic career. Perhaps even more than the record 2,000-yard season with Buffalo because that was more of an individual accomplishment. Beating UCLA, however, was a team accomplishment. My joy was no greater or no less than the other guys. This is what football is all about.

When the gun sounded at the end of the 1967 game, I was stunned. I saw guys doing flips on the field, and I couldn't understand why. I couldn't believe the game was over. I expected UCLA to mount a last-minute drive. I guess I expected the game to go on, probably forever. I almost wish it had.

The respect I had for UCLA that day was tremendous. If they weren't great, we couldn't have been great. We were all part of that moment. It has endured for all who were there. There were no losers. We just happened to have scored last. They were every bit as good as we were.

Whenever I see Gary Beban or any of the other Bruins, I realize we were all part of the same team that day—just teammates—and always will be.

O.J. Simpson
August, 1991

Foreword

For me, the UCLA-USC game is Mike Garrett walking into the Bruin locker room to congratulate us on a fourth quarter comeback victory in 1965, even though it meant he would never experience a trip to Pasadena on New Year's Day; Norm Dow, my teammate for two years, fulfilling a dream by quarterbacking and leading us to an unexpected victory in 1966; coming within one point of the national championship in 1967.

Many games and seasons have passed since I walked down the Coliseum tunnel, over a carpet of television and radio cables, and onto the field to hear the roar of 100,000 people. The passing of time has sharpened the thrill of Dick Witcher's and Kurt Altenburg's touchdown catches and Mel Farr's and Cornell Champion's touchdown runs, and dulled the disappointment of Pat Cashman's interception and O.J.'s legendary journey for a winning score.

Even today, when introduced to people, I constantly encounter the phrase, "I remember" or "I was there when . . ." Bruin and Trojan players are very fortunate to have participated in an event that is not forgotten and to have had the opportunity to contribute to the legacy of the UCLA-USC game.

Prior to the 1966 Rose Bowl game against Michigan State when we were a two-touchdown underdog, Coach Prothro tried to put the game in perspective for us by mentioning eight hundred million people in China who were not concerned with the final score of the game. He never made such a reference prior to a UCLA-USC game, so I have always assumed that they were interested.

To all of you who have said to a Bruin or Trojan player, "I remember" or "I was there when . . . ," thank you.

Gary Beban
August 1991

Acknowledgments

In the life of any university, there are countless numbers of interesting people, fascinating stories and captivating events. Add a second university and extend the time frame to 60 years, and the material becomes overwhelming. Without a lot of wonderful people taking the time and effort to provide a tremendous amount of crucial information, this book wouldn't have happened. So for those of you who opened your priceless archives, found your rare photos, supplied your invaluable books and shared your precious memories, some of them posthumously, thank you.

Our appreciation to: Pete Adams, Elliott Almond, Kurt Altenberg, Jon Arnett, Tom Asher, Robert Baker, Burr Baldwin, Sam Balter, Bill Barnes, Ray Bartlett, Kevin Baxter, Gary Beban, Owen R. Bird, Dennis Bitterlich, Bruce Bliven, David Bohrer, Norman Borisoff, Tay Brown, Paul Cameron, Al Carmichael, Cormac Carney, Sherman Chavoor, Sarah Comstock, Sam Cunningham, The Daily Bruin, The Daily Trojan, Aramis Dandoy, Anthony Davis, Terry Debay, James Decker, George Dickerson, Sam Dickerson, Terry Donahue, Norman Dow, Dennis Dummit, Norman Duncan, Bill Dwyre, Braven Dyer, Arnold Eddy, Vince Evans, John Ferraro, Bob Fischer, Jeff Fisher, Mal Florence, Mike Garrett, Al Gibson, Shav Glick, Marv Goux, Danny Graham, Pat Haden, John Hall, Andrew Hamilton, Ted Henderson, Rob Hertel, John Jackson, Thomas Jacobs, Jimmy Jones, Vic Kelly, Ellsworth Kissinger, Thomas Lambert, Jack Lescoulie, Hendrik Van Leuven, Lee Daniel Levine, Jerry Levitz, The *Los Angeles Times*, Paul Lowry, John Lynch, Johnny Lynn, Robert MacNeish, Ben Macomber, Edward E. Madigan, Robert Mannes, Todd Marinovich, Chaytor Mason, Ned Mathews, Nancy Mazmanian, Paul McDonald, John McKay, Rod McNeil, Don MacPherson, Dick Mesak, Bob Michaels, Tracy Morris, Brian Murphy, Jim Murray, Newsweek, Nick Pappas,

Pasadena Chronicle, Rodney Peete, Barbara Perry, Jim Perry, Tommy Prothro, Matt Purdue, Mike Rae, Tom Ramsey, Kathy Randa, Andrea Rich, J. Wesley Robb, C.R. Roberts, Bob Robertson, John Robinson, Rachel Robinson, George Robotham, David Saxon, Ambrose Schindler, Suzanne Schlosberg, Dean Schneider, Charles A. Schroeder, John Sciarra, Jim Sears, Manuel P. Servin, Gaius Shaver, Jade Shipman, Alice Short, Cliff Simpson, O.J. Simpson, Larry Smith, Annette Springer, Don Stalwick, Woodrow Strode, Lynn Swann, Ted Tollner, Eric Turner, UCLA Magazine, Dick Vermeil, John D. Weaver, Stephen Webster, Alfred Wesson, Charles White, Dr. Joseph P. Widney, Gwynn Wilson, Iris Higbie Wilson, Richard Wood, Sam Young, Paul Zimmerman.

Special thanks to: Marc Dellins, Tim Tessalone, Jan Klunder.

And to our agent Ed Novak and our editor Daniel Bial.

1

The Biggest Game
1967

Abroad, America was embroiled in Vietnam. At home, the country was in turmoil. But, on Nov. 18, the nation's focus was on Los Angeles. The year was 1967.

It certainly wasn't a good year, what with hundreds of soldiers dying weekly in the rice paddies of Vietnam, and dissension and civil unrest erupting on cities and campuses from coast to coast.

But even in the worst of times, there was always time for a big football game. And in the long history of USC vs. UCLA, 38 years at that point, none had ever been bigger. Nor have any approached it since.

At stake was merely:

1.) The city championship.
2.) The Pac 8 title.
3.) The Rose Bowl.
4.) The Heisman trophy.
5.) And, probably, the national championship.

At the student body level, it was also a battle of philosophies.

In earlier years, the students had confined their rivalry to the normal sophomoric pranks seen on most campuses. A prime target the week of the Bruin-Trojan game had always been Tommy Trojan, the large statue of a Roman gladiator that occupies a prominent spot on the USC campus.

A UCLA commando group, armed with a hacksaw and other tools, nearly succeeded in cutting off Tommy's head one year before being routed by police.

In the most creative assault on Tommy, a group of UCLA students once obtained a helicopter, loaded it with manure and dumped their load on the USC landmark statue.

Trojan boosters have hardly been content to stand on the sidelines and wring their hands at such shenanigans. They have used lime to spell out the letters "USC" on a grassy area in the middle of the Westwood campus. And USC students once formed their own commando squad to let hundreds of crickets loose in the UCLA library.

But those were in more carefree times. With the Vietnam War raging, students in 1967 were more interested in dropping a load of manure on the Pentagon.

UCLA undergraduate president Bob Michaels called for the formation of a California Federation of Students to "fight the common battle." Michaels was one of ninety-nine student leaders who signed a letter to President Lyndon Johnson, expressing serious doubts over the Vietnam War and stating that "unless this conflict can be eased, the U.S. will find some of her most loyal and courageous young people choosing to go to Canada rather than bear the country's arms."

While it certainly wouldn't be fair to characterize USC as pro-war, there seemed to be fewer doves flying around its campus. And with such former Trojans as John Wayne so visibly in the camp of the hawks, there was political tension between the two schools as well.

So although these two universities were divided by only a couple of miles, on November 18, 1967, they were split by a emotional chasm deep enough to have divided countries.

Despite the fact the Bruins and Trojans had only one loss between them, the two teams headed into this game from opposite directions.

UCLA was 7–0–1 and was coming off a 48–0 victory over the University of Washington. USC, 8–1, had suffered its only defeat the previous week, a frustrating 3–0 loss on a muddy field at Oregon State.

"We were one of the fastest teams to ever play," said Trojan fullback O.J. Simpson of his '67 team. "We just wore guys down."

But not that week in Corvallis. Heavy rains had inundated the field. The protective tarp had not been put on during the week, according to Simpson, leaving horrendous conditions.

"It was like running in a swamp," Simpson recalled. "Twice in the game, I broke through the middle, but slipped just as I was trying to get by the safety."

The result had been a slip in the ratings for the Trojans. The Bruins, on the strength of their record and their dominating win, had soared to the top of the rankings of both Associated Press and United Press International, the first time they had been so highly rated in both polls in 13 seasons. The Trojans, ranked No. 1 in both polls the previous week, had been dropped to No. 3 by UPI and No. 4 by AP.

The University of Tennessee was second in both polls at 6–1. Purdue was third in the AP at 7–1.

"I took the Oregon State loss real tough," Simpson said. "I was crying.

"I think we thought we were unbeatable. And when we lost, thank God there was UCLA the next week. No matter what had happened to us, they were still No. 1."

And dead ahead on the USC schedule.

This was the last week of the regular season. A win by the Bruins would obviously assure them the No. 1 spot, at least heading into the bowl season.

A win by USC would leave it with one loss, same as Tennessee and Purdue. And since the Trojans would have beaten the top team, they had a good chance of returning to the first rung on the ladder.

So no matter who won, USC–UCLA was probably for the No. 1 spot.

"It was so big for the seniors in particular," said Bruin quarterback Gary Beban. "When we were freshmen, we all said that by the time we were seniors we wanted to win a national championship. The game is always for [city] bragging rights, and it always seemed to be for the Rose Bowl, but this one superseded all that. Now, all the chips were on the table, including who was No. 1, and you couldn't ask to play for more than that."

Nobody needed a pep talk, but there were still plenty to be heard in the seven days before kickoff.

After a tough practice early in the week, Trojan linebacker and co-captain Adrian Young, fueling the flames that would grow into a bonfire by week's end, screamed at his teammates. "You guys read the papers?" he shouted. "Whose town is this? Bruin town? That's what they say."

They said plenty before it was all done. One would have to go to a Super Bowl to find as much pregame hype and speculation as there was for this classic matchup.

Simpson tried to stay out of it. He broke a personal habit and didn't even read the papers that week.

Few others had such discipline. The town had always reveled in the rivalry. And as the population grew, as the campuses got larger, as the electronic media came of age, as the print media increased in size, there were more and more performers involved in what became an annual publicity circus the week of the big game. It reached a new high that week in 1967.

And nowhere more so than the respective campuses. On the door to the USC practice field, someone had painted big blue letters that read: "UCLA No. 1."

In Westwood, no less a performer than Bob Hope was involved. The school's traditional Friday night pep rally served as an introduction for Hope's regular nationally televised comedy special. Hope's entire show was telecast from Pauley Pavilion with a preview of Saturday's game as the centerpiece.

Among those in the cast was actress Elke Sommer. As she pranced around in a miniskirt earlier in the week, practicing a dance routine on the floor of Pauley Pavilion, just outside the football training room, the Bruin players inside blacked out the mental pictures of their Trojan counterparts for just a moment.

"I know USC wants to win this game," said UCLA defensive back Andy Herrera with a chuckle, "but this is ridiculous."

Pictures of Trojan running back Orenthal James Simpson, best known as O.J., were prominently displayed in the Bruin lockerroom and the same for UCLA quarterback Gary Beban in the USC lockerroom.

Borrowing the phrase long before it got attached to a guy named

Gretzky, someone had labeled the pictures of Beban with the words "The Great One."

By midweek, Trojan coach John McKay had tossed another prize into the already bulging pot, declaring that the Heisman Trophy had come down to Simpson and Beban and the more impressive one Saturday should take it home.

By week's end, Prothro was not concerned with firing his team up emotionally. On the contrary, this was one of those rare occasions when a team didn't need to raise its adrenaline level, but rather lower it or risk choking on its own emotional juices.

"Everything was so helter-skelter," Beban said, "but we couldn't get caught up in it. This was not the kind of game where we needed hype to get up. We needed to settle down. We needed to be tranquilized, not pumped up."

It wasn't uncommon for a team to be shown a war movie the night before a big game. For the Bruins the night before the 1967 showdown, Prothro brought in a comedian.

O.J. and Beban.

The arm against the leg.

They were the sources of power that drove their teams and the centers of apprehension for other teams.

Coaches watched film of them until the grooves wore out, trying to find some way to stop them.

All Simpson needed was a tiny crack in the line, a glint of daylight, and he was gone, using the style, grace and speed that made him arguably the greatest broken-field runner in football history.

All Beban needed was the smallest defensive breakdown and he could whip one of his blistering quick passes or use his superior arm to throw one of the bombs that had sunk so many opponents.

Their styles and loyalties may have been at opposite ends of the spectrum, but their roots were surprisingly similar. Both grew up in Northern California without a great deal of money, but never short on talent or dreams.

Simpson spent his formative years in the Potrero Hill district of San Francisco in a fatherless home. His mother raised four children—two boys and two girls. It wasn't easy as his mother was among the minority locally in that she didn't depend on welfare for survival.

But to Simpson, there was no cause for pity. For him, Potrero Hill was a constant source of excitement and adventure.

It was also fraught with peril for a teen-ager. Simpson joined a gang, the Persian Warriors.

It was, he insisted, "a social club. The president might not have been the toughest guy, but he was the best athlete. Your status in my neighborhood was in direct proportion to your prowess as an athlete.

"I was always an exceptional athlete and always the captain. Always a motivated kid in athletics because that's where my status came from, my self-worth. So when guys got into trouble away from the field, it was usually through my leadership. Even though I would never get caught."

Trouble usually began at the pie factory.

"We lived in a very industrial area," Simpson said, "so it was easy to go down to this pie factory. They'd always open up the doors because they had to cool the pies. We'd hang and go in there and sneak off with a whole bunch of pies in what looked like a bucket brigade. If you were bored and wanted to make some money, you go 'hit the pie company.' Do it maybe once a month. Either sell the pies or gorge out on them. My favorite was blackberry."

Pies weren't the only source of profits. There was beef to steal, sardines from a neighborhood company and Cokes from trucks headed for the marketplace. "They knew the delivery schedule of those trucks," said Simpson of his friends.

Their toughest task was pirating away the slabs of beef.

"It was a bitch rolling those things down the hill," he said, "but there was no way one of those guys [the butchers] was going to chase anyone down into the projects."

At 14, Simpson had a path to athletic glory clearly marked out before him. But there were also disturbing signs, suggesting he was heading down a road toward self-destruction. Some of the credit for Simpson staying on a straight course must go to a man he had long worshipped from afar, a man who had seemed more mythical hero than flesh-and-blood athlete.

Simpson had just gotten out of a youth guidance center where he had spent a couple of days for fighting.

Or, as he conceded, "We might have stole some beer for a party we were giving."

Either way, Simpson's parents weren't too happy. His mother picked him up and informed him that his father, who didn't live with the family, would be coming over to see O.J. after work.

"That meant," Simpson said, "I was going to get a whippin."

He dozed off when he got home. When he awoke, it was to the sounds of voices in the other room. One of those voices belonged to his father.

"Oh," he thought, "here it comes."

His mother called for him to come out and, sure enough, there was his father. Along with the last person on earth he'd ever dream would be standing there—Willie Mays.

The San Francisco Giant centerfielder was the reigning superstar in town in those days.

"He was my absolute hero," Simpson said. "If he hit a homer, I hit a homer, from the time he arrived in San Francisco."

Simpson's elementary school was near Seals Stadium, first home of the Giants when they arrived in the city. So, Simpson and his friends managed to catch the final innings of more than a few games on their way home.

But what had caused Mays to catch up with the teen-aged Simpson? It turned out the head of a nearby community center knew Mays and was concerned enough about Simpson and his proclivity for fighting and mischief to get word to the superstar.

Mays asked Simpson's parents if he could take the kid for the rest of the day. Simpson held his breath waiting for the answer. He got the one he wanted. So for the next six hours, young O.J. Simpson was in heaven, driving around San Francisco with WILLIE MAYS.

There were no lectures, just small talk about sports.

"He went to the cleaners," Simpson said, "and had a meeting at his house. He never gave me any real speech.

"But I got to spend time with my hero and I saw he wasn't any different than me. He had his problems, some stuff in the cleaners that wasn't ready."

In other words, Willie Mays was just like anybody else. More importantly, O.J. saw that he could be like Mays.

"I was just as big as he was," Simpson said, "weighed as much as he did. I might have been as fast, or maybe a little faster than him. I saw that he was human. Before, he was like a god to me. I probably looked at him the way I looked at Jesus. A lot of people thought I was good, and I realized I could be this guy. I could *be* Willie Mays.

"I told myself it wasn't a dream. It was a reality that I could one day be like him, someone everyone knew and liked. I saw it wasn't an unattainable goal. I don't think I got in any real trouble from that point on. I got a little more focused."

The experience with Mays more than any other kept Simpson on the road to USC.

But still, it was hardly a straight road. Simpson's path to becoming a Trojan looked more like one of those zig-zag patterns he would later take to get to the end zone.

He didn't exactly sit around in high school and dream of a pro football career. Not after he got stuck on a team that didn't win a game in his junior year.

"My only interest in school was in getting out," he said. Especially after he failed to get a scholarship following his senior year.

"I was a little disillusioned at the time," he said. "I figured maybe I'd be a cop or playground director. I kind of liked the playground thing 'cause I figured I wouldn't have to go to college."

Simpson looked around and saw a lot of his friends dropping out of high school following the football season. Vietnam was heating up and many headed into the service. That seemed exciting to Simpson, whose favorite movie was "To Hell and Back" with Audie Murphy, the quintessential war film.

But Simpson's mother demanded he stay in school. By the time he graduated in June, Simpson was thankful he had heeded her advice. He saw a friend who had gone off to Vietnam return. Minus a leg.

"Before, Audie Murphy was glamorous," Simpson said. "Now, everybody hated soldiers. I had to be crazy to go there."

So what now?

Arizona State had sent a scout to look at Simpson, but he told the high school grad to go to junior college.

"I looked like a bad risk," Simpson said, "someone who would be tough to keep in school."

So off he went to City College of San Francisco where he got his chance to show what he could do when the two halfbacks playing in front of him got hurt.

And show he did, breaking enough tackles to break several national junior college records. Simpson rushed for an unprecedented 304 yards in one game on just 18 carries. He scored 36 points in a single game to set a new mark. In his two seasons at the San Francisco school, Simpson scored 54 touchdowns, and rushed for 2,552 yards, erasing the school records set by another pretty fair runner named Ollie Matson.

Yet with it all, Simpson's future was still undecided. For over two years, he had loved the Trojans. Watching USC play Wisconsin New Year's Day, 1963 in the Rose Bowl, Simpson, camped in front of a television, was captivated by a horse. After a Trojan touchdown, the traditional gallop around the sidelines by Traveler seemed like something out of a storybook for a poor kid from Potrero Hill.

Right then and there, Simpson knew where he wanted to go. His feelings for USC only had intensified by the time he was a high school senior.

"SC's pushing this guy, Mike Garrett, a black guy," Simpson said. "And then, he wins the Heisman Trophy. I'm thinking, 'Man, I like this school.'"

In his final game in his first season at San Francisco, Simpson and his teammates were playing Cal State Long Beach.

When it ended, Simpson walked off the field figuring he had played his final junior college game. He had decided to go to Arizona State.

Jim Stangeland, a USC assistant coach, was on hand to take a look at half a dozen prospects from Long Beach. But it was Simpson who caught Stangeland's eye with a tremendous game.

As Simpson got to the sidelines, Stangeland reached out and handed him a card. "I'm not going to bother you now," he said. "Here's my card. How would you like to be a Trojan?"

Simpson was stunned. The first thing he thought of was Traveler. Was his career about to take a storybook turn?

He showed the card to his best friend, Mike Taylor.

"Bleeping SC, man!" Simpson told Taylor, an incredulous look still on his face.

But it wasn't that simple. There was a matter of some grades to make up. Simpson worked hard on the books into the spring while also running track at San Francisco. But by summer, he was told he still needed another half semester to be eligible for SC. If he wanted to be a Trojan, he would have to stay at San Francisco another semester. That meant playing another season of junior college ball rather than moving up to the major-college level.

Simpson's first reaction: No way.

"I was, like, sick," he said. "This is my sophomore year, and I had broken all these records in JC. My whole offensive line was graduating. Who knows? I could come back and do nothing the next year. Or, be hurt."

So again, Simpson reverted to Plan B, Arizona State.

This time, he got as far as the airport where a Utah coach intercepted him and convinced Simpson to check out the Utah campus.

Confused, vulnerable and frustrated, Simpson changed his mind yet another time, signing a letter of intent while visiting Utah.

The deed was done, the decision made.

Or was it? USC assistant coach Marv Goux refused to give up. Attending a party in Palos Verdes on a Sunday afternoon, he received word of Simpson's change of heart. Goux called Simpson at home.

"Son," he said, "I just want to talk to you. You owe me that much."

Goux raced from the party to the airport and was in San Francisco an hour later. With another recruiter sitting outside Simpson's place, Goux marched right in.

"We're not going to offer you anything fancy," he told Simpson. "No fancy cars. No money. Just the opportunity to be a Trojan. If you could have the car of your choice, wouldn't it be worth waiting three or four months? Well, nothing against Utah, but this is the difference between a Volkswagen and a Rolls Royce. You're the one who wanted to go to SC. If that's what you really want, then isn't it worth just another three or four months of waiting?

"I don't promise you anything. But if you play the ball you're capable of, you'll end up with more than any of these schools will ever offer you."

Back to junior college Simpson went to get those grades. Cal still tried to recruit him, but this time, Simpson's decision was final. His first impulse had been correct. He was going to gallop with that big white horse after all.

While Simpson grew up in a large, fatherless family, Beban was born in San Francisco and raised in nearby Redwood City as an only child with a strong father figure to look up to.

And look up he did.

Even when he was a Heisman Trophy winner and a national star, Beban would still try to steer the conversation towards the accomplishments of his father, who spent 27 years as a shipping supervisor on the San Francisco docks.

Beban was proud of his father's ability to kick a football shoeless ("Dad's gotta be the best barefooted punter around"), his tour of duty as a gunner on a Navy boat in World War II and his boxing skills.

In his wallet, Beban carried a tattered, yellowed clipping from a Fresno paper. The article, or what was left of it, had been written in 1935. It read "In a rough-and-tumble heavyweight fight, Frank Beban, 198, knocked out Josh Woody, 187, in the third round last night . . ."

But the elder Beban's boxing career didn't last long.

"After he got out of the service," Gary said, "he snuck out for a few fights, but Granny (Frank's mother) put an end to that. He was strong, but a very kind man, a gentle bear. He's been a very significant influence in my life."

With such a role model, the younger Beban's course toward an athletic career was set. But Frank Beban nudged his son in that direction rather than forcefully pointing him.

"He did it in a neat way," Gary explained. "If I asked to go out and goof off, he always had plenty for me to do, from painting the house to pulling weeds. But if I told him I was going to play ball, he said, okay. He made it very comfortable for me rather than acting like some parents who are overly aggressive in trying to develop their kids in sports."

It took devotion. "There is a reason why Frank and I weren't able to take a vacation for five years," said Anna Beban, Gary's mother. That reason was Little League.

"I never missed games because of vacation," Gary said. "My parents just wouldn't go."

Beban's football career, however, didn't exactly begin with a moment a parent might want to preserve in a scrapbook. He started out in a Pop Warner league at age 12. Sent in to replace an injured quarterback, Beban immediately went for the trick play, a flanker reverse.

Bad move.

It lost 15 yards and brought his coach down on him.

"Beban," the coach yelled, "did you call that play?"

"Yes, sir," Beban replied.

"Ok," said the coach, "you're through."

Beban's high-school football career started out even slower. As a matter of fact, he didn't even play football in his freshman year at Sequoia High, devoting his time instead to basketball and baseball.

That didn't last. He was told that if he didn't go out for football, "there might not be a spot for you on the baseball team."

So Gary Beban became a football player. He didn't have any of the problems Simpson did in getting stuck on a winless squad. Just the opposite. When Beban joined the Sequoia varsity in his junior year, the team was riding a 29–game winning streak under Coach Joe Marvin. That was extended to 33 in a row, longest in the country, before Sequoia finally lost.

"Our line was larger than either Cal's or Stanford's," Beban said. "It was a real football factory."

By his senior year, Beban had narrowed his choices of a college to Cal, UCLA, Oregon State and perhaps Arizona. With Marvin being a former Bruin tailback, Beban looked seriously at UCLA. But he also became fascinated with Prothro. As soon as Beban met the Oregon State coach, he knew this was a man he wanted to play for.

But it was the mystique of UCLA *basketball* that finally tipped the scales.

Down in Los Angeles for a spring vacation, Beban got caught up in UCLA's bid for its first NCAA basketball title. When the Bruins won, Beban was down at the airport with hundreds of others, greeting the victorious players. Gale Goodrich and Walt Hazzard became his heroes and UCLA became his school.

Cal was also very interested, but Beban was looking for something farther from home. The Trojans also gave him a look, but weren't too impressed with what they saw.

"They said I was too small and too slow," Beban recalled. "Other than that, I was all right."

It wasn't the first time the 6-foot, 190-pounder had heard the label *slow* and Beban had an explanation for it. He figured it was the high-top shoes he wore, à la Johnny Unitas, that made him appear slower than he was.

Bill Barnes was the Bruin coach when Beban arrived, but not for long. On New Year's Day, 1965, Beban learned UCLA had hired a new head coach: Tommy Prothro.

"That just tells you how ironic life is," Beban said. "I was extremely excited when I heard Prothro was coming. This was the coach I had wanted to play for. I had gotten the best of both worlds."

That it was. Prothro and Beban would team up to bring UCLA some of its best teams and most memorable games.

But despite all their previous accomplishments, nothing could truly prepare Beban and Simpson for Nov 18, 1967. For them and everybody else on that field, it would be the game of their lives.

Despite UCLA's unbeaten record, USC was favored by three. Prothro, ever the master psychologist, reveled in the underdog role and milked it all week.

"Those cold gamblers," he said, "seem to be able to keep from getting emotionally involved in a game such as this, so I'd be inclined to go along with them.

"If anybody could prove the gamblers wrong all the time, he'd get rich very quickly."

Prothro looked for every edge. He was one of the world's best bridge players when he wasn't playing mind games. His remarks that week boiled down to, aw shucks these guys we're playing are so good, we're just happy to be on the same field with them.

Prothro even tried to build USC's loss the previous week into an asset for the Trojans.

"The pressure is off them now," he said, "and I think you'll see a difference in them when they play us. When you're unbeaten and favored to keep winning week after week, the pressure builds up so much that you tend to become a defending team. You keep telling yourself, 'I can't lose. I can't lose.' "

USC had two quarterbacks in Steve Sogge and Toby Page, but the brunt of their attack was Simpson, who took the Coliseum field that day averaging 150 yards a game.

In addition to the Beban-led multiple offense, UCLA had an another potent weapon in kicker Zenon Andrusyshyn. Andrusyshyn was a soccer style kicker, still a novelty in football in those days. But he would have stood out anyway with a leg that had already produced 11 field goals. One of those had come from 52 yards out and Andrusyshyn had barely missed another from 57 yards.

But despite the offensive firepower both sides were bringing to this fight, it didn't figure to be a high-scoring game because the two teams also came armed with excellent defenses. USC was fifth in the nation defensively, having allowed just 187 yards a game. UCLA wasn't far behind at 261 yards allowed.

On that November day, eight Americans were killed and another 31 wounded battling for Hill 1338 in the Central Highlands of Vietnam. The day before, 400 students had staged a sit-in outside the office of UCLA Chancellor Franklin D. Murphy, demanding more say in university policy. But for sixty minutes, a nation and a city put their troubles aside to watch a football game.

And were not disappointed.

November 18th was warm and clear in Los Angeles. The temperature was in the 70s, a 10–18 mile-per-hour wind pushing away any lingering clouds to leave a brilliant background for the 90,772 fans who crammed into the Coliseum. There wasn't a hint of smog, allowing the crowd at the top of the Coliseum bowl to see the few towering structures in downtown Los Angeles in vivid detail.

But the only details on the minds of the serious fans that day were on the field.

As Beban and offensive tackle Larry Slagle tried to make their way from the tunnel across the running track onto the grass of the football field, they found their path blocked by a jungle of television cables.

Beban looked around in wonder. He had never seen a stadium so crammed with cameramen and equipment and reporters and fans. And it was still a couple of hours before the opening kickoff.

"This one," Beban told Slagle, a knowing smile flashing on his face, "is going to be special."

It wasn't easy for Beban to smile that day because he was hurting before the game had even started. The UCLA quarterback had been speared in the ribs the week before against Washington, the hit coming after the whistle had blown.

"It ripped up my muscle cage," Beban said. "If I twisted the wrong way, the pain would tear across my stomach."

He twisted the wrong way often that afternoon, but refused to use the injury as an excuse.

The adrenaline was flowing in Simpson as well when he took the field. He had seen his first USC-UCLA game the year before, watching the Trojans lose, 14–7.

"It was amazing how down SC was," he said of the '66 game. "That night, I went to a party with a lot of guys who were going to UCLA the next year. I recall how UCLA ruled that night. The guys were talking crap back and forth. I remember thinking. 'Just wait. Just wait till next year.'"

At the start, it looked as if the Trojans were going to have to wait yet another year.

When USC punter Charles Aldridge, kicking from his own territory, had the ball go off the side of his foot and out of bounds at his own 47-yard line, UCLA had its first scoring chance.

And made the most of it, halfback Greg Jones climaxing a Bruin drive by scoring on a 12-yard run.

But the subsequent euphoria in the UCLA rooting section was short-lived. On the final play of the first quarter, it was the Bruins' turn to make a mistake. And USC's turn to cash in.

Beban was throwing what he later termed a "blooper pass" to Jones. Beban faked a handoff to Jones in the backfield, then looked right all the way as Jones headed out into the left flat before coming back to Jones at the last instant.

But Trojan defensive back Pat Cashman never bought the fake. He stayed on Jones and was rewarded for his effort with a soft spiral heading his way.

"They ran a throw-back pattern, something we've been working on defending," Cashman said. "When I saw Beban turn to throw, I just started to run up. I took it out of Jones' hands and all I could see was six points."

That's just what he got, racing 55 yards untouched as time expired in the quarter.

Prothro blamed himself. "I made the call on that play," he said, "and it was a terrible call."

Beban disagreed. "He can only take the blame," Beban said of his coach, "if he threw the ball. It was a very well-designed play. But Cashman was not where he should have been. If he had stayed in his position a little longer, it would have been different. But he saw something."

USC took a 14–7 lead in the second quarter, Simpson scoring on a 13-yard run that would later pale in comparison to the one he would be remembered for on that afternoon. But, to some, this 13-yard run was the more spectacular because seven Bruins had a genuine shot at tackling Simpson before he reached the end zone. All came up with nothing more to show for their opportunity than a handful of grass.

It was O.J. at his awesome best.

The touchdown had been set up by Earl McCullouch. The Trojan flanker, running a perfectly executed reverse, gained 52 yards to bring USC within reach of the end zone. But it was Simpson who got the Trojans there. He took the handoff in the backfield at about the 20-yard line. It was to be a sweep, but Simpson was forced inside. He got a block at the 15 and broke his first tackle.

"My only conscious memory," Simpson said, "was that the play broke down immediately. Even as the ball was coming to me, I could see that somebody had penetrated our backfield. My original instinct was to get back to the line of scrimmage. We were a running team, not a passing team, and it's tough to make up yardage."

At the ten, Simpson found himself surrounded by three Bruins. He sped past them, breaking his second tackle.

"He stepped through them," said offensive tackle Ron Yary, "and around them and underneath them and over the top of them somehow."

At the five, Simpson found three Bruins, but shed them all, breaking three tackles like a horse shooing off flies.

"It was a matter of trying to keep my legs moving," Simpson said. "SC does a drill of running in tires, throwing things at your feet to keep them moving and that's all I was trying to do. Getting to the end zone wasn't on my mind.

"I know I was going through a bunch of arms and legs and, finally, I could see the end zone."

But he wasn't there quite yet. At the three, two more Bruins got Simpson in their grasp. He dragged them to the one where yet another Bruin grabbed him and hung on for dear life, part of a human train heading for the end zone.

Finally, Simpson collapsed, falling across the goal line to culminate perhaps the greatest 13-yard performance ever.

Beban had yet to be heard from, but he made his presence felt in the second half with a 53-yard touchdown pass to George Farmer and a 20-yarder to Dave Nuttall.

But on the second TD play, Andrusyshyn's conversion kick was wide, leaving the score 20–14. The Trojans sensed a crack through which they could squeeze out a victory.

With ten and a half minutes to play, and UCLA still leading by six, the Trojans lined up at their own 36-yard line on a third and seven.

The designated play was a pass to receiver Ron Drake. But when quarterback Toby Page hunched over center to call the signals, he didn't like what he saw. UCLA had shifted to double coverage on Drake on the strong side.

No problem, Page figured. He'd send Simpson through the weak side. Page audiblized, calling for the 23 Blast.

Simpson was shocked. Page had just asked him how he felt. "Give me a blow," he said, worn out, as he had just run back a kickoff and felt like he had been in the arms of every Bruin defender at one time or another that afternoon.

"I couldn't even run a pass pattern," Simpson said. "I was so tired.

"I almost went into motion," Simpson recalled, "cause I wanted to say, 'No.' I thought, 'Not only am I tired, but that's a horrible call." But by then, the ball was snapped and it was all instinct."

But what instinct.

Simpson got the ball and off he went on one of the most storied runs in college football history.

Simpson burst through the left side of the line where tackle Mike Taylor and guard Steve Lehmer cracked some daylight.

"The hole opened up beautifully," Simpson said.

Fullback Dan Scott threw a block on linebacker Don Manning at the 40.

"Manning thought it was going to be a pass," Simpson said, "and hustled back to his pass responsibility. And I got right on Danny Scott's tail. I recall hopping, jumping in there, but since I was wrapped, I kept my legs moving."

Manning had reinjured his right shoulder three plays earlier, leaving him, in effect, a one-armed man on Simpson's run.

"The line backer (Manning) reached across with his left hand," Prothro said, "to try and get him (Simpson). He was hurt and shouldn't have even been in there. I learned a lesson from that."

At the 43, Simpson took a sharp left turn. Center Dick Allmon threw a block. So did Drake. Simpson took care of the rest.

"They had three guys on the run," McKay said, "and we had three blockers. If they go three-on-three against us, we're going to beat them. Now if they had the left end in there, we couldn't have blocked him. It would have been three-on-four and (the end) would have made the play. But we blocked those three and Simpson went through that thing like only he could do. That's about a five-yard run, but he turned it into something else."

Racing down the left sideline, Simpson swung back toward the middle at the UCLA 45.

"I could look at his eyes," said McKay, remembering the instant Simpson passed him, "and I knew that son of a bitch was going a long ways."

So did Simpson.

"I thought, 'I can score,'" he said. "Felt like I had a good, strong stride, but I didn't have a burst in that run. That's why I cut back to the middle of the field. I had no burst to get by those guys."

Several Bruins pursued, but they might as well have tried to catch the wind. The first touchdown had been scored by O.J., the power runner. This one belonged to O.J., the sprinter.

Tommy Prothro leaned over to an assistant and, referring to Earl

McCullouch, grumbled, "Isn't but one guy can catch Simpson now and he's on the same team."

Ahead loomed the open field, the end zone, the Rose Bowl, maybe the Heisman and perhaps even the national championship.

Simpson crossed the goal line and was quickly joined by hysterical teammates.

The scoreboard clock showed 10:38 still remaining to play, but this was a blow from which the Bruins would not recover.

Aldridge added the extra point, giving USC a 21–20 lead. And that's the way it would stay.

The Trojan defense, led by ends Tim Rossovich and Jim Gunn, turned back Beban and Co. three times in the final minutes. Two Andrusyshyn field goals were blocked.

"He kicked low, that sidewinder thing," McKay said. "He always pulled the ball to the left."

So McKay loaded that side of his line with five men, including 6-foot-8 Bill Hayhoe, who made the second block.

But when it was over, the play people would remember and still talk about two decades later was 23 Blast.

Simpson would go on to a brilliant pro career with the Buffalo Bills. He would be the first to gain 2,000 yards in a single season. But his name would always be synonymous with The Run as that 64-yard scoring play would simply become known.

"All things considered," Simpson said that day after gaining 177 yards rushing, "this is the toughest game I've ever played in."

It wasn't easy for Beban, either. Three times he was forced to leave the game with a painful rib injury only to return.

"The pain lasted only a very short time," said Beban, pretending to forget those moments when he was crushed by the powerful Trojan rush. "What bothered me most was the fact that I couldn't breathe properly. But USC is more the reason we lost than my ribs."

Despite his problems, Beban managed to throw for 301 yards and the two touchdowns. The 344 yards he generated in total offense was the most the Trojans had given up all year.

There was no depression in Beban as he walked off the field.

"We had been playing for a national championship and it wound up 21–20," Beban said. "I felt in pretty good shape. It was an awfully well-played game. It was not three yards and a cloud of dust. We both played wide open. I didn't feel the pain of the loss until later in the week."

As a consolation, Beban won the Heisman. Simpson had to wait another year before getting his.

Wrote Jim Murray in the *Los Angeles Times*: "The last time these many cosmic events were settled by one day of battle, they struck off a commemorative stamp and elected the winner President. . . . It was a four heart-attack feature. More fun than watching Sophia Loren getting ready for bed with the shades up. . . . They can send that Heisman Trophy out with two straws, please."

Colleague John Hall, in the *Times*, agreed the Heisman should have been given to both men. Wrote Hall: "They made a bum out of Frank Merriwell, knocked Cinderella out of the top 10 for good and turned the Hollywood dream spinners into straight men."

USC went on to beat Indiana, 14–3, in the Rose Bowl that year to wrap up the national championship.

But whenever members of either team talk about the 1967 season, they talk about November 18.

For once, all the pregame hype wasn't enough to adequately describe the game.

A note on the bulletin board in the USC lockerroom that day read: "Let's vow to make this a game that will forever be etched in the memories of those who will be fortunate enough to view it."

It was a vow both sides kept.

2

The First Games
pre–1929

Most of their names have been lost in time, but their common deed will forever echo through time.

Spaniards had founded the Mission San Gabriel Arcangel in 1771 nine miles from the Los Angeles River, then known as the Porciuncula. Ten years later, it was decided to start another settlement on the west bank of the river. Prospective settlers were rounded up down in Sonora and Sinaloa, current day Mexico. Eleven families totaling 44 people enlisted. The popular image of those pioneers is clear: Spaniards branching out into rugged, uncharted California, bringing European culture and ideas to the uninformed natives. Not exactly. There were, according to John D. Weaver in his book, *Los Angeles: The Enormous Village*, just two Spaniards. The rest were Indians, blacks or a racial mix.

There wasn't much fanfare on the night of September 4, 1781 when the group made camp for the first time in their new settlement at a spot that would later become the site of the Civic Center. There would have been a friar to recite the proper blessings and a flag to be planted by one of the four soldiers along for protection.

None of them could have dreamed that the little El Pueblo de la

Reina de Los Angeles (The Village of the Queen of the Angels) they had founded that night would become one of the great, sprawling metropolises of the world.

There was plenty of fanfare exactly ninety-nine years later, on September 4, 1880, when another historic moment in the history of the city occurred. And the names of those who took part that day have been preserved and honored.

The occasion was the founding of the University of Southern California. On a hot, dry day, dust in the lungs of those in attendance, 1,000 people took part in the ceremonies for the laying of the cornerstone of the new school. The entire population of Los Angeles at that point was around 12,000.

Progress in some areas had been excruciatingly slow. The streets still weren't paved. And there were no electric lights because, as explained in the book *Southern California and Its University* by Manuel P. Servin and Iris Higbie Wilson, such lights "attracted bugs, contributed to blindness and had a bad effect on ladies' complexions."

Lights or not, there wasn't much to see that first day at USC, just stakes in the ground. An onlooker at the opening ceremonies remembers "standing in the midst of a vast stretch of unoccupied, uncultivated plain covered with a rank growth of wild mustard, the unfinished building was indeed a lonely object to those who saw only the present."

The first structure was a two-story building with classrooms on the bottom and an assembly hall and offices on the top. It cost $5000 to build.

The land, 308 lots in all, was donated by Isaias W. Hellman, a Jew, Ozro W. Childs, an Episcopalian, and John G. Downey, a Catholic. Many pointed to that religious diversion as a sign that this university was destined to serve all who wished to enter its doors.

Fifty-three did that first semester, beginning on October 6, 1880. The first year, under President Marion McKinley Bovard, the school offered courses in the classics, philosophy and science.

Students were prohibited from using profane language, gambling or attending saloons. Liquor was not even permitted in their rooms. Nor were they permitted to leave town without the permission of the university president.

Despite the restrictions, the school grew steadily. From its modest beginning, enrollment increased to 110 students the second year, 154 the third and 248 in the fourth.

It wasn't long before the challenges of the classroom weren't enough for some students of the burgeoning university. Sometime in the mid 1880's—the exact date has been lost in time—USC played its first football game.

Well, sort of.

In *Cardinal and Gold*, Alfred Wesson writes, "Eleven sturdy young men sporting handlebar mustaches and padded vests drew lines on a vacant lot, erected wobbly goal posts and challenged all comers to contest in that new-fangled push-and-tug business called football."

The first opponents were the Los Angeles YMCA and a team from Pasadena, fittingly enough, future home of USC's ultimate annual game.

Things had become a lot more formal by 1888. In November of that year, USC played its first official game against the Alliance Athletic Club and won 16–0.

It still wasn't football as we know it. A touchdown was worth four points and the conversion another two. A field goal was good for five points. Tackling below the waist was a foul.

USC played only one other game that season, also against Alliance, and won again, this time 4–0.

The school's first, rudimentary steps into the athletic world came as L.A. was trying to take the final leap from pioneer settlement to big-time city.

Dr. Joseph P. Widney, dean of USC's first College of Medicine, wrote in 1888 that Los Angeles was "old as a picturesque, sleepy, free and easy Spanish pueblo, but new as a thriving, progressive American city. Old as a station where the solitary horseman stopped for a rest and refreshment. New as a railroad center, old as a Catholic Mission. New as a cosmopolitan city where 100 Protestant churches vie with Catholic chimes."

By the early 1890s, tuition at USC was $20 a term with a two-thirds reduction for sons and daughters of regular ministers and candidates studying for the ministry.

A year later, the USC football team, then known as the Methodists, played its first collegiate opponent, St. Vincent's (later to become Loyola Marymount), winning 40–0.

But even after a decade of football, USC still hadn't graduated to the ranks of the major powers. In 1898, the school played to a 0–0 tie and later suffered a 6–0 loss to Los Angeles High School.

The two schools played another 0–0 tie in 1900, but USC finally had its revenge in 1903, beating L.A. High, 10–0. By then, USC's big rivals were Occidental and Pomona.

The city was growing, too. The population had passed the 100,000 mark by the turn of the century. With fertile land and a thriving citrus industry, growers were netting a million dollars a year.

There was another sure sign the school was heading into big-time football—scandal.

In 1903, The Los Angeles Times accused the USC football team of "irregularities" in the way it played the game. Pomona College claimed USC was not adhering strictly to eligibility rules. And, in 1904, the *University Advocate*, the school paper, reported that a $25 check had been given to team captain Dan Caley for "services rendered." No one could quite explain what those services were.

It might seem mild compared to the shady, big-money dealings the NCAA would uncover in collegiate athletics around the country in later years, but it was no less shocking in those days.

"Has professionalism been present in our school and no one the wiser?" asked an *Advocate* writer, perhaps the first, but certainly not the last time that question would be asked of a collegiate program in the 20th century.

In 1905, USC met Stanford for the first time on the football field, losing 16–0, but beginning one of its great rivalries.

By then, USC has its first paid coach in Harvey Holmes. The school's first big-name coach was Dean Cromwell, whose forte later became track and field.

In 1910, his second season, Cromwell was undefeated, USC

finishing 7–0–1. True, three of the first four opponents were high schools. But USC finished against Redlands, Occidental, Whittier and Pomona, outscoring the four schools, 61–12.

So football had finally arrived at USC, right?

Incredibly, just the opposite. The USC football players were rewarded for all those big wins with a bigger loss—their sport itself. The glamour in those days was on the rugby field. That was the sport the big schools like Stanford and California excelled at and it was the sport USC wanted to be proficient in.

Quoted in *The Trojan Heritage* by Mal Florence, a USC spokesman explained, "We are looking for a foothold on an athletic ladder that would carry us, we hoped, to a level of competition to the proportion of our ambitious, restless, growing young institution."

Not quite. Rugby turned out to be a losing proposition, both athletically and financially, at USC.

About the only memorable thing to come out of the three years of rugby was the name Trojans. Credit goes to Owen R. Bird, a *Times* sportswriter, who, in 1912, wrote, "owing to the terrific handicaps under which the athletes, coaches and managers of the university were laboring, and, at the same time, appreciating their splendid fighting spirit . . . against the overwhelming odds of larger and better equipped rivals, the name *Trojan* suitably fitted the players."

Rugby didn't. Football returned in 1914 to stay.

In later years, the underdog image would hardly fit the powerful Trojans, but, in those days, they were a bottom-rung team in the hierarchy of college football, anxious to move up. And to do so, they couldn't continue to be satisfied playing the Occidentals and Pomonas. USC wanted bigger opponents. The Trojans scheduled California, Oregon, Oregon St. and St. Mary's.

Cromwell returned to coach for three more seasons, but there was a feeling the school wasn't going big-time as long as he was at the helm.

Arnold Eddy, a long-time figure in various capacities in the school's athletic program, recalled Cromwell's limitations.

"He was a track coach," Eddy said. "He wasn't a football coach. He was a real nice guy, very capable, a super salesman, but football coach wasn't his cup of tea."

With the end of World War I in 1919, USC found the straw to stir the drink. Elmer "Gloomy Gus" Henderson, given the nickname because of the way he downgraded his own players, ushered in a new era of prominence for the Trojans.

Despite the fact USC, just under 4,000 students strong, was taking on schools with four times the enrollment, the Trojans emerged victorious more often than not. The team was playing on Bovard Field which only seated around 6,000 until it was remodeled in 1920, doubling its capacity.

Gwynn Wilson, later a key figure in USC's athletic growth, remembers watching the Trojans at Bovard Field when he was still in high school.

An eight-foot fence served as the bleachers for Wilson and his friends. But at one game in 1911, too many fans used that fence and it came crashing down. Wilson was knocked cold. Upon being revived, however, he took a safer spot and watched the rest of the game.

In 1920, USC had an unbeaten six-game season against bona fide collegiate competition. The school was succeeding financially as well, its net worth up to $1,831,039.

The growth mirrored that of the city around it. At the turn of the century, Los Angeles encompassed 43 square miles. In 1923, it had grown to 392 square miles. Ben Macomber wrote in the *San Francisco Chronicle* that Los Angeles was "intoxicated with its growth."

In 1923, the USC football program was also growing in new directions. That year, the Trojans played for the first time in the Coliseum, beating Pomona, 23–7, in the inaugural game. Later that season, USC drew 72,000 for a game against Cal and climaxed the year by going to its first Rose Bowl where it beat Penn State, 14–3.

But through it all, Gloomy Gus lived up to his name. He once told *Times* sportswriter Paul Lowry that the Trojan line had so many holes, it would make Swiss cheese blush. Henderson referred to his center as the center of gloom.

But real gloom lay ahead for Gus.

By 1922, USC had been admitted to the Pacific Coast Conference. But the Trojans were never fully accepted by the conference's established powers like Cal and Stanford.

"We were a stepchild," Eddy said. "We were coming along fast, but they were jealous of us and they thought we were cheating on entrance requirements and things like that. We weren't. They were teed off with Henderson. They thought that he was rushing (recruiting) unfairly. They thought that because Henderson was bringing the team up so fast."

The muttering and grumbling about USC boiled to the surface in 1924 just prior to the Trojans' game at Cal.

Gwynn Wilson, who held a position at USC similar to today's athletic director, was called into an office on the Berkeley campus just prior to the kickoff. A Cal official gave him the shocking news.

"We like you, Gwynn," he said, "but not your university." He announced this was to be the final game of the series.

A stunned Wilson conferred with Harold Stonier, a USC vice-president, and they decided to go on with the game. But Cal also had the upper hand on the field, winning, 7–0.

With the sound of the final gun still echoing in his ears, Wilson also heard the other shoe drop. A Stanford official approached him and said, "We're not going to play you next year, either."

Enough was enough. Wilson looked him in the eye and replied, "Well, you're not going to play us *this* year."

Instead, the Trojans scheduled St. Mary's. But the rivalries were soon revived. Stanford came back on the USC schedule in 1925, claiming Cal had instigated the trouble. The Golden Bears themselves returned a year later.

But it was too late for Henderson. USC alumnus had been upset with him since he had lost the 1921 game to Cal, 38–7.

"They beat us on a single play," Wilson said. "It was like a screen pass. He just failed to react to this thing and had no remedy for it."

The brief breakup with Cal and Stanford merely exacerbated the situation, causing Wilson to fire Henderson after the 1924 season.

Henderson had two years remaining on his contract, at $10,000 a season. Wilson handed him a check for $20,000 and that ended it.

Henderson's successor was Knute Rockne. Really.

There was only one hitch. Rockne agreed to come west and coach the Trojans if Notre Dame would let him out of his contract. Of course,

Notre Dame wasn't about to do that, and Rockne stayed and became a legend.

So instead, USC got Howard Jones.

Not a bad substitute. Schools like Cal and Stanford may have been upset with how far Henderson had brought the Trojans, but, after a couple of years of Jones, they were longing for the good old days. Jones lasted 16 seasons, won three national championships, had three undefeated seasons and won five Rose Bowls.

"Howard was to USC," Eddy said, "what Rockne was to Notre Dame. Henderson put us on the map, but Howard Jones got us established as a football power nationally.

"Howard Jones was completely obsessed. When he took the practice field, he was in complete command. He got the kids to perform. He'd get right down on the line of scrimmage and show the tackle what he wanted him to do. Players would run through a concrete wall for him."

Jones' mind was so focused on football, he often didn't have room in there for much else. He would work the team until after the sun had set. Then he would stumble around in the dark, trying to remember where he had parked his car.

Paul Zimmerman, former sports editor of the *Los Angeles Times*, wrote that Jones "was so wrapped up in the game that he always came back from trout fishing trips with his pockets crammed with grid notes. Those trips were easy on the fish, but hard on the opponents next fall."

But Jones demanded mental sharpness of his players. When one of them fumbled on one occasion, Jones gave him the ball and told him to take it to class with him that week so he could learn to hang onto it.

"If you were a player," Eddy said, "and you were walking and Howard was walking on the same side of the street, you'd cross the street."

Under Jones, the Trojans became known as The Thundering Herd because of their relentless ground game.

"He just had that knack," Eddy said, "of taking the ball and rushing it down the other guy's throat.

"His theory was this: We kick the ball to the opponents. Then, we tackle them. If we just wait a little bit, they'll drop the ball. We'll pick it up and we don't have to carry it so far. Get them in their own territory and keep them there.

"Of course, we couldn't use a forward pass in those days like we do today. If you didn't complete one, you got penalized."v

Think of USC football and the first image that comes to mind is a tailback, whether it be Mike Garrett, O.J. Simpson, Charles White or Marcus Allen. It was Jones who first gave the ball and the importance to the man in that position, although, in those days, he was called the quarterback.

But from the Thundering Herd to Student Body Left, the Trojans were an army that attacked and conquered on the ground.

It was a time for memorable coaches and Jones wasn't the only one operating on the shores of the Pacific in The Roaring 20s. One of his biggest opponents, the Galloping Gaels of St. Mary's, were known in those days as the Notre Dame of the West. Their coach, Slip Madigan, was the Knute Rockne of the Pacific.

"There was a story going around," said Dick Mesak, a former All-Coast lineman for the Gaels, "that Slip was out on a recruiting trip when he came upon Wee Willie Wilkin (later a star tackle for St. Mary's) working with a plow in the fields.

"He asked Wilkin how to get into town. Wilkin picked up the plow with one hand and pointed. Madigan signed him right up."

The Madigan legend spread to the Coliseum when the Gaels came to play the Trojans.

Before one game, Madigan pulled out a flask. "In here, boys," he told his team, gathered around with eyes wide, "is holy water. I got it from an old monk lying on his deathbed."

It was later revealed Madigan had been seen filling the flask himself—at a Coliseum drinking fountain.

On another occasion, Madigan implored his team to win one for his five-year-old son, who was supposedly dying of some mysterious ailment. In reality, the youngster had the flu. He recovered sufficiently to walk into the St. Mary's lockerroom at the wrong moment—just as his dad had finished describing his son's "fatal" condition.

Characters such as Madigan and Rockne inspired enough stories to fill a library and kept college football in the headlines on the sports page in The Roaring 20s when people like Babe Ruth, Jack Dempsey and Red Grange were creating their own legends.

And USC, with heated rivalries against both Rockne and Madigan, prospered in the spotlight created by both men.

Another legendary figure appeared on the USC football team in those days, but his fame would have nothing to do with his skill on the field.

The year was 1927. The student manager, frantic over a missing player, rushed over to the student union to see Eddy. "Mr. Eddy," he said breathlessly, "the coach [Howard Jones] is very concerned. This is the second day of practice and Marion Morrison hasn't reported as yet." Morrison, a right tackle, was heading into his junior season pencilled in as a starter by Jones.

"Well," said Eddy, flashing the smile of a man who has the situation under control, "the boy's been working in the movies. I'll call up and find out what's going on."

Eddy got ahold of George Marshall, an executive at 20th Century Fox. When Eddy mentioned Morrison's name, Marshall's first reaction was to laugh.

"Well, Arnold," Marshall said, "you're going to have to tell the coach he's going to have to look for another right tackle because Marion Morrison is going to be an actor."

And thus ended the brief football career of Marion Morrison and began the acting career of John Wayne.

Howard Jones beat Knute Rockne before the USC coach had ever set foot on Bovard Field. In 1921, Jones, then the coach at Iowa, defeated the Fighting Irish, 10–7, ending a 21-game unbeaten streak by Notre Dame.

It was Gwynn Wilson, USC graduate manager, who first proposed a Trojan rivalry with Notre Dame.

The time seemed ripe in 1925. The Fighting Irish were playing Nebraska in the final game of their annual series. Wilson asked USC vice-president Harold Stonier if he could take a train to Nebraska where he would try to convince Rockne to put USC on the Notre Dame schedule. Permission granted.

But Wilson had one other request, a big one in those days of extremely limited travel budgets. "I'd like to take my wife, Marion, along," Wilson told Stonier. "We've only been married a year and have never been apart." Permission granted.

The rest of Wilson's plan, however, didn't go so smoothly. Rockne was too busy to talk before the Nebraska game. And too depressed afterward because the Fighting Irish lost.

Finally, on a train back to South Bend, Rockne met Wilson in the observation car. But the observations he gave Wilson were not what the USC envoy wanted to hear.

"Gwynn, it's not possible," Rockne said. "It's too expensive. It's too far. It takes the men away from their classes for too long. Besides, we can get all the games we want here in the Big Ten. Most of our alumni are around here. They can see us. I'd like to do it, but the answer is no."

Rockne had his own concerns to worry about. The Fighting Irish were already traveling so much critics were calling them the Ramblers. He didn't need yet another road game, one that would involve a week-long commitment.

Downcast, Wilson returned to his berth and told Marion what Rockne's response had been.

A mysterious smile crossed her face. "Go back in there," she told her husband. "Mrs. Rockne wants the game."

It turned out that while the men had been talking, so had the women. Marion had filled Bonnie Rockne's ear with the fine points of Southern California. And she, in turn, filled Knute's ear when he returned to his berth.

Back Wilson went to Rockne. And this time, when Rockne faced him, the Notre Dame coach had an embarrassed grin on his face. "Gwynn," he said, "what was this you were mentioning about these football games?"

Wilson offered a $20,000 guarantee.

On Dec. 4, 1926 at the Coliseum, the USC-Notre Dame rivalry, one of the great rivalries in college football history, began.

While USC was fighting for national recognition on the football field, UCLA was just fighting for its existence.

UCLA came into being in 1919 as the University of California, Southern Branch.

The school was the brainchild of Edward Dickson, then the 38-year-old political editor of the Los Angeles Express and the only University of California regent from the southern part of the state, and Dr. Ernest Carroll Moore, the 46-year-old president of the Los Angeles State Normal School, a two-year teachers' college. Dickson had a dream: a branch of the university in his home area.

In 1915, Dickson felt the time was right to form a full-fledged branch of the University of California. But others weren't so sure. A tough political battle ensued, with heavy opposition coming from the north.

What was working in Dickson's favor was the threat to start a separate university run by a brand new Board of Regents in Los Angeles unless the existing board expanded its territory. A separate state university would mean sharing tax dollars. Now, *that* made the regents sit up and take notice.

"The danger cannot be averted merely by resistance," Dickson told University of California president Benjamin Ide Wheeler in a conversation related in *UCLA On the Move* by Andrew Hamilton and John B. Jackson.

Wheeler advised Dickson to take the venture "a step at a time." Wheeler was worried a new university would take students, professors and funds away from the Berkeley campus.

So, Dickson started modestly with an adult education program in Los Angeles in 1916, followed by summer school sessions at Los Angeles High School in 1917.

Finally, the Dickson forces won over both the regents and the state legislature. On May 23, 1919, Governor William B. Stephens signed a bill establishing the branch.

Where would the new campus be?

A deal was worked out with Moore to take over the two-year teachers' college on Vermont Avenue, "out in the weeds and wild flowers," as it was once described. Included were buildings of brick, tile and stone on 25 acres, beautifully landscaped with giant eucalyptus trees dominating the scene.

The State Normal School had consisted mostly of women training to be teachers. The 1,338 students enrolled in 1919, the first year of the Southern Branch, formed an interesting mix. It was a predominately female class, the girls outnumbering the boys 6–1. The majority were seeking a teaching degree. There was a "federal" class, consisting of 175 servicemen who had come out of World War I with injuries ranging from standard bullet wounds to the horrendous effects of gassing.

In one class, the female to male ratio was 17–1. The campus newspaper, *The Club Californian,* told the male students, "Select your seventeen. Girls, start early and avoid the rush. And do your duty, boys."

The school began as a two-year institution, but gained accreditation as a four-year school in 1924, the enrollment having grown to 4,418.

Sports became a part of the institution right from its birth. The first meeting of the football team was held the day after school opened.

Reported the *Los Angeles Times:* "And now, the southern branch of the University of California lets out a yip to let the world know that it is up and doing in the world of football."

Well up anyway. Only 19 men turned out for that first meeting. The team played on a Vermont Avenue field that was a rough combination of dirt and sawdust.

Since it was a branch of the University of California, whose athletic teams competed under the name Golden Bears, it was only logical that UCLA would begin as the Cubs. But, as Hendrik Van Leuven points out in his book, *Touchdown UCLA,* the new school's name, Southern Branch of the University of California, was shortened to SBUC. Reverse the letters and that spells CUBS.

By any name, they weren't very competitive in those early years, hardy a surprise for a team that had trouble finding the manpower to fill out the squad. It could only go uphill for the Southern Branch after its opener. Facing Manual Arts High School after less than two weeks of practice and no scrimmages, the Cubs lost, 74–0.

Playing high schools, junior colleges, freshmen and service teams under Fred W. Cozens, the coach and one-man athletic department, the Southern Branch wound up 2–6 that first season. The price of admission was 11 cents.

In 1920, the Cubs moved up in competition to take on bona fide collegiate squads like Pomona and Redlands. And didn't win a game for two years.

As a matter of fact, in 1920, the team scored in only *one* of its five games. The season finale might have been enough to fold a lesser squad. Playing Whittier, the Cubs lost, 103–0.

When the school became a four-year institution in 1924, the team felt it had outgrown the name Cubs. Still respecting its origin as a derivative of the Golden Bears, the team took the name Grizzlies.

That respect was not always returned, however, according to John Jackson, a UCLA halfback in the mid 20s.

"Three good-looking guys in nice suits came and talked with Jimmy Cline (the head coach)," Jackson said, "and watched us play. What they were looking for were good guys to transfer to Berkeley."

They had already snared one player, Gordon White. "They convinced him to go up there and get a scholarship," Jackson said. "We didn't have any scholarships. It was an attitude that we were just the little brother to them. We were the farm team."

The first signs of respectability didn't come until 1925 with the arrival of Coach William Henry Spaulding.

He didn't have much of an act to follow. After a season of Cozens, three of Harry Trotter and two of Cline, the Southern Branch was a combined 6–29–4, including 0–5–3 the previous season. So imagine the amazement when Spaulding won his first three games of 1925, half the total the school had amassed in its history.

It began with conditioning. On the very first day of training camp, Spaulding had his players run wind sprints, ten yards up and ten yards back. Over and over until their tongues were hanging out. When they were finally done, the exhausted players headed for the gymnasium, visions of a cold shower splashing in their minds. Instead, they found the team trainer, on orders from the new coach, barring the door.

"No you don't," he told the players, "Around the track once for every one of you. And if you don't like it, it's three times."

Jackson figures he lost three and one-half pounds on that first day. He could ill afford it. At full strength, Jackson only weighed 136.

Spaulding had already been a head football coach for 18 years when he took over the Grizzlies. The last three came at the University of Minnesota where he became known as the man who stopped Red Grange because of a defense he came up with to cut down the yardage of the great running back from Illinois.

Spaulding knew he was going to need to pull a few tricks out of his bag if the Southern Branch was going to become anything more than tackling fodder for the opposition.

He used them all. He ran out of the single wing and the double wing. He ran reverses and double reverses. Spaulding would have his quarterback take off as though he were going to carry the ball, then softly lay it on the ground where an end would come around and pick it up. By that point, the defense had already committed itself, leaving the end plenty of open territory.

And when the other side caught on to this trick, Spaulding came up with a new wrinkle. He would have the quarterback fake as if he were going to lay the ball down, then keep it.

On defense, Spaulding is credited with being the first West Coast coach to cut back from the conventional seven-man or six-man line to one with just five men.

Spaulding beat San Diego State, 7–0, in his first game, then followed with a 16–3 victory over La Verne and a 26–0 shutout of Pomona, a school that had beaten the Grizzlies 50–7 the season before. Spaulding went 5–3–1 his first season, 5–3 his second and 6–2–1 in his third.

People began to take notice of the young upstart school, although at USC, they still referred to the Southern Branch derisively as The Twig.

In his first season, Spaulding had both St. Mary's and Stanford on the schedule, putting the Grizzlies in the big leagues of college football. A little prematurely, as it turned out.

The Southern Branch lost to the two schools by a combined score of 110–0. St. Mary's beat the Grizzlies, 28–0, then Stanford rolled over them, 82–0.

Jackson remembers being helpless on defense against Stanford as a running back blew by him for 40 yards. He got yelled at by the team captain, who was manning the other end. "What are you doing?" demanded the captain. He soon got his answer when Stanford tried his end with equal success.

When it was over, Spaulding conceded, "This game was scheduled too early because we weren't ready."

But Spaulding was confident his team eventually would be. He never let the early setbacks mar his long-term view. In that regard, he was the perfect coach for that time and place. Slow-talking and easy going by nature, Spaulding was calm on the sidelines, even when coaching in the face of a debacle. And he was upbeat with administrators, even when charting a future course for his team through a jungle of bureaucratic red tape.

Spaulding lost his share of games, but never his sense of humor. When a Washington punter kicked a ball 60 yards through the air against his club, Spaulding, his eyes still on the ball, leaned over to an assistant and muttered, "Angels, pull in your legs."

Spaulding's low-key approach extended to the lockerroom. No fiery halftime speeches for him. No pleas to win one for the Gipper or anybody else. Spaulding believed in working on fundamentals in practice, developing a solid, imaginative game plan and letting his players take it from there.

He could be found on a fall afternoon drilling his quarterback over and over on the importance of lofting a pass. "Just pretend," he would say, "the receiver is walking on stilts."

Spaulding didn't preach hate in the lockerroom and he didn't practice it. In the 20s, Stanford regularly whipped Spaulding's teams by huge scores. But after one such game, Stanford's coach, the legendary Pop Warner, came into Spaulding's lockerroom, impressed with some plays run by the Grizzlies' quarterback, Cliff Simpson.

Warner asked Simpson if he would explain the plays to him. Simpson, shocked at the thought of passing such classified information on to the enemy, looked to Spaulding for guidance.

"This man's a gentleman," Spaulding told his quarterback. "You help him. He will use what you tell him for the rest of his life."

If anything, Spaulding might have been criticized for being too nice a man. "He was a father to the whole group," Simpson said. "He probably could have been a little tougher. He didn't have an enemy in the whole world." A rare statement indeed when referring to a football coach.

A fanatical golfer who would spend every free minute with a club in his hands, Spaulding would often play with those who had the financial resources to aid his struggling young program. And he came away with more than just a good score.

"You can raise more money on a golf course," Spaulding once said, "than you can in a pool hall."

Spaulding used his quick wit the way he used his extensive playbook, to keep the opposition guessing. Spaulding's philosophy might best be summed up in the advice he once gave Simpson, his quarterback in the late 20s and later an assistant under him. When Simpson was asked to speak at an athletic banquet, Spaulding told him, "Entertain them as long as you can, but don't tell them anymore than you have to."

With enrollment continuing to soar, Dickson knew that the Southern Branch had the potential to outgrow the original tree. So a larger home had to be found for the school.

More than 100 possible sites were submitted to the regents. Finally, the list was narrowed to five: Palos Verdes, Burbank, Pasadena, Fullerton and Westwood.

Westwood became the top choice, the legend goes, because Fullerton was too far, because the temperature was over 100 degrees the day the Burbank and Pasadena sites were inspected, and because Palos Verdes was hit with a dense fog on the morning it was considered.

Supposedly, Dickson walked onto the Westwood site, looked around and announced, "This is the place."

The choice was made official at a San Francisco meeting of the regents held on March 21, 1925.

The land, which had first been occupied by Don Maximo Alanis, a Spanish soldier, once sold for 35 cents an acre. At one point late in the 19th Century, there were plans to construct the town of Sunset on the land. Railroad tracks were even built through it, but Sunset died on the drawing board.

As the fame of the Grizzlies grew, so did the anger of the Grizzlies. Because the Southern Branch Grizzlies had taken the same name as the University of Montana Grizzlies.

Again, it was time for a name change. Again, the Southern Branch looked for a derivative of the name Golden Bears. So, in 1926, the Grizzlies became the Bruins.

Now that *other* name had to go. The University of California, Southern Branch just didn't make it. The school sounded too much like a poor stepchild.

"Charles Henry Rieber [Dean of Letters and Sciences] said we would never be a full-fledged university," Jackson recalled, "a first-class university, as long as we're a branch. On his stationary, he put University of California at Los Angeles. He got his knuckles rapped by Berkeley officials who said, 'You can't do that.' "

But he kept doing it, as did others.

"We didn't want to be just a branch of anything," former Alumni Association president and Regent John Canaday was quoted as saying in *UCLA On the Move*. "We wanted to put our roots down and grow to full stature."

The name was not only demeaning, but confusing. David Barrows, president of the main university at Berkeley, visited Los Angeles and told a taxi driver to take him to the University of California. Barrows was dropped off at Universal City.

Finally, in 1927, the school officially became UCLA.

In September of 1929, UCLA opened the doors of the four buildings on its new Westwood campus. It was a heady time for the city of Los Angeles, one million residents strong.

In *Harper's Magazine*, Sarah Comstock wrote, "If we are a nation of extremes, Los Angeles is an extreme among us." She wrote about the city's new library, the Hollywood Bowl, the tremendous weather, and referred to the city's "hurly-burly of speed, noise, light," concluding that "what Los Angeles is to excess, all our cities are to some extent."

The city had also acquired a reputation it could not shake. Wrote Bruce Bliven in *The New Republic*, "I leave it to the sociologists to say whether cranks go to California or Californians become cranks. Whatever the process, the results are wonderful." But he wondered if a "real civilization" might not someday rise in Los Angeles where "today, not many civilized persons choose to live."

In 1928, UCLA had joined the Pacific Coast Conference. But the Bruins required more by 1929. Located in one of America's most exciting cities, housed in a beautiful new campus, UCLA needed something equally fresh and captivating for its football team.

The Bruins needed tradition to establish themselves. They needed an ongoing struggle to inspire them. They needed a rivalry to define them.

They needed USC.

3

The Worst Games
1929–1938

The Trojans and Bruins had never played each other and with good reason. USC was a powerhouse, UCLA was a patsy. USC boasted All-Americans, UCLA had trouble finding any players. USC initiated an historic matchup with Notre Dame, UCLA played high schools. But Gwynn Wilson, USC's graduate manager/prophet witnessed UCLA's meteoric growth from a small teacher's college to a major university in just one decade, and sensed the inevitable—someday, UCLA would be as highly regarded as USC. And, someday, Los Angeles, the fastest growing city in America, would stop everything to watch its two heralded universities play football.

On a winter day in 1929, Wilson took the street car to UCLA's Vermont Avenue campus, just before the school moved to its current site. Wilson stopped at the office of Steve Cunningham, UCLA's graduate manager, and made an intriguing offer.

"Let's play each other in football right now," Wilson said.

Cunningham was stunned. "That's crazy, you guys are too good for us."

"Look, Steve, we're going to be the biggest thing in this town sooner or later, so why not make it sooner?"

"Everyone will think I'm crazy. You guys were national champions last year. We're not in your league."

Wilson sold him on the idea, but he still had to sell his USC superiors and the alumni.

Among some alums, "there was a certain school of thought," Wilson explained, "that said that if we don't play them, it will take them that much longer to get ready, and that it's better to keep them down as long as we can, and if we start playing them, then we're helping them. I took the position of let's start it now."

Wilson had another reason to start the rivalry. "I figured if we start playing them now," he said, "our record would be a lot better against them than if we wait another two or three years."

Wilson won the argument. In 1929, the game was on.

UCLA had suffered from a split personality in 1928. Against Pacific Coast Conference opponents, the Bruins were outscored 129–19. But they romped over their old enemies in the Southern Conference, 152–7. In early September, UCLA formally occupied Westwood, and the football team prepared for its opening contest against USC (not until 1936 did they meet toward the end of the season).

In 1929, America's hopes were high. The talkies were gaining popularity across the country, the silent stars of yesteryear fading out. Economic prosperity had defined the decade, but the stock market crash was only a month away.

Throughout the week, UCLA worked hard in practice and looked impressive, prompting one sportswriter to proclaim that the Bruins "showed a lot of fight and promise in last Saturday's scrimmage and are not likely to be slaughtered as some folks suspect. I would not be surprised if there were no score in the first half."

The Thundering Herd, fresh from its potent 1928 season, didn't display much in workouts. Howard Jones, furious with the play of some of his first stringers, made three major substitutions prior to the Bruin game. "We'll do a lot more scrimmaging before Saturday," he told his squad as they left practice on Tuesday. "I can see I have been too easy on you chaps and it's hard work for all of you from now on. There will be a lot of varsity players warming the bench Saturday."

Playing UCLA didn't mean anything in the early days—Notre

Dame was the Big Game—but Gaius Shaver, USC's talented runner, recalls his teammates were highly motivated against the Bruins. "It was the first game of the season," Shaver said, "and that's always important because it gives you an idea of what the team is going to be like."

For USC, it was going to be another Jones masterpiece. For UCLA, it was going to be more Spaulding mediocrity.

USC breezed to a 76–0 triumph, and it could have been worse. Some rivalry.

The Trojans gained 712 rushing yards, the Bruins 99. USC collected 26 first downs, UCLA, four. The Trojans ran at will. The Bruins ran in place. By halftime, it was 32–0. For the 35,000 fans in the Coliseum the suspense had ended with the coin toss.

The parade of touchdowns included all of the Trojan stars, led by quarterback Russ Saunders, one of the original models for the Tommy Trojan statue. Saunders ran 50 yards late in the first quarter to start the slaughter. Subsequent scares by Erny Pinckert, Jess Hill and Shaver put it away.

The second half provided more of the same, as Jones substituted one All-American for another. Jones wasn't running up the score without mercy. But his second, and in some cases, third stringers had plenty of talent, and were anxious to earn more playing time.

"You can't keep the score down and tell a kid to not go out there and do something," Shaver said. "When you get something like that started, you can't stop. Everybody played. When we ran up big scores, it was because everybody looked good."

UCLA, on the other hand, stuck with its starters, even when the game spiraled hopelessly out of control. Quarterback Cliff Simpson never surrendered. He just ran out of energy. He intercepted a pass with about two minutes to go, and headed downfield, trying desperately to avert a shutout. But Simpson didn't get very far. The whole USC team caught him from behind. At least, it seemed that way to him. As Simpson got up, an official leaned over and told him, "Cliff, there are only a couple of minutes to go." The way his body ached, it seemed like an hour.

The game essentially magnified the differences between the two schools. USC had stars sitting the bench. UCLA had scrubs on the field.

"I think we had eight or ten people on our whole team," Simpson said, "who could have made their squad."

Still, Simpson and other Bruins who played in the debut game believe UCLA, lacking maturity and experience, might have been too intimidated by its more established foes to offer more than token resistance.

"I'd like to play that '29 game over again," Simpson said, "just to see if we were that bad, or they were that good."

After their debut confrontation, USC and UCLA continued in opposite directions. The Trojans finished 10–2, including a 13–12 loss to Notre Dame, in which they missed both extra points.

"Howard Jones would never give the players time to practice kicking," Eddy said. "He got all wrapped up in blocking and tackling." The Trojans didn't need to convert their extra points in the Rose Bowl; they clobbered Pittsburgh 47–14.

UCLA went 4–4, routing the Pomonas and Caltechs of the world while receiving similar disrespect from its PCC foes. The year looked like a turkey. Until Montana came to town on Thanksgiving Day.

The underdog Bruins captured a 14-0 triumph, their first against a PCC opponent. Simpson, who threw a touchdown pass that day, saw it as another big step for the Bruin program. Besides winning a conference contest, the game held even greater meaning for the future. "It helped us in getting kids to come to UCLA," Simpson recalled.

The Bruins were also able to eventually recruit talented teenagers who knew they would automatically gain significant playing time in Westwood, as opposed to the likelihood of riding the Trojan bench. So, year after year, as the Bruins proved they could compete at a higher level, more and more youngsters signed up; they no longer felt they were lowering their standards.

Still, the infusion of new talent and confidence made no difference against USC in 1930. Call it *Mismatch II*, the sequel.

This time, the Jones machine rolled past the Bruins 52–0, again dominating on the ground, gaining 421 yards to UCLA's 31. Orv Mohler, the Trojan sophomore quarterback, ran for 172 yards on 20 carries while Marshall Duffield added 89 yards and three touchdowns.

All-American tackle Raymond "Tay" Brown remembers an intense

Howard Jones before the game. "He was more fired up for that game than any game I ever saw," Brown said. "I think a couple of UCLA players had made some nasty remarks he didn't like."

Somehow, in the midst of another embarrassment, the Bruins found encouragement. Johnny Jackson, who remained close to the UCLA program, summed up the sentiment in Westwood: "We felt we could do better against them each time. If we had played the third game (in 1931) it might have been different. It might have been 25 to 0."

Nobody will ever know, because in 1931, the rivalry was put on hold. Gwynn Wilson says USC realized the games had been staged prematurely, that UCLA wasn't ready to compete at that level.

But Bill Ackerman, the Bruins' graduate manager, in later years, pinned the blame on Trojan stubbornness. "After those first two games," he said, "an argument ensued as to which school would host the first game in the Coliseum. USC believed it should have preference on dates because it regarded UCLA as only a young twig off the Berkeley branch. But I think the real reason is that USC didn't want to acknowledge a young school coming up. It felt that it was challenged in a city in which the Trojans were the dominant team."

UCLA also believed the game should be held at the end of the season to give its young squad a chance to mature. Southern Cal preferred the opening date. So, before UCLA could even score, before fans had a chance to relish the new annual battle for city supremacy, it ended.

For USC, it was time to conquer distant peaks, to beat Notre Dame, to win national titles. For UCLA, it was time to regroup, to climb one small hurdle after another, to build a football factory.

Each knew that someday, when both universities were ready, the rivalry would resume.

In 1931, both schools captured a city.

USC, staging a furious comeback from a two-touchdown deficit in the fourth quarter, upset the Fighting Irish 16–14 in South Bend. Notre Dame hadn't lost in three years—26 games—since USC had beaten the Irish in 1928.

Los Angeles went berserk, as about 300,000 fans greeted their heroes in a downtown parade stretching all the way to the campus. The city hasn't seen anything like it since. Five decades later, when the Lakers held almost annual celebrations, the crowds never exceeded 100,000.

Dr. Rufus B. von KleinSmid, president of USC, felt the urge to overstate, proclaiming "there is no more depression in Los Angeles."

"We were the only thing in all Los Angeles in those days," Ray Brown said, obviously discounting the newcomers in Westwood. "We owned Los Angeles."

The team in Westwood never received a ticker-tape parade. Yet, by defeating St. Mary's 12–0 in 1931, it had reason to cheer. St. Mary's was still a force in those days. Santa Clara couldn't beat the Gaels, and neither could California.

But the victory held special meaning for another reason. St. Mary's had knocked off USC 13–7 earlier that year. For the first time, UCLA had beaten a team that had beaten USC.

"That was the making of UCLA," said star fullback Norman Duncan.

One year later, the Trojans took their talent to an even higher level, especially defensively. The 1932 national championship squad yielded only 13 points—seven to California and six to Washington. It shut out Utah, Washington State, Oregon State, Loyola, Stanford, Oregon, Notre Dame, and Pittsburgh in the Rose Bowl. Yet Brown, six decades later, still dwells on the touchdown that should never have counted.

"At Washington," he said, "the guy was out on the one-yard line, and the referee threw his arms up (to signal touchdown) and the umpire told him no, but he wouldn't change his mind. That was no touchdown."

Brown wouldn't even dismiss the other score of the year without an excuse. "Cotton Warburton," he explained, "was covering a six-foot-six end."

The Howard Jones defense was simple. It didn't require a John Madden diagram or a fancy nickname. Just hard-nosed tackling. "Whip your man, and cover your territory," Brown said. "And don't let anybody through there. We had a method that we all worked on together. We'd get our shoulder and forearm under the guy's neck, lift him up, and keep control of him."

On offense, Jones was a diehard conservative. "We had about 100 plays," halfback Nick Pappas quipped. "Off tackle, off tackle, off tackle."

Jones only passed when the defense rushed everybody to contain the run. He quick-kicked on third down, and even kicked after the opponent had just scored. This was not an uncommon practice in those days. Football then, much more than today, was a battle for field position, trench warfare.

Jones won consistently. He set the tone for USC's entire football tradition. But few people ever knew Howard Jones. Not even his players or coaches. He protected his private life like a runner carrying the ball in the last seconds of a tight game.

But Jones, for all his intensity, was no Knute Rockne. "He didn't give pep talks," quarterback Amborse Schindler said. "His forte was being precise, and knowing how to position men."

Over in Westwood, Jones' counterpart and golfing buddy Bill Spaulding also avoided fiery sermons. Cliff Simpson, who both played and later coached under Spaulding, said his laid-back demeanor in the lockerroom and on the playing field gave the wrong signal to a young, undisciplined club.

"He was too much of a gentlemen," Simpson said. "He was easy to work for and honest, but I don't think he worked the kids hard enough. When we were getting beat 76–0, he'd cheer us up. He wouldn't say, 'you guys have to play better.'"

Low-key or not, Spaulding gradually narrowed the gap between the Bruins and the Trojans. In 1932, the Bruins (6–4) finished third in the PCC and, in 1935, they won four of five in the conference, tying Berkeley and Stanford for the championship.

Their five-year apprenticeship was over.

Bring back USC.

The Great Depression affected almost everyone. Students had to scrape together whatever cash they could to survive each week. At

USC, players took jobs as janitors and groundskeepers, earning 50 cents an hour. During the summer, stars from both schools moonlighted in Hollywood as actors in football pictures. They often earned $10 a day, which was excellent money.

"The movie people were very close to us," Brown said. "A lot of them used to come out to the fraternity just to be around us. People like Douglas Fairbanks, Jr."

Players even scalped tickets for extra money. Sophomores at USC received two tickets to every game. Juniors got three, seniors four, and the captain five. "We had people in the movies who would pay us $75 a ticket," Brown said. "They were just proud to be there."

Overseas, the world headed toward war. Adolph Hitler and Benito Mussolini established fascist dictatorships. Joseph Stalin purged all his enemies to consolidate his power in communist Russia. Americans, still weary over World War I—wasn't *that* supposed to be the last war?— favored isolationism. Feelings at college campuses grew tense, and the fear of communism, even in pre-McCarthy days, often ruled over academic freedom and individual rights.

In October of 1934, UCLA's chancellor, Dr. Ernest Moore, suspended five students he charged with "using their offices to destroy the university by handing it over to an organized group of communist students." Moore, angered over protests against the ROTC and genuinely fearful of a campus insurrection, believed UCLA had become a "hotbed of communism." He charged that a campus group, the National Students League, was merely a front to promote the socialist agenda.

Sympathetic students held loud demonstrations. Robert Sproul, president of the entire University of California system, conducted an investigation, found no trace of a communist presence, and eventually reinstated the students.

Thomas Lambert, one of those suspended, was "flabbergasted and stupified" by Moore's decision. In the five or six weeks he couldn't attend school "you would reflect, and think over your whole life." Lambert recovered from the attack on his reputation, and became a college law professor in Massachusetts. He remembers a distinct difference between his alma mater and Southern Cal.

"USC was sort of a gentry school for the well-born, the well-healed," he said. "UCLA was a red-brick university; you brown-bagged your lunch."

Campus turmoil would not go away; it never does. A new class merely inherits different issues. But, as America enjoyed seven more years of peace before Pearl Harbor, there were games to be played. Rivalries to be renewed.

In late 1935, Bill Ackerman met with Willis O. Hunter, the athletic director at USC, for lunch at the Beverly Hills Hotel. Heading their agenda was how to renew the series. They decided to hold the game at the end of the season, and let USC host the first contest.

"We worked the thing out," Ackerman said. "To keep UCLA from growing was like trying to stop the sun from coming up. Also, both schools needed the money. We had wasted five years."

Plus Los Angeles needed the stage to cement its role as a major city. In one decade, L.A. had more than doubled its population—to 1,238,048—to rank fifth nationwide.

This time, Howard Jones could not assume a battle with the Bruins would be a formality, a chance to play his entire roster and establish city superiority. Jones could no longer assume anything. His once-mighty Trojans had quickly fallen from the elite. From 1934 until their 1936 game with UCLA, there was no thunder in the herd; they went 13–15–2. Perhaps Jones couldn't adapt to the rapidly changing game.

Schindler, who joined USC in 1935, blames the decline on complacency. Even arrogance. "They didn't recruit," he said. "The alumni thought they could live on Howard Jones' reputation. Howard Jones was not a man who liked to recruit. He was so involved with the precise defenses and offenses that he devoted his life to that, and relied on other people to bring him good football players."

One ex-Trojan remembers a distracted Jones in those days. "He wasn't really with it," Pappas said. "He was concerned with things at home, and they were pretty tough. His wife was an alcoholic, and he didn't even drink. We used to take trains to games, and she'd come down in the car where the kids were and say, 'Let's have a beer.' And the guys would say, 'We don't drink,' and she'd say, 'Don't worry about Howard.' When she got taken care of, he came right back."

Once he put his personal troubles behind him, Jones, like football, finally graduated from the Stone Age. No more three yards and a cloud of dust. A pass, he realized, would not violate the sanctity of the game.

Jones also hired better assistant coaches, like Hobbs Adams and Jeff Cravath. In the early days, Jones delegated little or no authority to his assistants. He often ran into the middle of a practice, and got on the ground to demonstrate a play. His assistants just watched. That wouldn't work anymore. The game was getting too complex. Too much was at stake.

In 1936, the old Trojans resurfaced. They demolished Oregon State (38–7), Oregon (26–0), and Illinois (24–6) to start the season. But Jones' team, even the revamped model, didn't possess the old personnel. Heading into the encounter with the Bruins, USC stumbled in successive weeks, losing to California (13–7) and Washington (12–0). Dreams of another title and a Rose Bowl had to be abandoned. The UCLA game would be fought for pride.

That was fine with the Bruins. After all, they had never beaten the Trojans. A win would make their season, if not decade. Rose Bowls were fantasies for another time. The Bruins rolled into the Coliseum on a negative note, losing the prior week to Washington State, 32–7. Yet, at 6–3, they weren't going to concede anything.

"We had a great workout that week," said Bruin center Sherman Chavoor. "Spirits were high. Everybody was yelling and whooping it up. Everybody was on time. There was an extra determination. Coach (Spaulding) used that old cliché, 'They put their pants on one leg at a time, just like everybody else.' He didn't give pep talks; he just gave homilies."

Spaulding was anxious to finally defeat Jones. He had withstood the five-year layoff between games, and knew there would not be that many more opportunities. As the program improved, expectations only got higher. Even back then, alumni groups often interfered, presuming jurisdiction over all football matters. Spaulding was well-liked. But could he win? And how long could the restless fans wait?

This was no longer just another game. In 1929 and 1930, Southern Cal students and fans paid as much attention to the Bruin contest as the

Oregon State or Washington games. But, in 1936, students on both campuses recognized the beginning of something special.

They held pep rallies, and started the war of pranks. At USC, the Tommy Trojan statue was splashed with blue and gold paint by Bruin invaders prompting Trojan Knights and Trojan Squires, mens' campus organizations, to stand guard over their treasured sculpture until game time. They still guard it today. Meanwhile, the letters "SC" were burned on the lawn of the main quadrangle at Westwood.

The press sensed the changing atmosphere, too. On each day of the week preceding the Thanksgiving Day encounter, the newspapers were saturated with pre-game coverage. Injuries and strategies were dissected in more detail than an FDR address. Los Angeles took a time out from everyday life to focus its collective minds on a football game.

The week began with the standard Howard Jones pronouncement. This time, annoyed with the team's lackluster effort against the Huskies, Jones abandoned his two-team concept where he divided his players according to their offensive and defensive skills, in favor of putting the best eleven athletes on the field. In those days, substitutions were restricted, so teams frequently got caught with their best players on the bench. He wanted to shake things up, and that meant benching seniors who expected to play.

Spaulding, to contain the Trojan running attack, planned to install a six-man line. Teams normally went with seven-man up front, but that would have meant if a USC halfback got past the first wall of defense, there would only be four players with a chance to stop him.

"We never went into a game with only one defense," Simpson said. "We always had to be prepared for what they would do."

Game day arrived, and about 85,000 fans packed into the Coliseum—twice as many as had shown up at the last meeting in 1930—to see the Bruins (6–3) try to pull the upset against the Trojans (4–2–1). Before, only Notre Dame had generated such interest.

Both teams did little but punt in the first quarter. And then, in the second quarter, there was The Fumble. Ambrose Schindler will never forget it.

"Someone got a hold of me," said the USC quarterback, "and as I tried to pull loose, someone else hit me and the ball got away."

1888 team.

"Gloomy Gus" Henderson got his nickname because he was always pessimistic about his team's chances. He was USC's first successful head coach.

Tackle Duke Morrison quit college
football to launch his acting career. He
became better known as John Wayne.

Jeff Cravath, who coached USC from 1942-1950, was known for his strict and long practices. He once ordered the unthinkable—a practice on the day after a loss to Navy.

Forced into action because of injuries to USC's three top quarterbacks, fourth-stringer Dean Schneider carried the Trojans to a 21-7 victory over the Bruins in 1949.

Al Carmichael and Jim Sears combined to beat UCLA 14-12 in the classic 1952 match-up between undefeated powers. Carmichael's lateral to Sears for a 65-yard touchdown is one of the most famous plays in the rivalry's history.

Howard Jones, who coached USC from 1925 until his death in 1941, led the Trojans to three national championships. His legendary battles with Knute Rockne's Notre Dame put USC on the college football map.

Future NFL star and broadcaster Frank Gifford never played
a big role in the rivalry. He was usually injured.

An unknown assistant named John McKay arrived in 1960, and within two years returned the Trojans to the prominence of Howard Jones' days. In 16 years, McKay led the Trojans to four national titles.

Willie Brown never gained the accolades of his eventual successors, but he was the first outstanding tailback in the McKay era.

After backing up Mike Rae in the 1972 national championship season, quarterback Pat Haden led the Trojans to Rose Bowl appearances in 1974 and 1975.

O.J. Simpson gained plenty of accolades—and a Heisman Trophy. His 64-yard touchdown run to win the 1967 Bruin game, 21-20, remains one of the greatest plays in college football history.

Haden's favorite receiver was his best friend, J.K. McKay, the coach's son. McKay made numerous clutch receptions.

In one year, quarterback Vince Evans went from goat to godsend. After an awful performance in the 1975 Bruin game, Evans rebounded to lead the Trojans to an 11-1 season in 1976, including a Rose Bowl triumph over Michigan.

Replacing a legend wasn't easy, but John Robinson quickly won acceptance from Trojan fans. He brought a unique brand of enthusiasm to USC.

With good speed and punishing power, Ricky Bell found his place in the great tradition of USC tailbacks.

Rodney Peete chose USC over a pass-oriented school to win conference championships, and that's what he did in leading the Trojans to two Rose Bowls, in 1988 and 1989.

Todd Marinovich was supposed to set all kinds of career passing records at USC, but after two controversial years, he jumped to the pros, becoming the top draft choice of the Los Angeles Raiders.

UCLA's Chavoor, who had hyperextended his elbow earlier in the game but refused to come out, recovered the ball at the Trojan 40. In ten plays, capped by a two-yard plunge by Billy Bob Williams, UCLA took a 7–0 lead. It took seven years, but UCLA had finally scored against USC.

"I broke my nose trying to stop Williams," added Schindler, "and I probably wouldn't have done that but I was trying my best to stop what I had caused."

Schindler had more chances to atone. He engineered a 13-play drive in the third quarter to even the score. Jimmy Jones ran it in from the four-yard line.

And, as USC kept penetrating Bruin territory throughout the second half, it looked like Jones would maintain his mastery over Spaulding. Jones inserted a combination of seniors and sophomores in the second half, and they played much better than the original lineup.

"That 1936 team (of seniors) just wasn't that great," Schindler said. "I don't how many of them would have been good enough to play the next few years."

But the Trojans contracted fumbleitis down the stretch, losing the ball five times in all. They were also intercepted three times by UCLA's Merle Harris.

The game ended in a 7–7 tie. The yards gained were a lot closer this time. USC had 170 yards to UCLA's 139, and held the first-down edge, 9–8.

"We kept using this crossing pass," Schindler added, "but each time, we completed it to their safeties. The safety just stayed right in that zone every time. Howard Jones never let us use it again."

USC took the tie as a loss.

"I suppose those guys across the hall will be claiming one of those moral victories," said a disgusted Trojan. That was the best USC call of the day.

"It was a grand game," Spaulding said. "This is one of the happiest moments of my life. I've waited six long years to get another crack at my good friend, Howard Jones, at something besides golf and bridge. It didn't look like any 52-0 rout today."

As the final gun sounded, there was a mad scramble for the football. Most of the players on both teams swarmed on the field, and

it looked like there might be trouble. But referee Tom Louttit escaped with the ball.

After the game, officials from both schools decided to have the ball bronzed and made into a trophy to be presented each year to the winning team. This was finally a rivalry.

Football was changing on and off the field. The Bruins, frustrated with constantly losing superior athletes to their cross-town rivals, scored a coup with a kid from Lincoln Heights in Los Angeles, a middle-class white neighborhood. His name was Kenny Washington.

He could run. He could throw. He could box. He was an athlete Westwood had never seen before. He was also black.

According to his teammate, Woodrow Strode, who is also black, Washington was never seriously pursued by USC because of his skin color. "USC didn't rush black players," Strode said. "It was this superiority attitude. Back in those days, if you were black, you had to be twice as good to beat the white boy out."

Norman Borisoff, editor of the *Daily Bruin* in 1938, remembers one game in particular.

"When they played SMU," Borisoff said, "it seemed like every time he had the ball, eleven guys would converge on him, hitting him from every angle. It was aggravated assault, like watching the Rodney King tape. Was it a football game or was it a slaughter? I don't know how Washington survived. It was worse than watching a bullfight. And maybe the worst thing was that it was just accepted in those days. More than 50 years later, I still have the memory of that game. It made you sick to your stomach to watch."

Kenny Washington was that good. And opponents, especially ones with racist tendencies, resorted to any tactics to stop him.

Strode remembers an incident in a Washington State game. "They called him a nigger out there," he said. "He's running with the ball 90 percent of the time, and they wanted to break his concentration. You see, by calling you a nigger, that was supposed to upset you. When Kenny told us, I wanted to know who it was. I would always punch the guys out. I was like a hit squad."

Strode even accepted assignments on his own team. A tackle named Slats Wyrick, a kid from Oklahoma, wouldn't play with Strode.

According to Strode, Wyrick told him "I can't play next to a nigger because my folks would disown me."

A few of Strode's teammates told him Wyrick would punch him out if they got on the field together. Spaulding knew there was only one solution.

"He sent me right out there in front of Wyrick," Strode said. "On the first play, Wyrick called me 'a black son-of-a-bitch,' and I nailed him. Spaulding did that purposely cause Slats had no respect for Negroes. The bottom line was that he didn't have any guts to fight." Respect was earned, and the two became friends.

Generally, though, Strode experienced few racial troubles at UCLA. "Spaulding didn't get contaminated," he said. "We thought we were free, like everybody else. We thought this was normal. I really didn't find out about racism till later in life. I'm glad I didn't know then, because to play football, you cannot feel inferior."

In Washington's debut performance against Oregon in 1937, he sprinted 57 yards for a touchdown the second time he touched the ball. His key interception gave the Bruins a tie against Oregon State, and in the Missouri game, he intercepted a pass, raced down the sidelines, and lateralled to Johnny Ryland who scored. Against Southern Methodist, Washington hit Strode for a 45–yard touchdown. As a sophomore, he was already the most exciting player in Los Angeles, if not all of college football. Fans paid just to watch him. His uniform, number 13, was the first to be retired by the university.

The Trojans had their own gallery of stars—Ambrose Schindler, Grenville Lansdell, Don McNeil, Bob Hoffman. USC had rediscovered how to recruit, and their squads of the late 1930s rank up with the best the school has produced. Mediocrity wasn't tolerated at USC; failing to make it to the Rose Bowl was tantamount to disaster and the Trojans hadn't visited Pasadena since 1933.

But the Rose Bowl would have to wait. The 1937 USC squad, for all its talent, was raw, and couldn't get by California, Stanford, Washington and Notre Dame. The team entered the Bruin game with one prime motivation—to avenge the 1936 tie.

Robert McNeish, who joined the coaching staff in 1934, recalls another incentive. "The big thing," he said, "from our standpoint of coaching was: 'You're not going to be the first team to lose to UCLA, are you?' Everyone knew it was going to happen someday. You just didn't want it to happen while any of us were there playing or coaching."

There was plenty of pressure on Spaulding as well because the Bruins, despite the presence of Washington, were just 2–5–1 going into the USC game. Bruin alumni, after calling the 1937 season "disastrous," suggested that a committee be formed to probe into the coaching situation. The alumni praised the editorial of *Daily Bruin* managing editor Bob Reeder, who asked "why the Bruins played like champs at one time and dubs another." Spaulding had raised everyone's hopes, and now he was paying dearly for dashing them. Even an impressive 13–0 win over highly-regarded Missouri the week before the USC game wasn't enough.

For the Trojans, Spaulding would be without the services of Harris, the defensive hero in the 1936 USC game. The Bruins knew victory depended on their chances of shaking Washington and receiver Hal Hirshon loose off the weak side of the Trojan line. The week before against USC, Notre Dame's Mario Tonelli had streaked 70 yards to break up a tight game, paving the way to a 13-6 Irish triumph. UCLA needed a big game from Kenny Washington.

How about any game from Washington? According to Strode, Washington complained his ribs hurt so badly he wasn't sure he could play. He had taken a lot of punishment. "After every game," Strode said, "he would have to go to the Hollywood Hospital, and they would give him glucose to get the energy back so he could play the next week. We used to get jealous because he was there with the beautiful nurses."

USC (3-4-2) prepared for a healthy Washington. But Jones wasn't going to change course completely because of one player, whatever his credentials. "Rushing the passer in our day was of secondary importance," McNeish said. "The run was always the first thing, and even when it was obvious it was going to be a pass, the run was first considered."

Jones again looked like a genius. With nine minutes to go, USC held a 19-0 lead. It looked like game, set and match to the Trojans.

Washington displayed none of his normal effectiveness. In 51 minutes, UCLA had a measly 25 yards rushing and 46 passing. The Bruins had four first downs, none in the third quarter. And only once had they penetrated Trojan territory. UCLA seemed headed back to the days of the Southern Branch. Maybe the rivalry had been renewed too quickly.

USC sophomore quarterback Grenville Lansdell had emerged as the game's star with two touchdowns on the ground and one through the air. Lansdell, who had replaced an injured Schindler a few weeks earlier, entered UCLA territory as if he possessed a search warrant. The Bruins, whose defense was vulnerable all year, graciously got out of Landsell's path.

McNeish felt safe for another year. He was confident he would not be a member of the first Trojan team to lose to UCLA.

Schindler also figured it over. "We were trampling them," he said. "I realized I should go and get dressed. I started going through the tunnel and something said to me, 'Stick around.' Some voice told me to stay. I went back to take a seat on the bench. And in a few minutes . . ."

A legend was born. A stadium was stunned.

It started with a poor snap from USC's Don McNeil which hit fullback Roy Engle on the head, and was recovered by Bruin tackle Larry Murdock on the Trojan 44-yard line. So what? Surely this play would figure as one forgettable footnote in a day of USC domination. After all, Washington was four out of seven for 35 yards, not the kind of numbers to scare Whittier College. Spaulding had even replaced Washington briefly in the third quarter.

Hirshon tried a pass which was incomplete. But on the next play, Washington, faded back into his own territory and threw a spiral to the USC 10-yard line. Hirshon battled Trojan defender Joe Shell for the ball. Hirshon won. He scored. UCLA converted the extra point, and it was 19–7.

The Trojans didn't appear fazed by the sudden score. They dared UCLA to do it again. *They chose to kick off.*

Walt Schell returned the kick to UCLA's 28-yard line. Darkness was slowly covering the Coliseum, and, for the Bruins, defeat didn't seem far behind.

Washington took the snap, and quickly backpedaled to avoid the dangerous Trojan defense. Stepping up to his own 15-yard line, he spotted Hirshon deep, deep downfield. Washington let rip a desperation throw. Hirshon was too far away. Lansdell, covering one-on-one, gave up.

"In the dressing room after the game," McNeish recalled, "Granny bent over and asked me to kick him in the fanny. He told me, 'I didn't think anybody could throw it that far.'"

Nobody did. The ball arrived in Hirshon's hands between the Trojan 25 and 20-yard lines. It travelled a remarkable 61 yards in the air. Hirshon scored easily.

USC 19, UCLA 13.

"In the winking of an eye, black lightning struck the desolate scene," The *Los Angeles Times* would later report, referring to Kenny Washington. Kenny Washington was black lightning.

This time, Jones didn't kick off. Enough was enough. But the Bruins, sensing their greatest comeback in their brief history, forced USC to punt and took over on their 43.

Methodically, they moved. A Washington run to the Trojan 40. To the 31, the 24. First down at the 14-yard line.

First down: nothing. Second down: a couple. Third down: Hirshon from the tailback position threw to Washington coming out of the backfield. Washington was open. The ball was short.

"My pass was lousy," Hirshon said later. "I guess I just ran out of steam."

On fourth down from the 16, with just over a minute to play, Washington rolled out and spotted Strode on a hooking pattern. Strode turned around at the four-yard line. The ball arrived and dropped into his hands. And then . . . to the ground.

"Kenny would throw that ball so hard that if I didn't get it, nobody would," Strode said. "And as I made my turn, I was halfway around when it went right through me. It was too fast. If he had hesitated, I would have been in front. I guess it wasn't supposed to be. If we had won that game, there would have been statues to everybody at the Coliseum."

USC survived. Jones, who spent the last few minutes parading up and down the sidelines, knew what he had just been through. "We had to work all afternoon for our 19 points," Jones said, "and then they almost took it away in a few minutes. Yes, I suppose I'll find several new gray hairs when I get around to looking at myself in the mirror."

Spaulding, who some say saved his job that day because of the spirited comeback, tried to congratulate Jones after the game. He was met by a guard in front of the Trojan lockerroom who said the team was electing a new captain for next season.

Spaulding cracked: "Come on out, Howard, we've stopped throwing passes."

The Bruins, still inspired by their heroics in the USC game, started the 1938 season with a 27–3 triumph over Iowa. And, after a few midseason setbacks, they entered the Trojan duel at 5–3 with two shutouts in the last three games—6–0 over Stanford and 21–0 over Washington State.

The Trojans were 6–2. Sandwiched between a disappointing opening 19–7 loss to Alabama and a 7–6 defeat by Washington, they had rolled to six straight victories, holding opponents each time to seven points or less.

Now *this* was a Howard Jones team. Landsell was back, and Schindler was healthy again, although strong blocking back Bob Hoffman would have to sit out the Bruin game because of injuries. The highly-regarded recruiting class of freshmen who entered in 1936 had matured.

Before the game, it became known that this would be Spaulding's last game before taking over the job of athletic director. The stakes were immediately raised.

For USC, a win meant an excellent chance at the Rose Bowl. The Trojans would tie California for the conference title, but had defeated the Bears 13–7 earlier in the season. That would probably be the deciding factor if they could beat the Bruins.

For UCLA, a win meant Bill Spaulding's last chance against Howard Jones. As former Big Ten rivals, Spaulding had beaten Jones only once, when Spaulding coached Minnesota and Jones commanded Iowa. But at UCLA, Spaulding was 0–3–1.

The conventional wisdom was that Spaulding resigned. Simpson remembers it differently. "They forced him out," he said. "No question about it. They called him in and told him to resign."

At practice, Spaulding pushed his team harder than ever. "Whatever you do, hang on to the ball," he yelled. He didn't want to fumble his last chance.

On game day, USC made the first mistakes—two fumbles, one of which led to a UCLA touchdown, Washington to Strode from ten yards. The Bruins carried their 7–0 lead to the midway point of the second quarter.

Jones, who wouldn't tolerate subpar play for long, substituted nine reserves in the second quarter, and it made a difference. USC's Jimmy Jones broke loose on a 50-yard run to the UCLA two. From there, Jack Banta bounced over left tackle for the touchdown. A few minutes later, "Antelope Al" Krueger intercepted a short Washington pass and went 52 yards for a touchdown. The Trojans took a 13–7 halftime lead.

The second half was no contest. USC added nine points in the third quarter, and 20 more in the fourth.

Final: USC 42, UCLA 7.

"When the second half started," Jones said, "I sent in my first bunch again and they realized that they'd have to play football or give way to the second team again."

Lansdell gained 55 yards on 13 carries to lead USC. Washington had 36 yards in 15 carries for the Bruins. In total yards, USC outgained UCLA, 287 to 64.

USC went on to defeat Notre Dame the next week, 13–0, and captured the Rose Bowl from Duke, 7–3. Duke had not given up a point all year.

To finish out its season, UCLA defeated the Honolulu Town Team, 46–0, and the University of Hawaii, 32–7. There would be other big wins ahead, but they would come without Spaulding at the helm.

In 14 years, Spaulding had gathered a collection of rejects, and made them respectable. He beat St. Mary's, Stanford, Cal, all the challenges the Bruins couldn't pass in those first bleak years. A few breaks in the other direction—if Strode catches that ball, if Hirshon completes that pass, if . . . —and Bill Spaulding might have landed on a pedestal like Howard Jones.

But Bill Spaulding never beat USC.

4

The War Games
1939–1948

He was Bo before Bo.

He was a Bruin before he was a Dodger.

And he was a football star before he was a baseball legend.

Mention Jackie Robinson and all sorts of images appear: the pioneering days at Ebbets Field in the 1940s, the memorable Brooklyn Dodger victories of the 50s and the civil rights struggles of the 60s.

But before all that, Robinson was a Bruin. And a four-sport letterman who set new levels of athletic achievements. Robinson was the division's leading scorer as a member of the UCLA basketball team, the NCAA broad jump champion on the track team, an infielder on the baseball team and a star halfback on the football team.

Bo plays one sport at a time. Robinson would play two sports in a single day. One day while still in junior college, Robinson competed in the board jump, bounced out of the pit with a new record, leaped into the car of a friend and headed for the baseball diamond, changing his clothes on the move like Clark Kent heading into an alley.

"Those were good years," said Ray Bartlett, a close friend of Robinson and a fellow Bruin.

They were a lot more pleasant than the years of racial confrontation ahead, but Robinson was no wide-eyed innocent even then. He grew up with segregation in Pasadena and he didn't like it any more than he would in later years. Black children were only allowed in the public swimming pool one day a week and were limited to the balcony in theaters.

In his book *Goal Dust,* Woody Strode remembers a story Robinson told about being a kid in Pasadena. "I was out in front of the Pepper Street house," Robinson said, "sweeping up the sidewalk when a little neighborhood girl shouted at me, "Nigger! Nigger! Nigger!

"I was old enough to know how to answer that. My older brother, Frank, told me that, in the South, the most insulting name you can call a white person is "Cracker." This is what I called her.

"Her father stormed out of the house to confront me. I don't remember who threw the first stone, but the father and I had a pretty good stone-throwing fight going until the girl's mother came out and made him go back into the house."

Race was a motivating factor in Robinson picking UCLA over USC. "We figured we'd get a break," said Bartlett. "We felt if we played at USC, we'd probably sit on the bench because of racism."

Robinson had already demonstrated his football ability before arriving at Westwood. After attending Muir Technical High School, he went to Pasadena City College where he starred on the undefeated 1937 football team.

Describing the season opener that year against Loyola, the *Pasadena Chronicle* reported, "As the first half drew to a close, Jackie Robinson intercepted a desperate Loyola pass on his own 25 and eluded the entire Loyola team to chalk up the Pasadena TD."

Bill Ackerman, the UCLA athletic director at the time, told the *Daily Bruin,* "While Jackie was still at Pasadena, [Bruin football coach] Babe Horrell and I went out to the Rose Bowl to see him play. We stayed for about three quarters of the game. While we were there, he scored two or three touchdowns on 50 or 60-yard runs. When we left, we turned on the car radio and he scored an [85-yard] touchdown before we got home. We decided then that he was good enough for us to go out and get him."

Robinson played football for UCLA in both 1939 and 1940. He and

Bartlett felt they had truly become part of the team after an incident in Palo Alto prior to a game against Stanford in their first season.

The whole team was eating in a restaurant when the manager walked up to Robinson, Bartlett and the other black players. "I'm sorry," he said, "but *you* can't eat in here."

The blacks got up and walked out, hurt and angered. There was silence in the room for a moment. Then, one by one, the other players stood and looked at each other. One player picked up a glass of water and slowly poured it over his food. Then another. And another. When they had sufficiently destroyed their meal, the team marched out en masse.

From then on, the blacks had no doubt they were part of the team. And the pregame meal. "Either we would eat with the team," Bartlett said, "or they wouldn't eat there."

Robinson might have gained the support of his teammates, but he still had to battle the opposition. When the Bruins played schools like Texas A&M and SMU, Robinson found himself the main target. The racial insults were one thing. The pileups were another. When Robinson would be tackled and several other players would leap on, the opportunity would be used to pummel the helpless Robinson underneath the mass of bodies, beyond the view of the officials. "The game itself was rough enough without that stuff," Bartlett said.

The constant punishment may have been the key to steering Robinson away from football and into a baseball career. "I don't think he liked getting hurt," Bartlett said. "I don't think he liked the sight of blood."

UCLA nursing student Rachael Isum, who would later become Mrs. Jackie Robinson, met her future husband at the school. He was the campus hero, but she wasn't convinced the UCLA student body was that much more liberal than others. "I just think they made exceptions for stars," she said. "Many were not supportive or even aware of the plight of minorities. He [Jackie] was just so outstanding, he enjoyed their support. But if he had met these same people off campus in a social situation, I don't know that they wouldn't have treated him badly."

With Robinson and Kenny Washington, UCLA possessed the two

most dangerous weapons in college football. But were they enough ammunition to take the Bruins to Pasadena on New Year's Day?

Entering the 1939 USC game, UCLA was undefeated. Only two ties—a 14–14 deadlock with Stanford and 0–0 with Santa Clara—tarnished Horrell's debut season. He was already a hit on campus. Strode remembers Horrell as "high class, cultured and civilized. He always dressed right. He always talked right." But his biggest selling point was that he won.

The Bruins got their victories on the ground, averaging around 204 yards rushing. A lot of those came from Robinson, who played halfback and functioned as the man in motion. Yet defenses had to be constantly wary of Washington's arm. Howard Jones would never forget the near miracle of 1937.

Still, despite all the success, UCLA was the underdog again to another Jones juggernaut. The highly-touted USC freshmen of 1936—Schindler, Hoffman, Lansdell—had reached maturity as seniors. After an opening-game 7–7 tie with Oregon, the Trojans recorded seven straight victories, outscoring the opposition 160–26 to revive memories of the 1932 national champions who gave up a total of only 13 points.

The USC offense wasn't too shabby either, ranking second in the nation with an average of 320 yards per game.

Finally, the UCLA-USC matchup, a full decade after its inception, signified more than just a battle for city supremacy. For the first time, the Pacific Coast Conference title and the Rose Bowl were at stake, as was the opportunity for an unbeaten season and the possibility of a national title. For the Trojans, a tie would be enough to guarantee a return trip to Pasadena. The Bruins had to win.

Before the game even started, Jones had a serious problem to deal with, and it had nothing to do with unstoppable halfbacks or an impenetrable defense. All-American guard Harry Smith, fellow guard Ben Sohn, halfback Roy Engle, quarterback Ambrose Schindler and halfback Bob Robertson all caught the flu bug in the week before the UCLA game.

"We worked out on a high, wind-swept hill at a high school in Provo, Utah," Schindler said. "We should have been bundled up. We were goofing off and not taking care of ourselves. I had double vision throughout the whole game."

The flu bug wasn't the only thing terrorizing Jones. There was also Jackie Robinson. The Bruins frequently used Robinson in their single-wing attack. To adjust, coaches moved their defensive ends inside to clog up the middle.

Jones employed a different, far more daring strategy. He shifted his line to the outside, leaving a huge hole in the middle. Jones was gambling that Horrell wouldn't notice. "Jones turned around to us," Schindler recalled, "smiled and said, 'I don't think they'll ever find this hole.' They probably didn't have a play to hit that hole because that hole was normally jammed up tight."

How big was this game? A crowd of 103,303, still a record for the rivalry, jammed the Coliseum to find out which team would prove to be the greatest. "I had never played in front of a crowd like that," Bartlett said. "It was at a fever pitch."

From the start, neither side approached greatness. The Trojans put together the first serious drive, moving to the Bruin 11-yard line in the first quarter. But then Grenville Lansdell, bothered by a sore shoulder, fumbled at the two when tackled by Robinson and Ned Mathews. Strode recovered. And that, as it turned out, would be the only serious USC threat of the day.

UCLA couldn't do much better. Finally, late in the game, the Bruins, starting at their own 20, generated the kind of drive they had been struggling to put together all afternoon.

Robinson went around right end for 13 yards, slipping away from half a dozen Trojan defenders. Washington went for nine more. Washington passed to Don MacPherson, the ball reaching the USC 38.

Onward the Bruins moved, all the way to the Trojan three-yard line. First and goal and the Rose Bowl to go. Schindler and his fellow seniors saw their careers ending in disaster.

"We were all thinking they were going to score," Schindler said. "I've never been so agonized in my life. We used to have a saying, 'Hold your left one [testicle].' We were all literally holding the left one for luck and we needed it."

On first down, Kenny Washington was stopped for no gain. On

second down, 200-pound Leo Cantor got the call on a running play that had been successful all season. But this time, Cantor was tackled at the two by Bob Hoffman.

Cantor got the call again on third down, but Ben Sohn busted through the line and nailed the UCLA back for a three-yard loss. "We pulled a guard," Mathews, the quarterback, said, "and somebody forgot to block Ben Sohn."

Fourth and goal from the five. Mathews, who called the plays, had a decision—go for three or six? Today, there would be no choice. But in 1939, a field goal was far from automatic, even at close range.

Mathews entered the huddle. The noise in the Coliseum was deafening, the pressure almost unbearable. College football being what it was in Los Angeles in those days, especially between these two schools, success or failure at this moment might be carried for a lifetime.

Mathews didn't want to call this play on his own. He polled his teammates, but they were divided. Since play substitutions were restricted in that era, there was no help from the sidelines. It was Mathews' decision to make. Alone.

He went for six.

"We had beaten Washington, 24–7, the week before," MacPherson said, "and we missed all our points after. We would have hated to lose the USC game by another bad kick." To MacPherson, a tie with the Trojans was a loss.

Mathews called a pass play. He figured it would be too tough to gain five yards on the ground against the imposing USC line.

MacPherson wanted the ball. "I told Ned that I thought I'd be open," he said."Their backfield has a tendency to rotate to cover the man in motion. They had a big area to cover, so that's why I thought I'd be open."

But realizing the moment of opportunity would be brief, MacPherson tried to give some last-second advice to Washington, who would throw the ball from his tailback position.

"I'm too damn conservative," MacPherson said. "I wanted to stick my head in the huddle to yell to Kenny to throw it fast, but I was afraid I'd tip it off. So I just yelled, 'Throw it fast.' But he didn't hear me."

Robinson went in motion. Washington rolled out to avoid the USC rush and spotted MacPherson heading toward the right corner of the end zone. MacPherson was open. Washington cocked his arm and fired.

The Rose Bowl invitation hung in the air. Seemingly forever.

Until Bob Robertson shoved it beyond reach of the Bruins. He batted the pass to the ground. UCLA was denied again.

"Dammit, there was the Rose Bowl headed for my fingertips," MacPherson said. "I've played it over and over in my mind, and I've always caught it."

Not in Robertson's mind. "The cardinal sin is to let the guy behind you," Robertson said. "But, since they were so far downfield, I could play up. When the ball came, I saw a 100-yard return for a touchdown, but I got scared. I knew a tie would send us to the Rose Bowl. And if I had tried to catch it, I might have missed."

Afterwards, the Bruins were criticized for not attempting the field goal. "Maybe they thought they'd score no matter what they called," said Horrell of his players. "Anything Mathews did was good enough for me. The game is over. It makes little difference, don't you think?"

To the players, it will always make a difference. But Mathews doesn't question his call.

"The only thing I would second guess on," he said, "is that we didn't take time out."

Although UCLA lost the game, Bartlett felt the Bruins still won something important that afternoon.

"That team is the one that turned things around for the school," he said. "That's sometimes forgotten. That team gave [UCLA] respect."

USC, based on two ties to UCLA's four, went on to the Rose Bowl and defeated Tennessee, 14–0. Schindler was a hero that day with a touchdown pass in a game many think the Bruins should have played. "If they had given Kenny Washington the ball four times in a row," one ex-Trojan said, "they would have scored."

Some said the same thing about Jackie Robinson. A year later, the Bruins gave the ball to Robinson an awful lot. It didn't take a coaching genius to figure that out. Kenny Washington was gone. So was Strode.

And so was any chance UCLA had of being a decent club.

Robinson did his best, but, at times, he was a one-man team. He led the Bruins in rushing with 383 yards and 3.2-yard average, in total offense with 827 yards, in scoring with 36 points, in punt returns with a 21-yard average, and even in *passing* with 43 completions along with 444 yards gained through the air and two touchdowns.

But all the numbers didn't make up for the frustration. Take the season opener, for example. Facing SMU, Robinson returned a punt 87 yards for an electrifying touchdown. Great start. No finish. The Bruins couldn't generate any more offense and wound up losing, 9–6.

They lost a lot that season, but things weren't much better across town where the Howard Jones era was winding to a close. By the time UCLA and USC met near the end of the 1940 season, the only similarities from the memorable clash of a year earlier were the uniforms. The two teams had finished a combined 14–0–6 in 1939. In 1940, they would wind up 4–13–2.

The Bruins came into the game 1–8, having only beaten Washington State, 34–26. And to do that, UCLA had to come back after trailing 20–6 at the half.

Neither team had much of an offense. USC averaged 7.7 points a game, UCLA 7.4.

The Trojans entered the Coliseum that day 2–3–2. There was no national title at stake, no Rose Bowl, no conference championship.

But try telling that to the 70,000 fans was came out anyway. In the days before the Dodgers, the Lakers and the Kings, college football, in good years and bad, was king in L.A.

And so was the Trojans' Bob Robertson for the second season in a row. In the 1939 UCLA game, his heroics came on defense when he batted away Kenny Washington's last-ditch pass. In 1940, Robertson, the team's leading ground gainer with 667 yards, became the star on offense against the Bruins. The Trojans attempted just four passes and failed to complete a single one. No matter. USC rushed for 407 yards Robertson getting 170 of those and a touchdown. He also had a 60-yard kickoff return as the Trojans, who had previously failed to score more than 14 points in a game, doubled that with a 28–12 win.

The game marked the final appearance for two memorable figures in the rivalry. Robinson, after gaining just 56 yards on 13 carries that day, was off to Hawaii for a one-year stint with the Honolulu Bears pro football team before heading for the army and then on to his historic role, cracking the color barrier in major-league baseball and opening up the eyes and minds of a nation long overdue for the era of civil rights. Gone, too, from the scene would be Howard Jones. After 16 seasons at USC, seasons in which the school became a national powerhouse, Jones would follow the 1940 UCLA game with one more, a 10–6 loss to Notre Dame. Seven months later, he would be dead, the victim of a heart attack at 55.

The 1940s marked a new era in Los Angeles. The Arroyo Seco Parkway opened in December of 1940. Reducing the drive from Pasadena to downtown L.A. to 12 minutes, the six-mile stretch was called the "miracle boulevard." It was the first of what would later be called freeways.

Things were also changing in collegiate football. Over in Westwood, Horrell was attempting to install the T formation in the Bruin attack, allowing the quarterback to hunch over the center for the snap.

At USC, Justin (Sam) Barry was attempting an even bigger switch, taking over the coaching duties from the already legendary Howard Jones. Barry was no novice at coaching. He had been an effective assistant under Jones and a successful basketball and baseball coach.

But working under Jones was one thing. Following him was quite another. Especially without much talent to support him. Only Robertson's ballcarrying ability kept the Trojans in many of their games. But not even Robertson could keep the Trojans from losing six of their eight games prior to the UCLA showdown.

The Bruins were as inconsistent as their new offense, going 4–5 before meeting USC. But UCLA was a team on the rise. The new offense would eventually shake out the bugs and kick into high gear. And so would a talented young quarterback who, like his offense, had limited success in 1941, but an unlimited future. His name was Bob Waterfield.

So for the second season in a row, the Trojans and Bruins met while muddled in mediocrity. But again the fans would not be discouraged, 60,000 of them coming to the Coliseum that afternoon.

"There probably is no city in the nation," Paul Zimmerman wrote in the *Los Angeles Times,* "where football commands so much interest.

Even in these humdrum years like the last two, the fans refuse to stay away from these contests."

After a scoreless first half, Horrell decided to scrap his QT formation (a modified T with a wing) and go back to the single wing, a formation he felt more comfortable with.

That left USC exceedingly uncomfortable. With the Trojan linemen forced to stand almost erect to spot which formation UCLA was breaking out of the huddle with, the Bruins had gained both the physical and psychological edge. And quickly thereafter, the lead.

UCLA put together a 60-yard drive, culminating in an eight-yard run into the end zone by Vic Smith. Ken Snelling added the extra point. But, before the period had ended, USC answered with a scoring drive of its own, 63 yards in length, with Robertson going over from the half-yard line. Bob Jones' conversion kick tied the game. And that's the way it ended.

But just barely. The Trojans drove down to the Bruin 10-yard line in the closing seconds. On the final play of the game, Bob Musick threw a pass to Rick Heywood, standing on the one-yard line. It's a USC win if he catches it because he would have been able to fall into the end zone. It was nearly a USC win anyway even though UCLA's Ted Forbes intercepted the ball. Because Forbes' momentum carried *him* into the end zone. Trying to battle his way out, Forbes fumbled, the ball bouncing out of the end zone back onto the field where a fellow Bruin recovered.

If Forbes hadn't fumbled, USC probably would have won on a safety.

An era ended that day. The 7–7 tie was played on the afternoon of Dec. 6, 1941.

Even as the final gun sounded, guns were loaded with far more deadly intentions in the Pacific where Japanese warships were steaming toward Pearl Harbor. The attack that would reverberate through American history was about 18 hours away.

Life on campus, like life everywhere else in the country, underwent a radical change with the onset of World War II. There were victory gardens on campus, blood drives, bond rallies and a scarcity of cars due to gas rationing. Library books were moved into bomb-proof vaults.

"I can recall one class that had just three students and two teachers," said UCLA botany professor Charles A. Schroeder. "Many of the male students were either in training or in the service."

Because of a nationwide paper shortage, students were not allowed to destroy the cards they used in halftime stunts. Military training programs were set up at both USC and UCLA, and fraternity and sorority houses became military barracks.

In *UCLA On the Move*, Everett Hayes, then managing editor of the *Daily Bruin*, remembers keeping up with the 1942 UCLA-USC game while on a minesweeper somewhere in the Pacific. The ship's radio was broken, but Hayes, ever the faithful Bruin fan, overcame that problem by contacting someone on a nearby ship who was able "to send a play-by-play report on the blinker searchlight."

A total of 151 men and women from UCLA were reported killed in action. Among them was Charles Pike, an end on the football team who was killed in Germany, and cheerleader Hitoshi Yonemura, who died fighting in Italy.

When the U.S. government began the Manhattan Project in New Mexico to secretly build the first atomic bomb, UCLA, under the code name Project 36, was entrusted with the job of buying and delivering much of the crucial equipment needed. University professors engaged in research to find new ways to battle malaria, a scourge of the troops, and better ways of making gas masks.

The *Los Angeles Times,*in a Dec. 10, 1941 front-page editorial, told its readers, "This is a time for sensible, courageous, patriotic Americans to keep their heads clear, their chins up and their feet on the ground. For our civilian population to get rattled is not going to help anybody but Japan. But it will help her a lot."

The war had struck home, but never more literally than the predawn hours of Feb. 25, 1942. Two days earlier, a Japanese submarine had surfaced off the coast of Santa Barbara, firing several shells at an oil installation and leaving the entire West Coast jittery. So it was understandable, after word had been received of a possible attack on Los Angeles and radar had picked up an unidentified object over Santa Monica, that antiaircraft fire commenced a little after 3:00 in the morning on the 25th.

Thomas Jacobs, a UCLA chemistry professor who also served as a war gas officer in the West Los Angeles area, remembers that night. "I was dashing through the darkened streets wearing my hard hat," he said. "The streets were completely deserted. We had gas masks and were to decontaminate the area if necessary."

It wasn't necessary, but it was memorable. "The gunfire brought everyone to a window or front porch," *Newsweek* reported. "Golden tracers arched upward in the blackness. More than 1,400 three-inch shells were fired. Shrapnel whistled down to clatter on hard pavement or imbed itself in yards and houses. But no bombs were dropped."

Nor was any proof ever found that a single Japanese plane had invaded L.A. airspace. The Battle of Los Angeles was a one-sided affair.

The same could be said for the USC-UCLA rivalry up to that point. The two schools had met eight times in 13 years. USC had won five, and the other three had ended in ties. Amazingly enough, in the midst of all the terror and death and destruction of World War II, they found time to play football. And UCLA found time to finally make history.

The time seemed ripe in 1942 for the Bruins to break through against the Trojans. The T information was firmly in place and there would be no turning back now. Waterfield seemed firmly in command, beginning to flash the skills that would later make him a pro football star.

On the other hand, everything appeared out of whack at USC where, after a year, the Trojans still hadn't recovered from Jones' sudden death. Barry's one-year stint as successor had been a failure. His future at USC was decided by the war because he was called into the service before the start of the next season.

Next in line was Jeff Cravath, another former Jones assistant. Leaving the University of San Francisco where he had put together the best offense on the West Coast, Cravath came to the Trojans with the same plan already in effect across town: the T formation.

The season began at UCLA with none of the promise ahead evident. The Bruins lost their first two games, 7–6 to Texas Christian and 18–7 to St. Mary's Pre-Flight, a service team with a pretty good quarterback by the name of Frankie Albert, who went on to star with the

San Francisco 49ers. But then the Bruins put some touchdowns in the T and won six of their next seven heading into the USC game.

The T formation was a lot more erratic for the Trojans, who were 4–4–1 coming into the Coliseum to face the Bruins.

Yet despite the problems of both clubs, they were playing for the Pacific Coast Conference championship and a Rose Bowl bid when they met in front of a crowd of 87,000.

UCLA got the early lead on a two-yard touchdown run by Ken Snelling following an interception by Waterfield. "He went right over my back," said Bruin guard Jack Lescoulie. "I put [Trojan defender] Don Clark on his back."

The Bruins had been expected to take advantage of Waterfield's arm all afternoon, but, able to create holes for the running game, they wound up throwing only six passes all afternoon, completing two. One of those went from Waterfield to Burr Baldwin for 42 yards and UCLA's second touchdown, giving the Bruins a 14–0 lead heading into the final quarter.

"We were going towards the open end of the Coliseum," Baldwin said. "I went over to the center about 10 to 15 yards and the ball was right there as I crossed over the middle. The right cornerback was moving over too far and I just went into the end zone untouched. It amounted to the winning touchdown pass. It was a helluva big deal."

But, it wasn't over just yet. USC's Mickey McCardle scored on a 10-yard run to cut the margin in half, but the Trojans never got any closer. USC nearly tied the game in the closing minutes when McCardle fired a pass to a sprinting Hubie Kerns. The ball was just beyond Kerns' reach, however, slipping past his fingertips at the UCLA four-yard line to bounce harmlessly on the grass.

And finally, a goal that had long been beyond the collective fingertips of the Bruins was firmly in their grasp. They were going to the Rose Bowl for the first time after finally beating the Trojans in their ninth try.

In the *Daily Trojan*, the sports page was headlined "In Memoriam."

Underneath, it read:

Troy's Domination Over UCLA

BORN: Sept. 28, 1929

DIED: Dec. 12, 1942

UCLA lost to Georgia, 9–0, on New Year's Day. It had taken the Bruins a long time to get to Pasadena. But it would take another 22 years before they won there.

The Bruins didn't have to be content with merely whooping and hollering about their first-ever win over USC. They could also ring in the new era on the field with the first use of the Victory Bell. A tradition was born.

The Victory Bell was believed to have once been mounted on a locomotive. The UCLA Alumni Association obtained the bell in 1939 and presented it to the students. The bell was in the Coliseum on a Friday night in 1941 for the Bruins' season opener against Washington State. It was used to celebrate UCLA's 7–6 victory that night, with one ring for every point scored. When the game ended, the bell was loaded into a truck for its customary ride back to Westwood. About 26 students helped load the bell. Unfortunately for the Bruins, six of those were Trojan infiltrators.

One member of the USC group stole the keys to the truck. When the UCLA students discovered the keys were missing, it was suggested that some head for a nearby office for help while others phone the Automobile Club. Great suggestions, had they not come from the USC undercover agents. Once the UCLA students had departed, so did their USC counterparts, with the truck and the bell.

What followed was an espionage campaign exceeded only by those going on overseas. The bell was dismantled and moved constantly. To the Sigma Phi Epsilon House. To the Hollywood Hills. Under a hay stack. Out to Santa Ana. It even appeared in a USC fraternity newspaper on a junk pile with the idea that it should be turned into scrap metal.

All the while, UCLA students were conducting raids at USC, trying to find their precious bell. The battle between the two schools escalated. Tommy Trojan's sword was stolen. Paint was dumped into a UCLA office.

Finally, student leaders from the respective campuses—Bob

McKay from USC and Bill Farrer from UCLA—met to work out a truce. The USC captors agreed to surrender their prize only if the bell became a permanent trophy to be given to the annual winner of the UCLA-USC game. The two sides met in front of Tommy Trojan. A message was relayed that the bell could be found in front of a bar on Figueroa Street.

Ironically, the bell was returned in time for UCLA's first victory over USC. So, after an absence of 18 months, the Victory Bell returned to Westwood in triumph.

In 1943, travel restrictions dictated by the war changed the nature of the rivalry. There would be two UCLA-USC games each of the following three years, one at the beginning of the season and one at the end.

All teams were weakened by the constant loss of personnel heading into the service. The quality of play understandably declined, but more so at UCLA, it seemed.

Over the next two seasons, the Bruins would go 5–13–1. They lost both meetings with USC in 1943, leaving their historic win of '42 just a distant memory.

The Trojans won the opener, 20–0, and the second meeting, 26–13. The second game, played in front of a crowd of just 35,000, shows how poor the play became at times in those days. There were 14 fumbles—eight by USC—along with blocked kicks and even an intercepted lateral. Asked for his comment on the game, Cravath replied, "Everything I've got to say, I can say in three words: fumble, fumble, fumble."

It wasn't really so bleak for the Trojans. Despite all the players grabbed up by the military, they wound up winning eight of ten games in 1943, including a 29–0 whipping of Washington in a Rose Bowl limited to West Coast teams by travel restrictions. The Trojans were so dominating at the start of the season, they didn't give up a single point to their first six opponents and shut out seven of the ten. UCLA was 1–8 in 1943.

The 1944 season wasn't much different for either the Bruins or Trojans. UCLA and USC tied in their season opener, 13–13, the Bruins staging one of the most thrilling comebacks in the series' history to even the game.

With UCLA trailing 13–0, halfback Johnny Roesch scored twice in the final three minutes. The second touchdown came on an 80-yard punt return, the sound of the final gun echoing in his ears as he crossed the goal line.

In the *Los Angeles Times*, Braven Dyer wrote, " Roesch caught the ball cleanly on his own 20, shifted into high gear, sped down the sidelines nearest the Trojan bench, appeared to be cornered at midfield, broke loose again, stumbled near the 20, regained his stride and then swept into the promised land as pandemonium reigned."

Waterfield's conversion kick hit the right post, and ricocheted over the cross bar. "If this is the way they always play football out here," said Bronko Nagurski, the former pro football star who had become a Bruin assistant, "I'll never live through the season."

It was the last time that season the two clubs would be on equal footing. UCLA, losing Roesch to the military midway through the season, wound up 4–5–1. USC had an unbeaten season, finishing 8–0–2 with the second tie coming again Cal. The Trojans, led by quarterback Jim Hardy, hammered UCLA, 40–13, in the rematch. USC outgained the Bruins in total yardage, 403–148, and in first downs, 21–6. The Trojans ran up a 40–0 lead before the Bruins scored twice on the USC reserves.

The Trojans maintained their momentum into the Rose Bowl where they beat Tennessee, 25–0. In two straight Rose Bowl appearances, USC had a combined score of 54–0.

The 40–13 Trojan defeat was one of the most crushing in Horrell's career in Westwood. It was also his last. Impatience with the UCLA coach boiled over in the 1944 season. Sure, there was a war on and players were constantly leaving. But, critics wanted to know, was the war any less devastating across town at USC? Cravath was able to recruit from on-campus military training programs and take advantage of wartime rules that permitted the use of freshmen. Why couldn't Horrell?

"Babe was an easy-going guy," Lescoulie said, "maybe a little too easy-going." That became a common criticism of Horrell.

"Babe was the consummate gentleman," said lineman George Robotham. "He never swore, except for once. I remember we were going up to play Cal. The papers were writing about how much Cal had and how little we had. It got Babe all riled up. So before we broke practice to leave for Cal, he called us together and said, 'To hell with what they've got. Let's show them what we've got.'"

Not enough in the long run. Horrell resigned under pressure in January of 1945 after six seasons which included the Bruins' first win over the Trojans and first trip to the Rose Bowl.

Horrell's replacement was Bert LaBrucherie, a halfback under Bill Spaulding two decades earlier. LaBrucherie was head coach at Los Angeles High School and, upon arriving in Westwood, he equated his old job with his new one, high school ball with collegiate ball. Same fundamentals, he thought, same game.

Not quite. On his level, LaBrucherie was stepping into a brave new world.

And on a much bigger level, so was the rest of the planet. World War II was over. The Atomic Age had arrived with the dropping of two atomic bombs on Japan. U.S. Servicemen were streaming home to new jobs, new homes, new families and new lives. And some were coming back to play football.

That created an uneven mixture. For LaBrucherie, the mix didn't take right away. For one thing, LaBrucherie had a different personality than his predecessor and that created some hard feelings. "Babe was a super coach and a super person," said lineman Tom Asher. "He was a very nice guy. You couldn't say the same of Bert."

UCLA went 5–4 in 1945, losing both games to USC in the last season of the two-game arrangement. The Bruins scored first in the season opener against the Trojans, but not again, losing 13–6. In the rematch, USC prevailed, 26–15, before 103,000. The Trojans' ground game, led by Ted Tannehill's 107 yards and two touchdowns, proved more effective than the Bruins' speed and a passing attack which produced 225 yards through the air, but not enough points on the scoreboard.

It was not, however, one of Cravath's most dominating teams.

Going on to its third straight Rose Bowl appearance, USC lost to Alabama in Pasadena, 34–14, to finish the season 7–4.

"I guess," LaBrucherie said, "it wasn't quite my turn for the Rose Bowl yet."

But his turn was coming.

There was no doubt right from the start that LaBrucherie had a great team in 1946. Just ask Oregon State, a 50–7 loser in the season opener. Or any of the other nine opponents the Bruins mowed down en route to an undefeated regular season.

Quarterback Ernie Case led an offense that had outscored the opposition 282–66 going into the USC game. With quick runners like Skip Rowland, Jerry Shipkey, Ernie Johnson, Al Hoisch and Cal Rossi, power runners Jack Myers and Art Steffen, and receivers Burr Baldwin, Roy Kurrasch, Phil Tinsley and a future L.A. Rams star named Tom Fears, the Bruins averaged over 400 yards a game in total offense. It was an interesting group, war veterans playing alongside kids only a couple of years removed from high school.

"Many of the seniors were getting married," recalled lineman Tom Asher, "so those were less frivolous times, more low key. Many of us were in college to go to college. I don't know that we were much bigger, but we certainly had an older team than we usually would. In terms of guys gone off to war, the environment on the field was very serious. Things matured because of the war.

"UCLA, all of a sudden, was a very attractive school. It was discovered, so to speak, just as Southern California was found after the war. The G.I. Bill was paying for this. It brought in people who otherwise wouldn't have been brought in."

The 1946 Trojans weren't a bad team either at 5–2, but the oddsmakers figured their unbeaten string against the Bruins was finally over. Since their one and only victory over USC in 1942, the Bruins were 0–5–1 in the crosstown rivalry.

Los Angeles was underwater. Or at least that's how it felt to residents hit with the wettest November in nearly half a century. That left the Coliseum looking like a bowl of mud for the 1946 UCLA-USC game.

"I remember one play in particular," Asher said. "On one of our punts, I got off the line real fast and I was absolutely the lead guy down the field, which is strange for a tackle. Well, one of their little halfbacks caught it and I thought I was gonna cream him when my feet just flew out from under me and, I'm serious now, I must have skidded 20 yards. It was that muddy."

LaBrucherie decided conditions dictated that he turn the lever way down on his powerhouse machine and go conservative. His chief weapon? Not the run. Nor the pass. When in doubt, punt and wait for the breaks. And that's what he did, filling the rainy skies with booted balls. The Bruins kicked four times on first down, four more on second and eight times on third down.

It didn't take long for UCLA's hunker-down-and-wait, defensive game plan to pay off. In the first quarter, Bill Chambers blocked a kick by USC quarterback Verl Lillywhite. Fellow Bruin Don Malmberg picked up the loose ball, mud and all, at the Trojan 16-yard line and slushed his way into the end zone to give UCLA a 6–0 lead. The Trojans tied it before the half on Don Doll's four-yard scoring run at the end of a 43-yard drive.

Deadlocked at the half, LaBrucherie found himself at the center of a near mutiny in the lockerroom. "The boys wanted to quit playing defensive ball," he told the *Los Angeles Times*, "and go out after points. They gave me quite an argument, but when I ordered them to stick to our prearranged system of watchful waiting—playing it close to our belt and kicking early—they went right out and did it. But I admired their spirit in wanting to get out there and throw caution to the winds."

Finally, LaBrucherie's game of punt and pray paid off at the end of the third quarter. With UCLA on the USC 45-yard line, Case punted to the Trojans' Mickey McCardle, who received it on the goal line. But Hoisch's jarring tackle separated McCardle from the ball. UCLA's West Matthews fell on it at the USC five.

The referee blew his whistle. End of the play. End of the third quarter.

End of the mud pile.

The changing of the quarter meant changing ends of the field. And for the Bruins, that meant a big break because they were moving from the muddier side of the field to the drier, firmer side. It wasn't totally mud free, but it was much better for an end zone assault.

And that's just what they mounted. Myers up the middle for a yard. Hoisch off right tackle for three. And Case, behind lineman Don Paul, squeezing across the goal line. Case added the conversion kick, the UCLA defense held and the Bruins had a 13–6 victory, only their second win ever over USC.

The Bruins then beat Nebraska, 18–0, and headed into the Rose Bowl undefeated at 10–0, but were stunned by Illinois, 45–14. They had come a long way in two years under Bert LaBrucherie, but not far enough. Victory in Pasadena still eluded them. So did happiness in Westwood.

It was a strange time in college football, a time when war veterans who had been taking orders from field commanders under fire from fighter wings and tank formations were often listening to coaches whose only combat experience had come against single wings and T formations. On the Bruins, that meant trouble. The returning veterans constantly challenged the authority of LaBrucherie, creating dissension and a lackluster 1947 season.

UCLA was only 5–3 coming into the USC game, the Bruins back in their familiar underdog spot against an unbeaten Trojan squad that was 6–0–1 although Cravath, too, had his problems with returning veterans.

But, according to Don Clark, a USC lineman who came back from combat to play and later coach for the Trojans, the problem in that case was Cravath. "He was tough and firm when I played for him in 1942," said Clark of Cravath in the Trojan Heritage by Mal Florence, "but, when I came back in 1946, he was an entirely different man. He seemed to have a complex about the service. Whether it was because he couldn't get into the service, I don't know. But, for whatever reason, he took it out on some of the servicemen. I seemed to be one of his pet peeves. He always made comments to me about the service, guts and things like that. And he seemed to favor those players who stayed around USC in the Navy's V–12 and V–5 programs, or those who weren't called into the service right away."

John Ferraro, president of the L.A. City Council, has similar memories of his days as an All-American Trojan lineman.

"I came back in 1946 with a lot of veterans," he said. "I remember the discipline Cravath gave young football players. They had enough discipline in the war and didn't want any on the football field. They saw death on the battlefields, and football didn't seem quite as important. Some of the veterans had lost their drive for football. It was a combination of Jeff not adjusting and some of them having lost it."

Ferraro and Bruin lineman Don Paul achieved a unique distinction by playing in six USC–UCLA games. Their record was made possible by the fact the two schools met twice a season during the war.

In front of 102,050, USC scored the only points of the 1947 game on a 32-yard, second-quarter touchdown pass from Jim Powers to Jack Kirby.

The Trojans spent the rest of the afternoon turning back the Bruins. In the closing minutes, UCLA, starting at its own 35-yard line, mounted one last drive which brought it all the way down to the Trojan four-yard line.

Fourth down. Two yards for a first. Double that for the touchdown. Fifty-five seconds remaining. Quarterback Carl Benton called for a pass, with halfback Ernie Johnson designated to throw the ball in what would be his first attempted pass ever as a Bruin.

Phil Tinsley was the primary receiver. But he never got into his pass pattern, later claiming he was illegally held. Furiously, Johnson, having roamed out to his right, looked for an open secondary receiver. He spotted Bill Hoyt and fired.

Was the pass on the mark? Johnson will never know. Hoyt slipped and fell in the end zone, USC's Gordon Gray cutting over to grab the ball. Back on his feet, Hoyt nearly tackled Gray for a safety, but the Trojan defender slipped out of Hoyt's grasp and back out of the end zone to dash the Bruins' last hope and send USC back to Pasadena.

And disaster. The Trojans, hanging onto their unbeaten season despite UCLA's final charge,collapsed after that, letting their next two opponents charge over, around and through them. Notre Dame beat USC in the regular -season finale, 38-7, and Michigan topped that, trouncing the Trojans, 49–0, in the Rose Bowl.

LaBrucherie's collapse was complete in 1948. In two years, he went from an unbeaten regular season at 10–0, the Pacific Coast Conference championship and the Rose Bowl to 3–7, good for eighth place in the PCC.

Morale on the squad had sunk even lower when LaBrucherie fired popular assistant Ray Richards after the '47 season. Yet with all the problems, the Bruins put up quite a battle in 1948 against the Trojans, who entered the UCLA game 14-point favorites.

There were no Rose Bowl trips at stake this time. USC would finish the season 6–3–1. But this UCLA-USC game was still in a unique spotlight that distinguished it from all its predecessors. It was the first game of the series to be seen on that new rage sweeping the country—television. KLAC-TV showed the game in L.A.

USC, with the advantage both in its running game and defensive unit, ran up a 14–6 halftime lead. The crusher was the second touchdown, coming on a 60-yard scoring pass from Dean Dill to Jack Kirby with just two second left in the half. The Bruins never recovered. Both sides scored third-quarter touchdowns, the game ending with USC on top, 20–13.

Kirby had become the Bruin killer, having scored two of the three touchdowns as well as the only TD in the previous season's 6–0 Trojan victory. "I guess," said a smiling Kirby afterward, "I've just been lucky."

LaBrucherie was also smiling when it was over. It was hard not to when he emerged from the lockerroom to find a supportive crowd awaiting him. In behavior rarely if ever exhibited for a losing coach, the Bruin fans picked LaBrucherie up on their shoulders and marched around, yelling, "We'll be seeing you next fall, Bert."

Maybe so, but not on the UCLA sideline.

5

Red's Games
1949–1957

Bert LaBrucherie was supposed to become a legend, not a loser. Not after the unbeaten regular season of 1946. Not after whipping Stanford and USC in the same year. Something had tampered with the script. That something was the University of Illinois. "I don't think Bert ever recovered from that (the 1947 Rose Bowl) game," said Bob Fischer, who later became the school's athletic director.

But who would replace him? After all, UCLA was no USC. It possessed about as much national clout as Santa Clara. Before television, college football was a regional game. Folks in the South cared little about the West, and vice versa. Each sought the spoils of its own kingdom.

Before UCLA Athletic Director Wilbur Johns could begin an extensive interviewing process, famous sportswriter Grantland Rice intervened. Rice told Johns to check out a coach down South who had turned perennial also-ran Vanderbilt into a power.

Red Sanders wasn't the "name" the Bruins had hoped to find. Sanders had coached Vandy for eight years, compiling a losing record only in his rookie season. In 1948, he took his team to 12th in the national rankings.

Johns met Sanders at a coaches convention in San Francisco. The two clicked. The job belonged to Sanders. Vandy didn't let UCLA steal Sanders without a struggle. The school offered him a lifetime contract. With no official confirmation yet from Westwood, Sanders entertained second thoughts. He tried to contact Johns to postpone any formal announcement for a few days. Unable to reach Johns, he phoned Sports Information Director Vic Kelly.

Sanders asked him if he could locate Johns immediately. Kelly lied.

"I knew where he was," Kelly said, "but I wasn't going to tell Red. He wanted to get out of the commitment, at least for the time being. I told him the story of his hiring was going to go out that night, which was true. I could've turned him over to Wilbur, and that might have stopped it. But I didn't. We wanted him."

They got him. For nine years. For six wins over the humbled Trojans. For the first time that UCLA, not USC, owned Los Angeles.

At first, the city didn't tremble with the news of Sanders' hiring. According to one local newspaper account, "a male Caucasian, age 42, named Henry L. Sanders, was named head football coach at UCLA yesterday."

Sanders went to work immediately. He was credited with originating the 4–4 defense that was copied by many college and pro teams, and for inventing the "squib" kick as a substitute for the out-of-bounds kick. He changed the uniforms, from dark blue to powder blue. He changed the formations, from the T to the old-fashioned single wing. He changed the practice field from a cow pasture to a smooth training surface. Most of all, he changed the attitude in Westwood. Winning replaced whining.

"He got the most out of us," recalled defensive standout, Jack Ellena. "We were all overachievers. We had no superstars. USC got all the publicity."

Off the field, Sanders ran a loose program. No curfew. He was no Vince Lombardi. On the field, things were much different. UCLA became the West Point of the West. "You thought you were talking to General Patton," said Terry Debay, a linebacker and blocking back. "From the time you hit the practice field, nobody ever took a chin strap loose. Nobody ever took a drink of water. You ran between every drill, and you never sat down."

USC Coach Jeff Cravath also adhered to strict practices. Strict and long. Once, after losing to Navy, 27–14, in 1950, Cravath did the unthinkable. "Cravath was so upset about that loss," recalled running back Al Carmichael, "that on Sunday, the day after the game, he had us work out. For Cravath, you could be out there for four or five hours. He'd turn the lights on and keep going. Problem is we left it all out on the practice field."

The Trojans certainly didn't display much on game days. Their records in 1948 (6–3–1) and 1949 (5–3–1) were respectable, but respectable didn't make it at USC. The alumni, spoiled by the success of Howard Jones, craved perfection. Anything less, and the countdown to the next coach would begin.

For his first encounter with Saunders in 1949, Cravath had to fight without his best ammunition. Jim Powers, the first-string quarterback, had ended his season with an injured hip. His backups, Wilbur Robertson and Frank Gifford, were also sidelined with injuries. (Gifford was allowed to kick extra points). That meant using a sophomore, Dean Schneider, who had never played a down as Trojan quarterback, a kid who, realizing he wouldn't play much, had almost quit the game. "I told him it was up to him, and there would be no hard feelings whatever he wanted to do," Cravath said. "The boy missed one day of practice and then came to me and said, 'Coach, I've decided to stick it out.' "

USC developed a contingency plan in case Schneider caved in to the big-game pressure. The Trojans experimented in practice with the single-wing. The logic: If Schneider couldn't do it, there was nobody else to take the ball from center. Welcome back, "Gloomy Gus" Henderson.

For Sanders, though, the balanced-line single-wing was not some useless relic. At Vandy, he admired Tennessee's single-wing. He believed most defenses, normally prepared for more modern formations from other opponents, would be unable to adapt to the Bruin attack. The system also rewarded the versatility of UCLA's tailbacks, who, in split-second decisions, could run or throw. Linebackers could be frozen, defensive backs thrown completely off balance.

Sanders preferred the running game. Like Howard Jones, he wanted his defense to create scoring opportunities. The forward pass always carried risks. But Sanders was no dummy. He possessed an outstanding receiver, Bob Wilkinson, and he wasn't going to ignore him. Early in the third quarter against USC, Wilkinson caught a 12-yard scoring pass from Ernie Johnson to tie the game at 7–7. The Trojans had scored first on a nine-yard Schneider pass to Bill Jessop.

Despite his early success, Schneider was an emotional wreck. He could barely speak in the huddle, and that's not exactly the sign of a poised quarterback. For one play, Schneider whispered, "Oh, Christ," and took forever to mumble the play.

Finally, center Mercer Barnes couldn't take it any more. "Look, Dean, I don't care what you say, but just call the play," Barnes said.

At halftime, in case Schneider didn't get the message, Cravath repeated it for extra measure. "Dean, you got to shout those signals out," Cravath said.

"Gosh, Coach, I was shouting at the top of my voice," the teenager responded. "I can't yell any louder."

Somehow, in the second half, he found his voice, his arm, and his leadership. With fullback Don Burke doing the dirty work, the Trojans methodically drove downfield. On fourth-and-four from the 18, Schneider hit Johnny Williams for the clinching score.

UCLA was stymied the rest of the way, but USC wouldn't sit on its lead. The game was over, but with two seconds left, Burke blasted over for the final touchdown in a 21–7 triumph. That last score angered some Bruins. "I didn't like that," recalled Wilkinson. "I didn't think it was necessary."

Wilkinson and his teammates wouldn't forget it. Schneider denies the Trojans tried to pour it on. "You can't tell guys to lay down," he said.

Overnight, he had traveled that unlikely route from scrub to stardom. He finished 13 of 26 for 127 yards. And, more significantly, he gained automatic access to the Big Game's enduring lore.

Red Sanders had also become an overnight hit. Players, sportswriters and fans all loved him. UCLA finished 6–3, and the future looked even more promising.

Yet Sanders wasn't satisfied. USC, despite several subpar seasons, still considered itself the only show in town. Especially when it came to recruiting highly-touted California talent. When Donn Moomaw starred at Santa Ana High in 1948, Cravath told Sanders that Moomaw naturally belonged to the Trojans. Sanders saw it as another sign of USC arrogance. "They think they have a divine right to everybody in Orange County," Sanders said. "We're here in town. We have a right to get people, too."

Sanders got him, and it was no fluke. Others, like standout tailback Paul Cameron, followed. The Trojans no longer possessed a near monopoly on home-grown talent, and never would again. Sanders, by the mere force of his charisma, overcame USC's prestige. It also didn't hurt Sanders to have cocky assistants such as Tommy Prothro. "Well, do you want to go to USC and then get beat every November?" Prothro asked recruits. "Or do you want to go to UCLA?"

Bruin coaches played hardball. At USC, they told high schoolers, you'll struggle to make the starting lineup. At UCLA, you're guaranteed to play. Some UCLA alums feared that the single-wing would discourage players more accustomed to the "T" formation in high school. But Sanders wouldn't budge. He felt he could teach the system to anyone.

But would he be around to teach it? In 1950, the University of Florida courted Sanders, initiating an almost annual ritual. In later years, Air Force and Texas A & M made serious bids for Red, but each time, he chose to remain in Westwood, though not before alarming an anxious student body.

Meanwhile, the UCLA campus had other Reds to worry about. The fear of communism had once again shown up in Westwood. A few miles away, in Hollywood, the House Un-American Activities Committee hunted for communists in the entertainment world.

In June 1949, the California Board of Regents moved the search to the academic community. It passed a loyalty oath requiring faculty members from all the branches to deny, in writing, membership to the Communist Party. By the summer of 1950, dozens of faculty members throughout the system refused to sign the oath. Three UCLA teachers, including Dr. David S. Saxon, assistant professor of physics, were dismissed because of their non-compliance. Saxon had no involvement with left-wing or right-wing causes. He opposed the oath because he felt it was inconsistent with academic freedom. Saxon was soon vindicated.

The California Supreme Court ruled against the oath. Saxon rejoined the faculty, and from 1975 to 1983, became the school's president.

Across town, as the 1950s unfolded, the mood at USC was very serious, especially after the Korean War ended in 1953. "They were concerned with careers," said J. Wesley Robb, a religion professor in the 1950s. "They didn't care about activism." That generalization of the USC student would be repeated often in the 1960s.

In the fall of 1950, UCLA and USC were headed in opposite directions. UCLA had a strong voice—Sanders—who instilled confidence from the starting quarterback to the third-string linebacker. USC had a weary voice—Cravath—who clearly wasn't getting the most from his team of stars.

UCLA opened the season with successive shutouts: 28–0 over Oregon, 42–0 against Washington State. Even a 35–0 rout by California the week prior to the Trojan contest couldn't dampen Red's second impressive season in a row.

USC lost three of its first four, and entered the Big Game at 1–4–2. Cravath was kaput. Still, the Trojans, with stars Jim Sears and Al Carmichael, had gained 427 yards in total offense the week before against Washington.

In practice, Sanders announced he had relied too much on the passing game all season, and would try to run against the Trojans. But, several days before the game, football strategy suddenly lost all meaning. LaVon Hansen, wife of UCLA's senior running back Howard Hansen, died after a long illness.

Sanders decided Hansen should sit out. But, for the first time, the player wouldn't obey the coach. "I'm going to play Saturday," Hansen told Sanders. "She would've wanted me to."

"No, I can't allow that," Red said.

"I'm going to play, and that's it," Hansen said.

"The sportswriters would crucify me," Sanders insisted, "saying I was trying to exploit the situation."

Sanders called the team together, and it was agreed that Hansen should be allowed to play. So a team still hurting from its 21–7 loss in 1949 to the Trojans now had its Gipper—win it for Howard! And the

Bruins did, going away, 39–0. It was the worst conference loss ever suffered by the Trojans, the lowest moment of the lowest of seasons.

Once again, Frank Gifford couldn't play, and but his presence wouldn't have mattered. The game belonged to Ted Narleski, who, at the beginning of the 1950 season, had been rated fourth among Bruin backs. All Narleski did was rush for 138 yards and three touchdowns. Hansen chipped in with 61 yards. Altogether, UCLA ran for 337 yards to USC's 30. The Trojans never penetrated past the Bruin 20-yard line.

"The amazing thing about that game," Prothro recalled, "was that Narleski could not pass much, and we had to have a running attack. Nobody ought to ever beat USC with a running attack, but we did."

Carmichael, who led USC in rushing with 13 yards, said the Trojans never had a chance. "We couldn't do anything that day," he said. "I remember in the third quarter, I looked at Sears and his nose was running blood all down the front of his jersey, and mine was the same way, and we just held our hands up, like 'What's is going on here?' "

A rout, that's what. And, for the first time in the Sanders Era, it was USC who feared UCLA. "I think that was the toughest team I ever played against," Sears said. "They knocked you down every place. I had heard so much about Notre Dame, and then, all of a sudden, we ran into the Bruins. We were playing Notre Dame instead of UCLA that day."

Sears felt that UCLA, motivated by the Hansen tragedy, was a team possessed that afternoon. He forgot to mention the Bruins wounds still festering from the 1949 loss, and the unnecessary final touchdown with two seconds to go.

Sanders hadn't forgotten. "A lot of people," Vic Kelly said, "asked, 'Why did Red pour it on?' He explained that, 'Look at our record going back against USC. We've had a lot of close games, and if we had won this game by a field goal or one point, they'd say that SC's still the top dog. We had to destroy that image with a big game.' "

Sanders substituted plenty of reserves, but he certainly didn't rein them in. Cravath won the final game of the 1950 season, beating Notre Dame, 9–7. But it was too little, too late.

Like UCLA two years earlier, many USC alumni craved a "name" coach—someone like Bud Wilkinson or Paul Brown, the highly successful coach of the Cleveland Browns. Other names mentioned were General Bob Neyland of Tennessee, Bob Woodruff of Florida, and Fritz Crisler of Michigan. When word spread that former Trojan football star Jess Hill—he scored in the first game against UCLA in 1929—would assume the role, some alumni made a last-ditch effort to stop him. They weren't crazy about a guy whose coaching experience had been confined to high school, junior college and the Trojan frosh taking over the varsity job.

"They really wanted another Howard Jones," Sears said. "They wanted us all to get together to say Jess wasn't good enough to be the coach, but the players wouldn't do it. Jess was from the USC family."

Hill got the job, and made an immediate impact. "With Jess," Carmichael said, "we'd have an hour and 45 minute workout, but you ran all the time. We were always confident we could wear the other team down. Halfway through the third quarter, you could see the other team dragging, and we were still up."

Hill, like Sanders, was a master tactician. He delegated a lot of control to his assistants, while he played battlefield general, mapping out the precise troop movements necessary to conquer each week's opponent. He was a quiet man who didn't swear, who kept his composure all the time.

In the first six weeks of the 1951 season, Hill made the alumni forget about the futile search for a more famous coach. The Trojans were undefeated, including wins over Washington and California. Gifford (162 carries for 757 yards), moved to tailback, had become a star. Linebacker Pat Cannamela anchored the defense. Even a 27–20 loss to Stanford couldn't nullify a remarkable turnaround in Trojan fortunes. Entering the UCLA game, USC (7–1) was ranked sixth nationwide by Associated Press.

The Bruins were unranked. But the respect earned by a Red Sanders team would never be questioned again.

"When Sanders came in there, we realized there was a definite change in the style of play," Carmichael said. "They were hitting harder; you couldn't move the ball as easily, and their defensive line was tough. A lot of teams you'd play would hit you, and then they'd slide off you, but it seemed like every time you got hit by a guy from UCLA, they got a good piece of you."

The Bruins (4–3–1) were still very dangerous, especially with sophomore tailback Paul Cameron. Going into the Trojan game, Cameron needed only 41 yards of total offense to break Kenny Washington's single-season school record of 1,394. Still, Sanders considered starting Narleski, the hero of the 1950 game, because he didn't quite trust first-year players in tough contests.

Sanders went with Cameron. And Cameron went crazy. With 40 yards on the ground and 88 in the air, he broke Washington's mark, and carried the Bruins to a 21–7 triumph.

Gifford carried 16 times for *17* yards, and threw just one pass, which was almost intercepted. Despite his much-celebrated college, pro, and announcing careers, Gifford never made much of a difference in the USC-UCLA rivalry. His only points came from his foot. It seemed he was either injured or ineffective whenever the Bruins were the opponents.

Sanders simply outcoached Hill. He put in a new defensive wrinkle which completely confounded the unprepared Trojans, who rushed for only 33 yards. Each time USC had the ball, the Bruin line formed a V-shaped wedge which didn't dissolve until the Trojans jumped into their positions on the line of scrimmage. UCLA would then deploy its defense according to whether USC came out into a T, a single wing right, single wing left, or punt formation.

"It kept us from jumping around, changing places at the last moment," Sanders explained. "And it kept them from knowing what kind of defense we'd drop into or who would be where."

The win guaranteed the Bruins sole possession of second place behind Stanford in the PCC. USC finished fourth. And for the first time since the rivalry began in 1929, UCLA won back-to-back games over the Trojans.

Sanders didn't confine his competitive spirit to the football field. He wanted to win everywhere. "We were playing golf," recalled former assistant coach Bill Barnes, "and we had a bet on the 18 holes. Red gave us all four strokes a side, and so at the end of the first nine holes, two or three of us had him down. He said 'We're changing the bet. The boss is right.' "

The boss was revered. His players formed deep emotional bonds with him they hoped would last a lifetime.

Sanders could be strict in practice, but some discovered his sensitive side. "I never knew if he knew my first name," Debay said, "but I had a job in the cafeteria with Bob Heydenfeldt. We're down there at 7:40 in the morning after our last game as seniors, and Coach Sanders walks in. We realize we shouldn't feel too intimidated. We just played our last game. He can't hurt us.

"He walks in, and says, 'Bob and Terry, I want you to know how much you have meant to me, and I want you to call me if there's anything I can ever do for you.' You sensed there was that side to Red, but you wouldn't let yourself think it because it was never let out on the field."

In the early 1950s, the Bruin players found out about another side to Sanders. It would test their loyalty like never before. Red Sanders loved to drink. Nobody quite remembers when it began, and to this day, most of his players and coaches refuse to talk about it. They protected him then, and they still protect him now. But what does emerge is the portrait of a man who, despite outward appearances, faced a lot of pain.

Ironically, Sanders, upon arriving in Los Angeles, had been most concerned about the new west coast lifestyle corrupting his staff. "He didn't have any problems at Vanderbilt," Prothro added, "and when we came to UCLA, he met with all the assistant coaches and warned us about the fast living in California, and that we shouldn't let it get to us. He was the only one it got."

It was the staff which had to watch *him*. Kelly was often assigned to escort Sanders on speaking engagements to make sure he returned home safely. When the assistants couldn't find Sanders, they divided the town to search his favorite watering holes.

One such hunt took place the night before an important game against Stanford. It was about 11:00, and there was no sign of Sanders. The coaches, worried the pressure might make him drink, looked everywhere. Finally, about 2:00 or 3:00 in the morning, Prothro found him in a room at the Beverly Hills Hotel. He threw him in the shower to sober him up. A few hours later, Sanders met the players as if nothing had happened.

For years, he managed to keep his drinking problem away from the practice field and game day. He walked the sidelines with total ease, as if he didn't have a worry in the world. But after Sanders was picked up by the police for drunken driving, he couldn't keep silent any longer. He called a meeting to clear things up. "Men, I've embarrassed you, myself and the university," Sanders said. "I apologize to you, and I apologize to the university, and I assure you it won't happen again."

It did happen again, but Sanders never lost the respect of his players. He earned it on the field, and he earned it in real life. "We went back to Illinois once," Debay recalled, "and we were in the hotel when someone told us, 'The niggers can't eat here.' Two minutes later, Coach Sanders finds out and you have never heard a tongue-lashing like this. He protected all of us, black or white, like it was messing with his family."

The 1952 USC-UCLA matchup promised to be a classic. Nobody in the crowd of 96,869 ever asked for a refund. For the second time in the rivalry's history—1939 was the other—everything was at stake for both teams: The PCC title. The Rose Bowl. An undefeated season. A possible national championship.

The Trojans (8–0) were dominant all season, especially defensively, once again drawing comparisons to the 1932 squad, which had yielded only 13 points. With standouts such as Marv Goux, George Timberlake, and Elmer Willhoite, USC felt confident it could contain UCLA's explosive offense, led by junior Paul Cameron. Just one week earlier, the Trojans had humiliated star Washington signal caller Don Heinrich in a 33–0 whitewash.

The Bruins (8–0) were equally impressive. They beat Stanford, 24–14 (Cameron threw three touchdowns), California, 28–7, and tuned up for USC by thrashing Oregon State, 57–0. But could the Bruins beat the Trojans three times in a row?

UCLA got the first break of the game when Sears fumbled and Myron Berliner recovered on the SC 32. Cameron and Don Stalwick picked up nine yards between them. A few plays later, Pete Dailey kicked a field goal from the 22—the first ever in the rivalry. UCLA, 3–0.

In the second quarter, controversy—never a stranger in this series—showed up again. Al Carmichael was about to be tackled by Berliner on his own 36, after a simple six-yard gain. But somehow, he pitched the ball to Sears who ran untouched 65 yards for a Trojan touchdown.

Some Bruins felt cheated. Either they thought Carmichael's forward motion had been halted, or that he tossed a forward lateral. But the play stood. It could be considered a fluke play, except for the fact Carmichael and Sears, best friends, had spent hundreds of hours preparing for fluke plays. They practiced laterals over and over. "As I was on my way down," Carmichael said, "I saw someone out there and I thought it was Sears, but I wasn't really sure. I just took a chance."

Four decades later, Bill Barnes admits UCLA didn't really have a case against the call. "It looked to us like he was stopped, but we couldn't really see," he said. "The only reason we said it looked like he was stopped was because we got beat."

The Bruins scored on a safety. Harold Han fumbled the pass from center, and, when he went back into the end zone to retrieve it, he was tackled by Berliner and several other Bruins. USC 7, UCLA 5.

The Bruins had scored in every fashion but the most obvious. And they got the touchdown when Bill Stits punched over from the one, climaxing a short 30-yard drive. UCLA 12, USC 7. And that's the way it stood at halftime.

Both teams had reason to be pleased. UCLA had overcome a momentum builder, the lateral. USC had kept the Bruin offense in check.

Early in the third period, the game turned around for good. UCLA marched with the kickoff to USC's 18. Another touchdown would give UCLA a 12-point lead, perhaps insurmountable even for the powerful Trojans. Cameron, trying for the kill, rolled out to his left. He looked for Ernie Stockert. But Stockert was knocked down at the line of scrimmage, and never had a chance. Cameron was hit just as he released the ball, and it fell into the hands of All-American Willhoite who was out of position on the play. He returned the interception to the Bruin eight.

A few plays later, Sears hit Carmichael on a fourth-down play that Jess Hill had specifically designed for the Bruin game. Carmichael pretended to be a blocker, drawing the defensive back in, and then he released just at the right time. Sears hit him in the flat for six points. USC 14, UCLA 12.

A quarter and one-half remained, but UCLA was finished. Cameron injured his shoulder a few minutes later, and didn't come back. The most important game of the rivalry's history was taken by USC.

Sanders, as usual, was gracious in defeat. "This is the best team I ever coached," he said, "but SC's was the best defense any team of mine ever faced."

Moomaw wasn't as generous. "I suppose I shouldn't say this," he said, "because it'll sound like sour grapes, but I think we'd beat them six more times if we played seven more times."

The final statistics were fairly even: UCLA outgained USC in passing yards 115 to 88, and in rushing, 84–80. UCLA went home, its dreams of a perfect mark dashed. USC lost the following week to Notre Dame, 9–0, and then beat Wisconsin, 7–0, in the Rose Bowl.

Still, the wounds haven't completely healed. "To this day," Stalwick said, "you won't convince me that we didn't get beat on two fluke plays. We should have won all three years I was there."

The Bruins didn't carry the USC disappointment into the 1953 season. With Cameron, Stits, and Berliner they had the key personnel to play both offense and defense.

The rulemakers had decided to reinstitute the single platoon system which had been abandoned during the war. The players had to be in better shape, and Sanders made certain of that. UCLA whipped their first four opponents: Oregon State 41–0; Kansas 19–7; Oregon 12–0, and Wisconsin 13–0. Maybe this team was even better than the 1952 version.

That possibility was erased when the Bruins visited Stanford. The two schools never got along. "There were those of us," Prothro said, "who had more of an animosity toward Stanford than SC. Stanford always had this attitude that all the rules 'are for you guys. Not for us.'"

They certainly didn't make up in 1953. On the night before the game, the Bruins sat down to dinner. Instead of offering New York steak, the inn hosting UCLA served huge pieces of prime rib. Sanders was furious, worried the meal would fatten up his players and make them lethargic for the game. He told them to eat moderate portions, but, in this case, Sanders was powerless. "It was the biggest piece of meat I've ever seen," Debay said. "I promise you it was at least two inches thick. It was just great. Everybody couldn't resist."

The same thing happened on game day. This time, the Bruins devoured gigantic pieces of steak. "In twelve hours, we had two of the worst meals you could possibly eat," Debay said. From then on, they would eat only fish on Friday nights.

To Sanders and other Bruins, the heavy food was part of a deliberate plot to sabotage UCLA's chances in the game. It worked. Stanford escaped with a come-from-behind 21–20 victory, spoiling Bruin hopes for a perfect season and teaching Sanders a lesson he would never forget.

With UCLA leading, 20–7, late in the third quarter, Sanders installed his second string. By the time the starters could return— substitutions were only permitted every 15 minutes—Stanford had taken the lead. Sanders would never substitute prematurely again. After the game, Stanford fans heckled the Bruins as they headed for the locker room. When the team arrived in Los Angeles, Sanders consoled his disappointed players. "I don't know what's going to happen," he said "but I'll tell you this, we're going to play them next year. Remember that."

First things first. UCLA had a season to salvage. Wins over Washington State (44–7), California (20–7), and Washington (22–6) set up the Trojan showdown. The Bruins entered the USC game fifth in the polls. A UCLA victory would earn a Rose Bowl bid if California tied or beat Stanford.

USC (6–1–1), ranked ninth nationally, was having another fine season, but under the no-repeat rule, the Trojans were ineligible for the Rose Bowl. The battle with the Bruins would be for pride, never an insignificant motivator. Pride and a touch of arrogance. "We haven't lost a game in the Coliseum since Notre Dame beat us in our final 1951 start," a Trojan said, "and UCLA isn't Notre Dame."

Pride couldn't compete with the Paul Cameron Show. Cameron scored a touchdown as UCLA won, 13–0. (He broke Bob Wilkinson's season record of 48 points, but fell just 19 yards short of Kenny Washington's three-year total offense record.)

The Trojans had no heroes, only horrors. Three fumbles. One serious scoring opportunity. Only 38 yards passing. And worst of all, another loss to a Sanders squad.

UCLA would up the regular season surrendering only 48 points, ranking second in the nation behind Maryland which allowed 31. The team had rebounded from the Stanford setback to play its best football of the season. Cal tied Stanford, and the Bruins headed to Pasadena. Yet 1953 was only a hint of things to come. And even a 28–20 loss to Michigan State in the Rose Bowl couldn't derail the Bruins from their imminent rendezvous with greatness.

It started in spring practice and lasted all through winter. Nobody could touch it or define it.

In 1954, a magical sense came over the Bruin camp that this year could be historic, as if all the previous Sanders seasons had been tasty appetizers preparing Westwood for the main course.

Cameron had graduated, but plenty of top-notch talent remained: Debay, fullback Bob Davenport, right half Jim Decker, left tackle Jack Ellena and guard Sam Boghosian.

And then there was the religion factor. That year, coincidentally, the Bruins had a large contingent from the Campus Crusade for Christ. Many players felt that the Lord would guide them to greater heights. "I'm not saying it had anything to do with our won-lost record," Prothro said, "but it does indicate the type of team we had. We had no smokers, no drinkers, never a problem with curfew. There was no hell-raising or barnstorming."

The first two games didn't prove anything—UCLA overpowered the Naval Training Center of San Diego, 67–0, and Kansas, 32–7. But the third contest would demonstrate if that preseason sense was real magic or just an illusion. Defending national champion Maryland was due in town. Terrapin Coach Jim Tatum's team was known for its outstanding running attack and pass defense. The Maryland secondary had intercepted five Kentucky passes in its opening 20–0 victory.

Both teams recognized the game's importance. During the summer, Maryland sent its assistant coaches to clinics to learn as much as possible about UCLA's single wing. Sanders, meanwhile, quizzed other coaches, looking for schemes to dethrone the nation's number one team.

"We spent all spring practice working against Maryland," said Prothro. "We felt that whoever won that game was going to win the national championship."

Entering the season, the only spot of serious concern for the Bruins was the tailback position. Could Primo Villanueva replace the legendary Cameron? The answer came in the Maryland game. Yes.

Villanueva, relieved of calling signals by Sanders who prefered blocking back Terry Debay's composure, made a lot of big plays, including a critical third-and-six run to set up Davenport's clinching touchdown. UCLA won 12–7.

After a 21–20 scare over Washington, the Bruins' adrenaline was flowing at a season high. Higher even than it had for Maryland. Dead ahead on the schedule lay hated Stanford. This time, there would be no prime rib and heckling fans. No ill-conceived substitutions and late-game heroics. This time, there would only be a rout for the ages.

UCLA won, 72–0, and the game might not have been that close. The Bruins gained 359 yards to Stanford's 54. They intercepted eight passes, including a few from a promising quarterback named John Brodie. It was a payback Stanford would never forget.

Because of their arrogance, Prothro recalled, "we would have gotten 172 if we could have. We wound up playing third string, but we kept trying to score."

Added Debay, "We had the greatest week of practice, and we just said to ourselves, 'It's either going to be us totally destroyed or them totally destroyed. We were as emotionally prepared for combat as any team I've ever seen. Everybody was so ticked off that it didn't matter who was in there. Nobody said anything. We just walked out on the field and did it."

The Bruins then breezed through the next three weeks, outscoring Oregon State, California and Oregon by a combined 129–6. Next up, the Trojans and another chance for a perfect season.

To the players, this was their bowl game. Again, the no-repeat rule stood in the way of a showdown for Pasadena. Nobody liked the rule. Both the Bruins and Trojans always suspected the rule was pushed through the PCC by the Northern conference members who resented the traditional dominance of USC and the rising greatness of UCLA.

USC (8–1) was headed to the New Year's Day game, and would be a formidable PCC representative. Its only loss was to Texas Christian, 20–7. But the Trojans, if they could beat UCLA, would prove they belonged at the Rose Bowl, instead of merely getting there by default. Armed with an impressive arsenal of running backs—Jon Arnett, Aramis Dandoy, Lindon Crow—and quarterback Jim Contratto, the Trojans were given an excellent chance of upsetting the nation's number one team.

For the first three quarters, an upset looked very possible. UCLA led by only a touchdown, 7–0, courtesy of a Villanueva 48-yard bomb to Heydenfeldt midway through the first quarter. And when USC drove to the Bruins' 8 yard line late in the third period, it looked like 1952 all over again. When it most mattered, would the Bruins choke again?

Not quite. James Decker intercepted Contratto's pass on the two-yard line, and, while a clipping penalty deprived him of a 98-yard interception return for a touchdown, the Trojans had let their best opportunity slip away. The would not get another one. "When they didn't score down there," Debay said, "it took the wind out of them. The dam broke, as if 'maybe these guys *are* better than us.' The change of momentum was incredible."

Said Dandoy: "I was able to run against them for a while, but then they just started killing us. They were unbelievable." In the fourth quarter, UCLA scored 27 points, coasting to a 34–0 triumph.

The Bruins (9–0) had finally attained perfection. It was a magical season. And one UCLA has never repeated. Ohio State was judged national champs by the Associated Press, but the Bruins were recognized as number one by UPI. In three seasons, UCLA had gone 25–3, and was very close to 28–0.

USC went on to lose, 23–17, to Notre Dame, and, 20–17, to undefeated Ohio State in the Rose Bowl.

Two questions faced the rivals in Los Angeles as they approached the 1955 season. What would UCLA do for an encore: And could USC win the town back?

There were many new faces in Westwood. Gone were Villanueva, Debay, Ellena, and Prothro, who left to fill the head coaching vacancy at Oregon State.

USC, meanwhile, would return with much of its firepower,

including Contratto and Arnett. There were faster and stronger runners than Jon Arnett, but none who possessed his uncanny sense of balance. Just when he seemed hopelessly trapped in the backfield, he would slip one guy, then another, and soon, he was 20 yards downfield. A choreographer couldn't have made his runs any more artistic. Arnett had seriously considered attending UCLA. A star at nearby Manual Arts High School, he was heavily recruited by Sanders. One night, the Bruin coaching staff took Arnett out to dinner. That's when he made his decision. "I remember Sanders got really drunk, and his head was drooping in his salad," Arnett recalled. "I was a 17-year-old kid, and you expect the guy to be pretty straight with you."

UCLA had its own marvel. He was Ronnie Knox, a tailback with perhaps more raw talent than anyone since Kenny Washington. In a 33–13 win against Iowa, Knox ran for one touchdown and threw for another. Against the College of Pacific, he boomed an 82-yard punt.

Even with Knox, the Bruins couldn't repeat 1954's greatness. They stumbled against Maryland, 7–0, and only a last-minute Jim Decker 35-yard field goal gave them a 19–17 win over Washington. But in the Husky game, Knox suffered a broken bone in his right leg the first time he carried the ball. The Bruins quickly had to implement Plan B.

All year, they had practiced plays designed for Knox against the Trojan defense. To counter another powerful Trojan defensive line, the Bruins had assembled a formidable passing attack. Without Knox, UCLA would be forced into a battle in the trenches. "We really don't have any good passers outside of Ronnie," Sanders lamented.

During practice, they tried Sam Brown, Doug Bradley and Gerry McDougall. Each looked inept. Still, the Bruins (8–1) had already secured a trip to Pasadena while the Trojans (5–3) had lost to Washington, Minnesota and Stanford.

Another game for pride.

Jon Arnett took the opening kickoff on his 3-yard line, scooted up the middle for a few yards, shook off a desperate grasp by John Hermann at the 15 and sprinted to the end zone. USC 6, UCLA 0.

The Trojans went berserk. They would not be denied this year.

Oh yes, they would. USC was ruled offside on the play, and the run was called back.

Arnett was furious. "That was a fluke," he said. "They usually give you a warning, and certainly should have before the game. The referees blew it."

UCLA's next kickoff was deep in the end zone, and Arnett had no alternative but to down the ball. "I was told by a couple of coaches," Arnett said, "that they saw the team go absolutely flat after that penalty. I heard one of them say jokingly later that the reason we didn't win the game was because I didn't run the next one back."

Arnett was largely ineffective the rest of the game. He carried only eight times for 24 yards, and was used mainly as a decoy for the other Trojan runners, C.R. Roberts and Gordon Duvall. He didn't understand the strategy then, and 36 years later, his original evaluation stands. "We didn't do real well with it," he said. "I was the lead tailback. It didn't make sense."

UCLA's Brown, meanwhile, had the game of his career. He rushed 27 times for 150 yards and a touchdown, leading the Bruins to a comfortable 17–7 victory. Without Knox, the Bruins completed only two passes for 50 yards. Plan B was a success.

Jess Hill, perhaps showing the strain of three straight losses to the Bruins—the first time in series history—was less than complementary after the contest. "This is the weakest UCLA team of the last three years," Hill said. "No, I can't say they are the best team we have faced. They beat us worse than Stanford, but Stanford is very good and it would be quite a game if they played now."

USC recovered to defeat Notre Dame the following week, 42–20. The Bruins were once again beaten by Michigan State in the Rose Bowl, 17–14. But with five wins in six years against USC, Red Sanders had made Trojan fans feel what it must have bene like for Bruin fans in the mid-1930s.

College football changed in 1956. Not on the field, but in the boardroom.

The Pacific Coast Conference finally decided to police itself, focusing on the under-the-table money paid by university booster clubs to the schools' football players. The practice had been going on for many years. Periodically, someone would ask questions.

"I remember we were freshmen," Debay said, "and Coach

Dickerson told us that some guy might ask us questions about much money we get. We told him they shouldn't talk to us because we'd tell the truth. He told us not to come around the office for a few weeks, so we didn't."

Players at UCLA and Southern Cal struggled to pay their bills. They were paid $75 a month for campus jobs, but that didn't cut it, especially for Bruin athletes who couldn't live in cheaper on-campus dormitories. So clubs at both schools were set up by alumni to give players an extra $40 a month to get by. Even that was barely enough.

The penalties were severe, and almost all PCC schools were involved. UCLA was eventually placed on three years probation with all its athletic teams ineligible for any championships or even postseason play. USC was put on two years probation with similar restrictions.

For many Bruin and Trojan followers, the penalties were viewed as a conspiracy by the weaker teams in the conference to punish the two Southern California schools for their success on the field. "There was this feeling," Vic Kelly said, "that Red had stepped on a lot of toes, and was winning too much. A lot of people thought UCLA was getting too big for is britches."

Added Prothro: "They wanted to discredit Red and the program every way they could."

But it was the players who suffered the most. The rules for the penalized schools got really crazy. Seniors at USC and UCLA, in 1956, were only allowed to play five games, and they had to be consecutive. In 1957, seniors couldn't play at all.

"The things that caught were so minor," said Nick Pappas, then a USC scout. "We didn't buy cars. It wasn't like today."

Many players lost their futures. C.R. Roberts, an outstanding USC runner, claims the penalties cost "me a lot of my living. I had a shot at the Heisman Trophy" in 1957. Instead, he jumped to Canada to play professional football for the Toronto franchise. He later made money in the NFL, but will always wonder what might have been.

For Sanders, the handicap only heightened the challenge. "He always said, 'I will rise and fall on what our assistants do,' Vic Kelly said.

Heading into the Trojan contest, the Bruins were 7–2, losing only to Michigan, 42–13, and Oregon State, 21–7. Prothro obviously had no pity for his ex-employer. For the third year in a row, UCLA had defeated Stanford and John Brodie, this time, 14–13. Sanders called it his greatest win ever.

USC (6–2) proved just as gutty. The Trojans started strong with four consecutive victories. Arnett, believing the early schedule was stiffer, elected to play the first five games. He gained 625 yards in 99 carries before he became ineligible.

Both teams suffered chemistry problems. Younger players, accustomed to starting positions became understandably resentful when they had to give way to seniors who had missed the first five games. In some cases, seniors even lost jobs because of their absence. "It was always like having a new team," Roberts recalled. "It definitely hurt the team."

Said Arnett: "We could have been 10–0 if we had all played together."

According to Roberts, there were other underlying tensions in Trojan camp. Racial tensions. Roberts, who is black, claims Arnett, who was white, was better treated because of his color. Instead of trying to run faster than Arnett on the practice field, Roberts said he surrendered to the racist expectations of white society.

"I could have beaten Arnett any day of the week," Roberts said, "but I knew that if I did that, I would have had to race him every damn week. They wouldn't have accepted the fact that I had won."

He found other ways to show his anger over Arnett receiving more playing time. "The only way I could protest," he claims, "was to fumble the ball."

He believed Arnett, by receiving the ball deep in the opponent's territory, got all the glory by scoring the points while he took the pounding by carrying the ball when the Trojans had poor field position.

Arnett said he is surprised by Roberts' anger and never felt there were any racial problems on the team. Roberts, as one of only two black football players at USC, had to face a lot of abuse. He got plenty of hate mail. "They'd say, 'Nigger, you can't play at this white boy's school,'" Roberts said. "At UCLA, there were a lot of black guys and they told me blacks can't go to USC, and I think that's why I went to USC."

The 1956 USC-UCLA game lacked the drama of previous match-ups. Only 63,709 showed up at the Coliseum. But the Trojans didn't care about drama. They settled for beating the Bruins for the first time since 1952. And it was the first loss for UCLA at the Coliseum since that 14–12 struggle.

Roberts said it best. "I'm not for saying a lot of words," he told a mob of hysterical SC rooters outside the dressing room. "But I'll say this—now we can live in this town."

That's because a solid performance by USC quarterback Jim Conroy and the rugged Troy line carried the Trojans to a 10–7 victory. The game also featured the first USC field goal in the rivalry, a 32-yard kick by Ellsworth Kissinger. It was Kissinger's first successful kick ever—that includes high school and college.

Conroy brought back memories of Dean Schneider. A fourth-string quarterback at the beginning of the season, Conroy moved up because of injuries and the five-game restriction. He had few opportunities for mistakes as the game was won on the ground. The Trojans gained 314 yards; the Bruins just 23. USC employed a basic 6–2–2–1 defense. The Bruins fumbled four times.

"We were told that if we could handle their guard (Esker Harris) and linebackers," said Monte Clark, USC's 246-pound sophomore tackle, "that we could whip 'em."

Pappas, who had scouted UCLA numerous times, helped develop the strategy to beat the Bruins. He told Hill to avoid off-tackle or end run plays. The key was to wedge them, or run up the middle. It worked with Roberts doing the bulk of the running.

"I'm walking off the field," Pappas recalled, "and Sanders comes up to me and says, 'In all the time I've coached, nobody ever wedged against me before. Nice going.' I walked into that locker room and I was ten feet tall."

In six years, Jess Hill proved he would never be another Howard Jones. So in 1957, Don Clark, an assistant coach, came in to try to revitalize the program. Three or four losses a year was acceptable for Oregon or Washington, but not for the Trojans. USC was about winning championships.

USC would win nothing in 1957, certainly not respect. In the first five weeks, all losses, the Trojans were outscored 81–32. They finally won the next week against Washington, 19–12, but then lost to Stanford and Oregon leading up to the Bruin matchup. In eight games, USC had fumbled 37 times.

At Westwood, however, Red Sanders pulled one last miracle. The Bruins, after early victories against Air Force and Illinois, stumbled against Oregon, 21–0. But they were 7–2 entering the Trojan game, which Sanders claims he never expected. "I privately thought we'd have trouble breaking even this year," Sanders said, "and would have been delighted if somebody had guaranteed we'd win five or six games."

Would you believe eight? That's what the Bruins finished with after beating the Trojans, 20–9. USC wound up 1–9.

USC started strong, driving to the Bruin 28-yard line after the opening kickoff. But the familiar enemy—the fumble—came back to haunt them again. This time, the culprit was left halfback Don Buford (later of Baltimore Oriole baseball fame). USC had bobbled its chance to make an early statement.

"The one game we won this year, Clark said, "was when we scored first. This team hasn't been able to come from behind, and when our touchdown drive was stopped right off the bat, it gave UCLA a terrific psychological boost."

So did Don Long. Long, the junior tailback who got more playing time because of injuries, threw two touchdown passes, scored another, and intercepted a Trojan pass when the game was undecided. For good measure, he also caused a safety. He completed nine of 13 passes for 181 yards as the Bruins outgained USC 338 to 226. One of his touchdown throws, from 57 yards, went to star receiver Dick Wallen.

UCLA's season was over. The Trojans later wished they were that fortunate. They lost the following week to Notre Dame, 40–12.

In December 1957, UCLA officially announced what had been speculated for months: So long, PCC. Along with Cal, the Bruins set their formal exit for July 1959. USC would later make similar plans. The penalties had created irreparable damage at Southern Cal and Westwood. From the moment they were imposed, it was only a matter of time before the conference was doomed.

Soon afterwards, it looked like Sanders, too, might be changing loyalties. Texas A & M made a strong bid for the UCLA coach. The rumored offer included a $15,000 annual salary, a $5,000 expense account, and stock in an oil corporation. Additional inducements included a new station wagon every year and an air-conditioned, rent-free home with all food supplied.

It was very tempting, but Sanders cared about more than material goods. Sanders was working on the second year of a 10-year pact but Westwood officials immediately tore up the contract and presented him with a new 10-year deal. He told Texas A & M, thanks, but no thanks. "I'm very, very happy at UCLA, he told his supporters. "I want to spend the rest of my days here."

Unfortunately, there weren't many left. Sanders died of a heart attack on August 14, 1958. Sanders had gone to visit William T. (Pop) Grimes, a retired commercial hotel owner who lived at the Lafayette Hotel. Sanders then complained about the heat, and shed his coat and shirt. When Grimes left the room to get cool soft drinks, Sanders collapsed.

After Grimes departed, Sanders, according to newspaper accounts, began talking about football to Ernestine Drake, a woman in the hotel room.

"He kept talking football and asked me if I'd seen many games," Drake said. "I said I hadn't." Suddenly Sanders clutched his chest and fell to the floor. He was dead when medical help arrived. He was 53.

Westwood went into shock. Even today, four decades later, his former players and coaches still dearly miss Sanders. They miss the man whose magnetic personality turned young boys into mature men. He never won a Rose Bowl, but he won practically everything else.

One coaching legend in Los Angeles passed away. Another would take his place two years later. His name was John McKay.

6

The Political Games
1958–1966

Leading the UCLA Bruins was a dream job. Following Red Sanders could be a nightmare sentence. For George Dickerson, one soon turned into the other. A Bruin player under Bill Spaulding, Dickerson had been a UCLA assistant for a dozen years when he was named to replace Sanders. A hundred years in Westwood might not have been enough to prepare Dickerson to be the *next* Red Sanders. Ask Gene Bartow, who was put in the position of being the next John Wooden. Or Heartley (Hunk) Anderson, who was selected to be the next Knute Rockne.

But replacing Sanders was only one of Dickerson's problems. He was also faced with having his seniors play just five games because of the lingering punishment from the illegal payment scandal of a few years earlier. He was stuck as a lame duck in the Pacific Coast Conference, a conference the Bruins were leaving at season's end.

And, what was perhaps most aggravating to him, Dickerson felt recruiters from other schools were taking advantage of Sanders' death to try and lure away players the late coach had already secured. According to Bill Barnes, who would succeed Dickerson, other coaches would approach UCLA's recruits and tell them, "You don't want to go to UCLA now. Red's gone."

It was more than Dickerson could handle. "I was pretty disturbed," he admitted. So he singled out Cal, the school he felt was the most blatant, went up to Berkeley and confronted head coach Pete Elliott.

Embarrassed, UCLA officials censured Dickerson for going over their heads. But, the coach, by making a public scene, accomplished his goal. "I just wanted to make sure," he said, "that they didn't steal any of our players. In one fell swoop, I was able to keep them from getting our kids. We didn't lose a boy. Did not lose a one. It was probably the smartest move I ever made."

But a costly one. The battle to keep his team left Dickerson physically and mentally exhausted. UCLA officials suggested Dickerson get away for a few days with his wife, Betty. But Betty soon called the school in distress. "He doesn't sleep," she said, concern and anguish in her voice. "He just wants to talk so much." Dickerson was soon hospitalized and Barnes was appointed temporary coach.

"I had a father who had a nervous breakdown," said Vic Kelly, the UCLA sports information director, "and I saw him go through it. Then, later on, I saw George Dickerson start out the same way and yet, I did not recognize it. The symptoms [are] compulsive talking, compulsive actions. The mind was racing so fast with ideas. It was incredible and not one of us saw it."

Dickerson returned for the season opener against Pittsburgh, but the Bruins lost two of their first three games and Dickerson continued to get worse. "I remember one occasion," Barnes said, "where we had quite a few people in for training table and, after the training was over, George got up to talk and it just didn't sound like George. It was kind of spooky.

"I said to Ducky Drake, the trainer and track coach, 'There's something wrong here.' It got worse and worse. So, he [Dickerson] was taken to the hospital. From the time it started, it rolled so fast."

Dickerson was suffering from manic depression. At 45, his head coaching career was over after just three games. "Who knows what happened," Dickerson said. "I don't know."

Could it have been triggered by the pressure of trying to live up to the Sanders legend? "Very possibly," Dickerson said. "I always wanted to be a coach. I tried the best I could. I was just trying too hard and it caught up to me. I got all excited. It was just one of those things.

Actually, it was one of the best things that ever happened to me. Otherwise, I would have wound up an old football coach."

Instead, after effective treatment, Dickerson went into the construction business where he carved out a successful career over a quarter century. He retired eight years ago at age 70 and now lives in Laguna Hills.

Was Dickerson ever tempted to try coaching again?

"Hell no," he replied.

Talk about tough jobs to fill, Bill Barnes took over a UCLA club that had lost two coaches in two months, was about to lose its seniors (who could only play five games), and had already lost two games, as many as it had lost all of the previous season.

Barnes needed something to provide a quick lift. So he reached into Sanders' old bag of gimmicks and came up with the W formation. It was actually a spread out single wing, giving the Bruins a chance to operate in a wide-open offense. And Barnes had the perfect man to trigger it in Bill Kilmer, who could either run or pass.

By the time UCLA met USC, the Bruins had failed to do either very successfully, losing six of nine games. It was a mediocre year for the Trojans as well, USC splitting its eight games.

While most ties leave both sides exiting the field in frustration, this one, which ended 15–15, at least produced satisfaction for the crowd of 58,507. They may not have seen a winner declared, but they got their money's worth in the exciting fourth quarter.

Leading 8–7 heading into the final 15 minutes, the Bruins added to their advantage when UCLA's John Brown intercepted a lateral from USC quarterback Tom Maudlin, who reportedly had an ailing shoulder, and raced 45 yards to a touchdown. Jim Steffen's conversion kick gave UCLA a 15–7 lead.

But only for a moment, because USC's Luther Hayes ran back the ensuing kickoff 74 yards for a touchdown. Maudlin kept the ball on the conversion attempt, went to his left, dove head first and landed about an inch inside the end zone. USC was even.

The Trojans might have even pulled the game out if Don Clark had saved a timeout. USC reached the Bruin 19 with the final seconds ticking away. But without a way to stop the clock, the Trojans couldn't get their kicker on the field. Instead, Maudlin tried to get one more play off, his efforts stopped by the sound of the final gun.

USC outgained the Bruins, 359–148, but fumbled the ball away five times to destroy any chance for momentum. After all their troubles, the Bruins were happy to at least end the season without a loss to the hated Trojans. But, mostly, the Bruins were just happy to end the season, a season of death and disaster.

There was a new beginning for UCLA in 1959. For one thing, in Barnes, they would have the same coach for an entire season. For another, the crippling probation was finally over. So were the Bruins' and Trojans' membership in the PCC. Both joined the new Athletic Association of Western Universities.

With Barnes' system in effect from the beginning and with Kilmer having a season of experience behind him, UCLA figured to be good.

With no speed and a quarterback with a bad shoulder in Willie Wood, USC figured to be bad.

So go figure.

The Trojans won their first eight games, including three shutouts, to move to No. 2 in the nation. The Bruins were a .500 team coming into their annual crosstown showdown, going 3–3–1.

Outweighing UCLA by around 20 pounds a man on the line, USC was favored by nine and a half points. But the Bruin defense was equal to its Trojan counterparts and the game was tied, 3–3, in the fourth quarter.

Then Bill Kilmer, who missed the first half with a bruised ankle, came up with the most important gain of the day for UCLA—on an interception.

On second and 17 from the Bruin 47–yard line, Kilmer threw a bomb towards teammate Marvin Luster. But before the ball came down, Luster was joined by a pair of leaping Trojans—Wood and Jerry Traynham.

Wood came down with the ball. But UCLA came up with possession when field judge George Wilson ruled pass interference on Traynham.

"I don't remember," Traynham said, "whether I grabbed at him [Luster] or not."

The call advanced UCLA 46 yards to the USC seven-yard line. Ray Smith was then given the ball three straight times, taking it in from the three-yard line on his final carry. Ivory Jones added the conversion kick and UCLA had a monumental 10–3 upset win.

USC lost again in its final game, falling to Notre Dame, 16–6. And then the Trojans suffered an even bigger loss when Clark, their coach, resigned at age 36 to go into business.

Who replaced Don Clark? For some, that was an answer, not a question. When Clark's successor was picked, one L.A. paper announced, "SC Names Mr. Who." Abbott and Costello would have loved it.

John McKay didn't mind it, either. Considering his roots and his early career goals, he didn't care what they said as long as he had a signed contract in hand.

A product of the coal-mine region of West Virginia, McKay had been handed bigger responsibilities. Like helping to support his family at age 13 after his father died. That McKay did, doing everything from washing out bathrooms to delivering wet concrete in a wheelbarrow. He figured his future was going down a dark hole, straight into the coal mines. Until he discovered a way out.

McKay played football and basketball at Shinnston High School and came up with what he considered an ambitious career goal—to someday replace Mickey McClung, his high school coach.

After serving as a tail gunner in World War II, McKay went to Purdue, where he played freshman football, and then on to Oregon where he became an All-Coast halfback, operating in the same backfield with future pro football great Norm Van Brocklin. McKay stayed on at Oregon after his playing career ended, serving as an assistant coach for nine years.

Nick Pappas, a USC assistant, was highly impressed with McKay and suggested him for a job on Clark's staff when an opening came up in 1959.

Why in the world would McKay give up his seniority at Oregon to hook on with a team that had gone 1–9 in 1957, 4–5–1 in 1958 and was still on probation? McKay asked himself that same question.

Clark assured McKay the Trojans were going to get some speed and get competitive. Besides, McKay's wife, the former Nancy (Corky) Hunter, was from Southern California and liked the idea of going home. "If my wife had been from Hoboken," McKay said, "I probably would have gone to Hoboken."

In his first season at USC, the Trojans went from 4–5–1 to 8–2. The only new face on the coaching staff was McKay, whose basic responsibility was running the offense. So, although he insists he didn't make any significant changes, some felt McKay was the difference. "I probably got more credit than I deserved," McKay said. "We could beat anyone that wasn't real good."

But despite all the accolades, McKay wasn't thinking about his future at USC. He was thinking about getting out. Clark was 36 and, as far as McKay knew, not going anywhere. John and Corky had four kids and he was making $9000 a year. His old backfield mate from Oregon, Norm Van Brocklin, had told him he would be in line for the head coaching job with the Philadelphia Eagles if Buck Shaw retired. If Van Brocklin got it, he wanted McKay as an assistant. McKay agreed.

Shaw didn't retire. But Don Clark did.

The decision in the USC hierarchy was unanimous. At 36, John McKay was to be the new Trojan head coach.

A sportscaster mistakenly announced that "Jim McKay" had been selected. That was the name of McKay's brother. "He was a colonel, flying 52s out of Spokane," McKay said, "and he wired me that he wouldn't take the job."

McKay got a one-year contract. "It was not typical," he said, "but it was acceptable."

A couple of games into the season, it seemed regrettable to USC loyalists. The John McKay era had begun with a whimper rather than a bang. In his first three games, the Trojans scored a total of six points and lost all three.

A combination of lack of speed and lack of health made it a rough season for USC. By the time the Trojans stumbled into the UCLA game, they were 3–5. And John McKay was in deep trouble. "It looked like we were going to get fired," he admitted.

Things were going a lot better for the Bruins who were 5–1–1 when they trotted onto the Coliseum field to face the Trojans. Kilmer had been brilliant at times, like in the Purdue game when he threw three touchdown passes and scored another on the ground. Kilmer was fourth in the nation in total offense coming into the USC game. He had completed 54 percent of his passes and gained 447 yards rushing. UCLA led the AAWU in both offense and defense.

USC's most noticeable numbers came in the injury department. Fifteen Trojans had been hurt during the season. Eight would be out for the Bruin game. But those that suited up were more than UCLA could handle.

USC raced out to a 14–0 lead by the second quarter on a 21-yard touchdown pass from sophomore quarterback Bill Nelsen to end Marlin McKeever and a two-yard run by Hal Tobin. Then, the Trojans dug in for the expected Bruin assault. But defenders like McKeever, Jim Bates, Mike Bundra, Roger Mietz, Jerry Traynham and Carl Skvarna turned back Kilmer and his crew time and again.

Kilmer gained just 29 yards on the ground, completed only four of 17 passes for 80 yards and had three intercepted. Toward the end of the game, the USC rooting section chanted, "We killed Kilmer." Not totally. He scored the only UCLA touchdown on a two-yard run in the fourth quarter as USC prevailed, 17–6. He survived long enough to have a Hall of Fame career with the Washington Redskins.

"They had tough luck all year," Barnes said, "but they had a good team. They just outhit us. They outweighed us by 27 pounds per man and they just hit harder than we did. They were bigger and stronger and that had a lot to do with it."

The Trojans outgained the Bruins, 333–171, and had 20 first downs, double the number for UCLA.

Big win for USC?

Said McKay, "It only saved my job."

McKay was given a two-year contract which took some of the pressure off him when the Trojans struggled again in 1961.

But though he wound up just 4–5–1, that may have been the most important season of all for John McKay. It was the season he started using the I formation. It was the season he put Willie Brown at tailback, the position that would become synonymous with USC football over the next three decades. "We called it the shifting I," McKay remembered. "People said we stole the I. We never stole the I."

But then McKay didn't invent the I formation, either. Nor did he claim to. He saw it for the first time back in the early 50s, being used by a junior college coach in Washington. The coach was Don Coryell, who would later bring his expertise to the pro game.

When McKay went to the I, he instituted one big change that made his unique. He stood the tailback up prior to the snap from center, hands on his knees, eyes straight ahead studying the defense. "If we're going to run the daylight out of the football," McKay said, "the tailback should see the defense as the quarterback sees it."

Standing up gave the tailback perhaps a crucial extra second to read and react. The results made Trojan history.

But not at first. In the beginning, critics called McKay lots of things for using his new formation, but "genius" wasn't one of them. In his book, *McKay: A Coach's Story*, the USC head man recalls sportswriters saying the I in I formation stood for "incompetent, " "ineffective" or "intolerable."

McKay unveiled it on a limited basis against Georgia Tech in the '61 season opener and lost, 27–7. In the next game, against SMU, Brown, running from the tailback spot, scored on 93-yard run, USC gained 285 yards rushing and won, 21–16. A season of experimentation, however, led to inconsistency, the Trojans going in against UCLA 4–4–1.

The Bruins were 6–3, spearheaded by runners Bobby Smith and Mike Haffner. Smith led the AAWU in total offense with 874 yards and in scoring with 95 points. Haffner led in rushing with 620 yards.

For the first time in nine years, a Rose Bowl bid was on the line when UCLA and USC met. Neither had been to Pasadena in five years.

As it turned out, the ducks would have had a better chance of winning this one. Not the Oregon Ducks, but the natural variety. The skies were filled with rain, the field with mud on a miserable day at the Coliseum.

All UCLA could manage in in the first half was a 31-yard field goal by Bobby Smith. Pete Beathard's 52-yard punt return off a quick kick gave USC a 7–3 halftime advantage.

But, in the third quarter, UCLA defensive lineman Mel Profit tipped a Beathard pass into the hands of Bruin teammate Joe Bauwens, who rambled 15 yards to the USC 33. UCLA put together the winning drive from there, the deciding touchdown coming on a six-yard run by Smith, who, battling mud and tacklers, just made it across the goal line before being shoved out of bounds.

USC came close to tying the game before the quarter was over. As close as the width of a goal post. Carl Skvarna's 38-yard field-goal attempt hit the left goal post and bounced the wrong way for the Trojans, back onto the field. Final UCLA 10, USC 7.

"They didn't do anything we didn't anticipate," McKay said, "except beat us."

The Bruins went back to the Rose Bowl for the fifth time, but the results were the same as the other four—a loss. This time, Minnesota beat UCLA, 21–3.

It was 1962, the year John McKay had waited for all his life. Finally McKay had the team he'd waited for all his life.

Two seasons earlier, a sportswriter had said that "USC's backs run as if their shoes are too big and laced too tight."

No more. Now the Trojans had plenty of speed, on both offense and defense. They had two effective quarterbacks in Beathard and Nelsen, and star receiver Hal Bedsole to throw to. Nobody was making fun of Willie Brown or the I formation anymore. McKay was able to run his team effectively to either side. Student Body Left and Student Body Right became McKay's twin methods of terrorizing opposing defenses, the basic weapons of a sometimes unstoppable offense.

And few seemed able to do much against a USC defense modeled after the Arkansas system. The Trojans allowed only 16 points in their first four games, surrendered just seven touchdowns and outscored the opposition, 219–55, in the regular season. USC shut out three opponents and beat them all, going 11–0 to win the national championship, its first in 30 years. In just three seasons, McKay was already being compared to the legendary Howard Jones.

Things weren't going nearly as well over in Westwood where the

Bruins were struggling through a 3–4 season when they met the Trojans. While the I was thriving at USC, Barnes had put the T formation back in at UCLA, but it wasn't enough to offset the inexperience of a young Bruin squad.

While the game may have lacked the talent level on UCLA's part to make it as big as many of its predecessors, there was nothing lacking in the spirit department. Early on the morning of the game, $4,000 worth of cards for the Bruins' rooting section were stolen from a Coliseum storage room. Guess who was suspected.

The day before the game, McKay had learned that his team, win or lose, had already been invited to the Rose Bowl. He decided to keep the information to himself. It wouldn't hurt the Trojans, he reasoned, to think they were still fighting for a berth.

By the time they played USC, the Bruins were without a reliable quarterback. Barnes benched Larry Zeno, who had thrown 11 interceptions, and went with first-year letterman Carl Jones. In the *Los Angeles Times*, Paul Zimmerman wrote, "This might be called desperation." But with a little over 10 minutes to play, it was USC who was desperate. Zeno, though not quarterbacking, had accounted for the only points of the game on a 35-yard field goal.

The Trojans had already been stopped once at the UCLA one-yard line, inches from a first down that would have almost guaranteed a USC touchdown. The Trojans, with all their talent and all those flashy numbers, were suddenly staring down into the abyss, their unbeaten status and national championship about to be swept away by their archrivals.

But instead, USC hung on with the same tenacity Willie Brown showed in grabbing the game's most crucial pass. On a fourth-down play from the UCLA 26, Nelsen lofted a pass intended for Brown. Even Nelsen figured it wasn't going to get there, that the Trojans were going to have to surrender the ball.

"When I let go," said Nelsen in the postgame lockerroom, "I didn't think he was going to catch it. I thought the ball had taken off."

But so had Brown. "I didn't know I had it until I came down with it," he said. "I didn't see the ball at first. He [Bruin defender Al Geverink] hit me as I caught the ball, I think."

Geverink stopped Brown at the two-yard line. Ben Wilson scored from there and Beathard later culminated a USC drive by going over from the one to give the Trojans a 14–3 victory, keeping them unbeaten.

But nobody was gloating. "We coaches knew before the game we were going to the Rose Bowl," McKay told a group of USC rooters when it was over, "and our team played like we already were in the darn thing.

"A lot of you people thought we were in trouble out there. Well, we were."

The Trojans went on to whip Notre Dame, 25–0, and then survive one of the wildest Rose Bowls ever, outlasting Wisconsin, 42–37.

It was a lot easier playing UCLA in 1963. Having perfected his weapon in 1962, McKay got the ammunition in 1963 with a new running back named Mike Garrett, the first of his Heisman Trophy-winning, superstar tailbacks. With a Willie Brown in there, the I formation was effective. With a Garrett, it was deadly.

Although just 5' 9" and 185 pounds, Garrett had both speed and power. He ran for a then-NCAA record 3,221 yards and 25 touchdowns in his three seasons in cardinal and gold, averaging 5.3 yards a carry. He also scored four more touchdowns on passes and two on punt returns, averaging 11.3 yards per punt. In all, Garrett set 14 NCAA, conference and school records.

And he loved doing it for McKay. "He was the greatest coach I ever played for," Garrett said. "He could be a taskmaster, but we were always well prepared. We were always in great shape and we never thought about being outcoached."

While Garrett was racking up the yards, the 1963 Bruins were racking up the losses. With only three seniors and musical chairs at quarterback, Barnes, the UCLA coach, shuffled his lineup and his game plan, even giving the Bruin offense a pro look at times. Nothing seemed to help as UCLA came into the USC game at 2–7. The Trojans, enjoying the services of both Garrett and Brown along with key members of the national-champion squad of the previous year, had won six of nine games, a good season, but not good enough for national championships or Rose Bowls.

The game was scheduled for Nov. 23, 1963. But twenty-four hours earlier in Dallas, President John F. Kennedy was assassinated. While the NFL went ahead with its schedule on Sunday, including a Ram game at the Coliseum, the USC–UCLA game was postponed for a week.

It didn't prove to be much of a game anyway. Certainly not for Bruin fans. For once, the old cliché about throwing the records out the window when these two met didn't hold up.

The Trojans, still harboring hopes of a Rose Bowl berth, were a 13½ point favorite and played like it. They ran up a 13–0 lead and cruised to a 26–6 victory. No surprise considering that UCLA came into the game averaging only 76 yards a game rushing. Garrett alone was averaging 71.

USC rolled up 530 yards in total offense to the Bruins' 314. Garrett collected 119 yards rushing. Beathard completed 14 of 22 for 152 yards. The UCLA offense basically consisted of the Zeno-to-Kurt Altenberg passing combination, good for eight completions and 166 yards.

Being on the winning side in this annual game meant a lot to Garrett. "You knew them," he said of the Bruins, "and often worked out with them during the summer. So, you wanted to beat them real bad. UCLA talks a lot of trash when they beat you. You didn't want to live in the city all year after being beaten by them."

But the joy of beating the Bruins in 1963 was muted for Garrett and his teammates. When it was over, the Trojans learned that Washington, a 22–7 winner over USC earlier in the season, had gotten the Rose Bowl bid.

McKay said it was like losing "a million dollars."

Things weren't much different in 1964. The Trojans, with Garrett still running wild, wound up with the same 7–3 record. The Bruins, with Barnes still trying to find the right personnel, improved slightly from 2–8 to 4–6.

But they didn't improve enough to beat USC. It wasn't hard to figure out why. The Trojans had the best offense and defense in the AAWU. The Bruins had the worst.

Sure enough, USC dominated the game, winning 34–13. It was not only the Trojans' third straight victory over UCLA, but their most lopsided win over the Bruins in 20 years.

Garrett gained 181 yards rushing, and quarterback Craig Fertig added another 124 passing, completing six of 11 with three touchdown passes. In all, USC outgained UCLA, 463–260.

Of the downturn in the Bruins' fortunes, Sid Ziff wrote in the *Los Angeles Times*, "Their alumni are probably a little tired of it. But I've got news for any alumni hotheads. Lemme see you take your club champion and beat Arnie Palmer. . . . It takes the horses and UCLA has been playing with ponies."

But not much longer.

By 1965, the Bruin slide was intolerable. They hadn't been to a Rose Bowl in three years. They hadn't beaten USC in three years. They hadn't even had a winning season in three years. They needed help. They needed someone like . . . Red Sanders.

They got the next best thing.

The losing streak ended Barnes' coaching career. In his place came Tommy Prothro, a link to the great UCLA teams of the past. A Tennessee native, Prothro had played for Sanders at Riverside Military Academy.

Prothro continued playing football at Duke. Then, after serving in the Navy, he renewed his acquaintance with Sanders at Vanderbilt where Prothro served him as an assistant coach. The pair continued their relationship at UCLA, Sanders bringing Prothro with him to Westwood. In 1955, Prothro became head coach at Oregon State, leading the Beavers into the Rose Bowl in his second season.

Prothro seemed the logical successor to Sanders immediately following his death, but Prothro didn't go after the job. "I've always believed," Prothro explained, "you never follow the man that led them out of the woods."

Prothro also had his doubts about following Barnes, but for a different reason. "Bill Barnes was my high school pledge father at my high school fraternity," he said. "As a matter of fact, I had an opportunity to go to UCLA to replace Barnes a year earlier [after the 1963 season], but I turned it down."

Prothro figured Barnes still had a chance to turn things around.

When he didn't, Prothro decided it was finally time to go to Westwood. "I knew they were going to make a change," Prothro said, "so I thought I might as well take it if he was going."

The result was one of the most memorable eras in UCLA football. Prothro himself was pretty memorable. Possessor of a brilliant mind, he was equally at home among the best bridge players or the best football players.

Prothro always seemed to have a new wrinkle. For example, he noticed that Washington's defensive players kept their heads in the huddle too long. They would only pop out when the other team's offensive players came out of their own huddle to head to the line of scrimmage, not paying attention to anything that might have gone on before that. The Huskies seemed too concerned with what they were going to do and not concerned enough with what the other side was doing. Prothro filed the information away and, when the Bruins found themselves in a tight game with Washington, he took advantage.

Prothro had receiver Dick Witcher come over to the very edge of the sidelines between plays. Under Prothro's plan, Witcher engaged in conversation with several teammates as though he were out of the game, gabbing on the sideline.

But, Witcher wasn't out. He had never actually stepped out of bounds and, when the ball was snapped, Witcher streaked down the sideline and caught a key touchdown pass.

"He always had trick plays," said Gary Beban of his coach, "and they always seemed to work."

When Beban came out for spring ball in 1965, he started fifth on the depth chart at quarterback. But as Prothro began to install his own system, it became obvious to him that Beban had the ability to become the key ingredient. Prothro was going to a wing-T, resembling in some ways the single wing with the tailback directly behind center serving as quarterback. Beban was familiar with the single wing, having run out of it in high school. And, Prothro figured, Beban had the running ability, the arm and the intellect to run the new offense.

With his trademark briefcase and booming voice, Prothro was a striking figure on the UCLA sideline. "Tommy was different," Beban said, "but you don't realize how special he was until you look back. He was not close to his players while they were playing. There was a certain aloofness. But there was always respect. We knew we were well coached and he always treated us as men."

While the image of Prothro might be akin to an absent-minded professor, brilliant but eccentric, always diagramming new formations and gimmicks in his mind, Beban says there was a lot more to Prothro than that. "You might talk about bridge with him," Beban said, "or chess, or the parliamentary system. He allowed us to be football players, but he also allowed us to be students."

It was bridge, Prothro said, that altered the obsession he once had with football. "Bridge probably hurt my football," Prothro admitted. "People don't understand how dedicated football coaches are. When I started playing tournament bridge, I didn't spend every waking hour on football." But no one questioned his intellect or football knowledge.

"I think any time you say a person is a real good bridge player," McKay said, "you're indicating a high intelligence level. My wife's a very good bridge player . . . but has a hell of a time with the checking account."

While Prothro's aloofness and intelligence didn't leave him very emotional, he knew how to motivate his teams when necessary. Playing at Tennessee in a homecoming game for him, Prothro was angered to watch his Bruins fall behind, 21–0, by halftime. "I'm embarrassed to be your coach," he told his players. "This is my hometown and I'm embarrassed to be here." The Bruins went back out fired up, staged a furious rally and almost caught Tennessee, losing, 37–34.

Prothro could also take a lighter touch and be philosophical as he was with Beban in the lockerroom at the Rose Bowl prior to the 1966 New Year's Day game against Michigan State.

"I was nervous," Beban said. "It seemed as if I were in a different world." Prothro, sensing his quarterback's apprehension, approached him and, in that easy drawl of his, said, "Now just remember this: there are 800 million Chinese over on the other side of the world who don't give a damn about this game."

Beban nodded and replied, "Yes, sir, but what about the 180 million Americans who do care about this game?" Nevertheless, the point was well taken. Beban went on to score both touchdowns as UCLA won, 14–12.

Prothro could also be tough when he had to be. Like the time Beban was late for a bus waiting to take the Bruins to the airport. Finally, Prothro, tired of waiting, told the bus driver it was time to go.

"But," an assistant coach reminded Prothro, "Beban's not here." Prothro nodded and replied, "If you're going to make an example of somebody, make it a first-stringer."

But what was the deal with the mysterious briefcase? Prothro clutched it to his side all those years. What dark secrets did it contain? Everybody has an opinion.

McKay: "We spent most of our time trying to figure out what he had in that bag. Turned out to be a peanut-butter sandwich."

Barnes: "Probably some puzzles. He loved to work on puzzles."

Beban: "We still don't know. He never opened it. If you find out, let me know."

And finally, the ultimate source, Prothro, reveals the truth: "I had things in there I hoped I never had to refer to, things to jog my memory. There were substitutions, game situations, what you wanted to do if this happened, what you would do if that happened. In the excitement of a contest, sometimes you forget things."

But he never did open it. "Fortunately," Prothro said, "I never forgot things."

Maybe Prothro *should* have opened the briefcase for his first game as UCLA coach. Facing Michigan State, the Bruins lost, 13–3. "I just want you to know, you were not well coached," Prothro told his players. "They're better than we thought they were, but you're better than you showed."

As the season moved along, the Bruins showed a lot more. They won their second game, beating Penn State, 24–22. And they didn't lose again, coming into the USC game 6–1–1.

Which was the same record the Trojans, with Garrett better than ever, brought into the game. Garrett had 1,118 yards rushing and was averaging 139.7 yards per game when he sunk his spikes into the Coliseum grass to face UCLA.

But the Bruins had the aerial game to match USC's ground attack. Beban had gone over 1,000 yards through the air, completing 57 passes for 1,079 yards and seven touchdowns.

It was just like old times. Both teams were unbeaten in the AAWU, leaving the Rose Bowl berth to be decided by these two familiar rivals.

The Bruins broke into the scoring column when Mel Farr broke open for a 49-yard first-quarter run. But two touchdown passes by Troy Winslow and a field goal by Tim Rossovich gave USC a seemingly comfortable 16–6 lead that held up until just four minutes remained.

It was especially comfortable since Beban was suffering through a most uncharacteristic afternoon. He had thrown two interceptions, had fumbled twice, completed only two of eight attempts and lost 33 yards on the ground.

Then, following a Winslow fumble, the Trojans' fifth of the day, Beban hit Witcher with a 34-yard touchdown pass and came right back to connect with Byron Nelson on the two-point conversion. "It was not a good day," Beban said, "but the throw to Witcher, that gave us a shot."

It was 16–14, Trojans still on top. Four minutes to play. Prothro went to his playbook and ordered an onside kick. Kurt Zimmerman booted it and his teammate, Dallas Grider, recovered on the USC 48.

"Sometimes," Beban said, "things just happen in the stars."

Things seem to happen on the Coliseum turf as well when Beban had the ball in his talented hands. UCLA got down to the USC 38, then was pushed back to its own 48.

"There was no way it would slip away," McKay said. "We had the game won. We played a three-deep secondary. We told our safeties to stay in the middle of the field. They [the Bruins] can roll left or right. We don't give a damn. You know a five- or ten-yard pass won't kill you. The game is over if you stay where you are."

It was time for a Beban miracle. He faded back to pass, scanning the field, looking for an opening he hadn't found before.

"We had tried the play earlier and it was intercepted," Beban said. Surely, the Bruins figured, the Trojans wouldn't expect them to try the same play again.

"The idea," Beban said, "was for Kurt, the split end, to run a post pattern, and the back, Mel Farr, to swing behind him. When I dropped back, Mel was the primary target."

But Altenberg had other plans. "All Prothro wanted was a swing pass to Mel to get us in position for a field goal," he said. "I lined up near the sidelines, right next to Prothro. He kept yelling, 'Run,

Altenberg, run.' That doesn't help you when the defensive backs are listening only five yards away.

"Prothro didn't care because his idea was to dump the ball to Farr. But that wasn't my idea."

When the safety coverage, despite McKay's admonitions, broke down, the determined Altenberg blew past two defenders to get open. "I just did what I was trained to do by Tommy and Pepper [Rodgers]," Beban said, "throw it up and let the receiver run under it."

It was perhaps the biggest throw of Beban's career, but he never saw the ball after it left his hands, never saw Altenberg, just ahead of defenders Mike Hunter and Nate Shaw, take the ball over his right shoulder at the ten-yard line and race into the end zone. "I was down on the ground at the time," Beban said, "with one of those SC guys rolling on top of me. The crowd let me know he had caught it."

Altenberg didn't need anyone to let him know. "I never doubted," he said, "that I would catch it."

A two-point conversion attempt failed, but so did the Trojans' bid to regain the lead in the remaining two minutes and 39 seconds. They had outgained the Bruins in total yardage, 424–289, but it didn't matter. Final: UCLA 20, USC 16.

"They didn't belong on the same field with us," McKay said. "We kicked the bejesus out of them, but we got beat. So when you get beat, you shut up and go home."

The verdict had to be particularly galling to Garrett. He had gained 210 yards rushing against the Bruins, but, as a senior, had run out of time, denied in his final opportunity to get to the Rose Bowl.

Did he sulk? Hardly. Instead, Garrett went into the UCLA lockerroom to congratulate the players and wish them well in Pasadena. Beban would later say Garrett's gesture defined the word "class" for him.

"It was a game where we should have beaten them," Garrett said. "But Gary was spectacular throughout. He was so poised for an underclassman. I respected how he played and I wanted to tell him. They beat us. Whether it was luck or not, they were a very good team. I thought, 'Gee, these guys are on a hot streak where they could beat Michigan State [in the Rose Bowl], as tough as Michigan State is.' They could do something I never got to do. I knew going in to see them was the closest I could get to playing in a Rose Bowl."

Garrett went on to play pro football with the Kansas City Chiefs and the San Diego Chargers. He may not have gotten to the Rose Bowl, but he made it to the Super Bowl. "Making All-Pro and getting to the Super Bowl," Garrett said, "let me know I was a good player. Sure, it was a disappointment not getting to the Rose Bowl, but it doesn't gnaw at me."

It bothered McKay. "That was probably my fault," he said. "We just didn't get it done when he was there. Mike Garrett was the best player whoever played at USC who didn't go to a bowl game."

Replied Garrett, "That's easy for him to say, since everybody else did.

"It was just great playing in great games like [the '65 UCLA game]. It was not that you won or lost, but that you had the opportunity to play in games like that."

As great as Garrett was, his star was soon eclipsed by an even brighter one—O.J. Simpson.

"O.J. had more talent," McKay said. "Garrett was a hell of a runner. He did things I didn't think anybody could do. But he never played with the cast that O.J. did."

No argument from Garrett. "Not for one moment," he declared, "would I say I was as good as O.J. You could win with O.J., but you could also win with me. And that's the big test."

The Bruins found they could win with Beban. Their losing streak against the Trojans had ended. So did their Rose Bowl drought. UCLA went on to beat Michigan State, 14–12, on New Year's Day, 1966, the Bruins' first victory in Pasadena on their sixth trip there.

But even a season as successful as that one could not kill the stereotype. It was still "the gutty, little Bruins" beating the odds and the big, powerful Trojans to get to the Rose Bowl.

It's an image McKay refused to buy into. "Those gutty Bruins," he said, "the only way they could win was if their coach outcoached the other coach. I thought it was nonsense and I said it about 1,000 times. I just felt UCLA had very fine players, very fine coaches. Where that gutty, little Bruin thing got started I don't know. I coached against them at Oregon. I don't know how they got so little. They looked pretty good to me.

"They had such terrible players," he said facetiously, "like Mel Farr, who couldn't do anything. A small guy, about 210 pounds, and he ran the 100 in 9.1 [seconds]. Couldn't do much else."

Prothro had his own ideas about the Bruin image. "I preferred little hitters over big hitters, little guys who could maneuver more than slow guys. I don't buy the 'gutty little Bruin' thing at all."

Every school seemed to have a stereotype image, McKay said, and he certainly didn't appreciate the one the Trojans got branded with. "Everybody at Stanford had an IQ of 199 and we [Trojans] were all just paid athletes," McKay said bitterly. "We were the only ones being paid.

"I was there a long time and nobody every investigated us. If we had been investigated for five seconds, Dr. [Norman] Topping, [school president] would have fired the whole staff and Dr. Topping would have kicked my ass all the way up and down the whole street."

By the mid 1960s, there were more important battles to worry about than UCLA vs. USC. The war in Vietnam was heating up in Southeast Asia while the debate was heating up at home.

War protests were becoming commonplace on college campuses, but far more so at UCLA than USC.

Here, too, there were images in the public mind. USC was the campus of John Wayne, UCLA of Angela Davis.

Chaytor Mason was a World War II Marine fighter pilot who became a psychology professor at USC and was on campus in the Vietnam years. He remembered going to an event at UCLA and noticing that someone had spray painted some gold drapes in the midst of a protest.

"We were utterly shocked," Mason said. "They would never do a thing like that at USC.

"We generally commented on the goings on at UCLA in those years and the lack of them at USC. There was so much more vehemence and vitriol at UCLA and I think there are reasons for that. USC is not a place where people are generally working their way through school on their own. They feel they owe something to their family for bankrolling them. They feel a certain amount of duty not to drop out, not to waste their time while they're here."

ROTC classes were still big at USC during the Vietnam War, according to Mason, despite the anti-military feelings so prevalent on most campuses.

"We never had demonstrations against ROTC," he said. "There was never any catcalling. ROTC was accepted as a way of life in the United States. Also, there were a lot of courses taught for the military here. So there were lots of military people on campus, from first lieutenants through generals."

The military programs also attracted foreign students from the Orient, many of whom believed more strongly in the Domino Theory than in the theories of the Chicago Seven. The result was a campus often muted while upheaval exploded around it.

"There was not the rebelliousness you would find on other campuses," Mason said. "In many cases, it was blind rebellion [elsewhere], people making noise and damaging things with not a lot of deep thought about what it was all about.

"USC looked upon UCLA as being sort of childish, the kind of school where they'd go cover statues with blue paint."

Across town, the opinions may have been 180 degrees different, but the words were astonishingly similar, proving that the rivalry could be just as fierce, if not more so, in politics as it was in football. UCLA vice-chancellor Andrea Rich, a student during the protest years, said of USC, "They always seemed so smug, so rich, and so childish."

But, according to Rich, even UCLA was not always so vocally anti-war. "In early 1965," she said, "the free-speech movement began with Mario Savio at Berkeley. That was the hot school for sit-ins. But UCLA, at that point, couldn't quite get it together from the student activists' point of view. It was a commuter school and students who wanted to sit in had to get home by 5:00 because their parents had dinner on the table. It was Berkeley that was hot stuff.

"The late 60s was the time the war took hold and things got very, very serious. The notion of the draft and the casualties hit students hard. There were a lot of demonstrations here, vandalism, protests, lighting fires."

At one wild point, it was so bad the police took over the campus.

There were sharpshooters on the roofs, helicopters overhead, and students beaten with clubs and arrested. "It got very nasty," Rich recalled. "The playful demonstrations in the early 60s when kids came to college to get involved in issues became a horror in the late 60s.

On a grassy area, UCLA students erected tombstones with their own names on them, along with a sign that read "Happy Graduation." In the middle of much of the controversy was Angela Davis, an assistant philosophy professor who conducted a public battle to remain at UCLA despite her admitted membership in the Communist Party.

"It was a time when students had to make choices," Rich said, "and consider what they stood for. There was no buffer point anymore. You had to make a stand. It was around you all the time. It was a very polarized time."

But football still had its place. Students could march and protest and riot about life and death issues, but, on Saturday afternoon, they could still put down their "Stop the War" signs and pick up their "Stop the Trojans" banners.

For those in the Coliseum seats in those emotional years, football was a perfect release. They would argue with classmates until they were hoarse about whether or not the U.S. should be battling enemy forces in Vietnam, but there was no argument about the enemy forces on the opposing sideline. Whether at USC or UCLA, students were at least united in their desire to do battle on the football field.

Mike Garrett was gone in 1966, but USC, behind the best defense in the AAWU, remained a powerful team, coming into the UCLA game 7–1. The Bruins boasted the best offense and an 8–1 mark. But the Trojans were favored by 7½ points. Why?

Because Beban, the heart of that Bruin offense, was only going to be a spectator against the Trojans. He had broken an ankle the week before against Stanford, leaving the quarterbacking job to Norm Dow, who had played a total of 58 minutes in three seasons as a Bruin, understandable for a player stuck behind Beban.

Three days before his first game as a freshman, Dow hurt his knee, went into surgery and had been waiting to start a game ever since.

"I felt I was very fortunate to be at UCLA," Dow said. "If you're going to be second string, it might as well be behind a Heisman Trophy winner. I could have transferred out, but I liked UCLA."

It was a nervous seven days for Dow, waiting for the Trojans. There was a rumor that Mel Farr was going to play quarterback. No way, Prothro said. He had long admired Dow's work ethic and wasn't about to deny him his chance for the spotlight.

"If we play as a team as hard as Norman Dow has practiced all year," Prothro told his players, "we will win this game."

UCLA officials asked the media to leave Dow alone in that crucial week, but when he went to his first class on Monday, he found an unexpected visitor—a reporter looking for an interview.

It was the last class Dow attended all week.

"I was quite nervous," he said. "It appeared the game was going to be for the Rose Bowl and it looked like they [the Trojans] were coming out for revenge for the year before. Boy they were upset, and the word was they were going to take it out on us. There was a lot of pressure."

Until the first time Dow got hit. Then, it was just another game. But for Dow, it was the game of his life.

It wasn't easy, especially playing in an offense so geared to Beban. "It was the perfect offense for him," Dow said. "It was fair for me. But then, I wasn't as good an athlete as he was."

The game was scoreless in the first half. Then, USC quarterback Troy Winslow went out with a charley horse and Dow went to work. He led the Bruins on a 42-yard drive to their first score, getting it himself on a sweep around right end. "[Rich] Deakers and [Rick] Purdy put two guys down in front of me," Dow said, "and I went in untouched."

Before the quarter was over, USC had tied the game on a one-yard plunge by Dan Scott.

Dow was a key figure in the winning drive, keeping it alive on a second-and-27 with a 26-yard scramble. "Three guys had Dow," an exasperated McKay later said.

The Bruins had the first down on a one-yard lunge by Mike Bergdahl. Two plays later, from the Trojan 21, Dow started right, then handed off to Cornell Champion on a reverse. One man to beat—Nate Shaw at the 10—and that Champion did with a fancy move that left only the end zone ahead. Final: UCLA 14, USC 7.

In the delirious Bruin lockerroom, a teammate whispered to Dow: "If you don't get laid tonight, you never will."

Dow finished with 82 yards on 19 carries and a day he'll never forget. He called it "the greatest 60 minutes of my life."

Beban was almost as excited as Dow. "For two years, he supported me," Beban said, "and never let out the emotion that he must have felt that he should have been the starter. He got his day in the sun, to say the least."

And it's still a shining moment for Dow a quarter century later. "It was a fairy tale ending that I'll never forget," he said. "It's a feeling 99.9 percent of the people in the world never feel."

But other feelings were soon unleashed. Ugly feelings. Two days later, the AAWU voted to send USC to the Rose Bowl. Although UCLA finished with a 9–1 record to USC's 7–2 and had beaten the Trojans, USC went based on a better conference mark. Having played one more game, USC was 4–1 to UCLA's 3–1.

Rather than calling the upcoming Rose Bowl by its familiar name, "the grandaddy of them all," an angry Bruin supporter suggested this one be called "the grand *mother* of them all."

The bitterness that the best team had not gone to Pasadena grew even more in the ensuing weeks when the Trojans were whipped in their final regular-season game by Notre Dame, 51–0, then lost to Purdue in the Rose Bowl, 14–13.

Dow was as angry as anybody. "We had feelings of betrayal," he said. "Everybody knew it was a joke. I think they voted that way just to deny [Prothro] another trip to the Rose Bowl. It was very unjust.

"But it couldn't take away what I'd accomplished. Nothing could take that away. I'll take that to the grave."

Furious UCLA students took their anger to the streets, with as many as an estimated 2,000 persons blocking traffic on the nearby San Diego Freeway, shouting obscenities and starting bonfires. The protest lasted a little over seven hours and resulted in 30 arrests.

Vietnam? For one afternoon, USC–UCLA was even bigger.

7

Playing McKay's Game
1968–1975

On a clear June evening in 1968, harsh reality came to Tinseltown. It's one thing to watch teenagers die in living color in a war thousands of miles away, in between "Merv" and "Get Smart"; it's quite another to watch the shining hope of millions in a divided nation extinguished in your backyard.

Robert F. Kennedy, moments after delivering his victory speech in the California Primary, moving him that much closer to the presidential nomination, was killed by an assassin at the Ambassador Hotel in Los Angeles. Camelot was dead—again. So were the dreams of so many white and black Americans searching desperately for an end to the cycle of violence and disorder. First, John Kennedy. Then, Martin Luther King, Jr. Now Bobby. Two months later, Chicago.

College students across the country didn't give up. One martyr replaced another. Each week demanded a new crusade. Burn the bra, ban the bomb. Life on campus was rarely boring. But, as administration buildings were seized, and Vietnam War teachins took students from the classroom, much of the normal collegiate experience remained intact. Especially athletics.

"In college you are practicing for three hours and going to class and trying to hit the best party," said former USC quarterback Mike Rae. "You don't have time to think about the guy in the jungle three thousand miles away."

Supporters of USC and UCLA were still buzzing over their historic 1967 matchup. O.J. Simpson's 64-yard run had already passed into myth. Gary Beban's brilliance in the air granted him similar sainthood in Westwood. In college football, however, nostalgia only lasts until next season. Lose to Oregon, and last year's victories are a dim memory.

Entering the 1968 season, the Trojans felt more secure; their legend—Simpson—was coming back for his senior season. Over at UCLA, Beban graduated, taking his Heisman Trophy and game-rescuing ability with him. Beban edged out O.J. in the tightest Heisman race ever, which never fazed Simpson. He didn't expect to win the award. "I grew up in San Francisco," he said. "I was a Beban fan."

But, a year later, Simpson craved the Heisman. He remembers his first impression of the statue. He was at Mike Garrett's house for a party after the 1968 Rose Bowl, and so was *it*. All night long, Simpson kept finding excuses to return to the trophy. He couldn't take his eyes off of it, imagining his name carved underneath. He suddenly realized how close he had come to winning it in 1967, and knew he had only one more chance.

"So whenever we won a game," in 1968, "I'd look at the paper and see what Leroy Keyes (Purdue) or Terry Hanratty (Notre Dame) did," Simpson said.

USC had O.J., but not much else that season. Steve Sogge was, at times, a gutsy, efficient quarterback, but certainly not one to spearhead a deadly passing attack. So the Trojans would run, run, run. And usually score, score, score. But their defense was young and inexperienced, and, unlike 1967, there would be no easy games.

In four games, USC was tied with its opponent at the end of three quarters. In another, it trailed. Against Minnesota, Simpson had to score the winning touchdown with 3:31 left. Final: USC 29, Minnesota 20. Against Washington, O.J. scored with five minutes to go. The Huskies drove the length of the field, fumbling at the Trojan nine-yard line. Final: USC 14, Washington 7. And against Stanford, the Indians had the ball on the USC 41, trailing by just three late in the game. A pass to Gene Washington was two yards short of the first down. Final: USC 27, Stanford 24.

"We had glaring weaknesses," Simpson said. "McKay did his best coaching job with that team. We were the worst undefeated team in the history of college football." Still, they were undefeated (8–0) and ranked No. 1 by both wire service polls. They were known as the Cardiac Kids.

UCLA, meanwhile, had lost six times entering the Trojan contest—more defeats than in the prior three years combined. After opening with wins against Pittsburgh (63–7) and Washington State (31–21), the Bruins lost three in a row to Syracuse, Penn State and Cal. They beat Jim Plunkett's Stanford squad, but then got crushed by Tennessee and Oregon State. This was not one of Tommy Prothro's finest.

UCLA simply couldn't replace Beban. Neither sophomore Jim Nader nor junior Bill Bolden could throw with any consistency. Greg Jones was a solid tailback, but hardly the kind of singular threat to intimidate the Trojan defense, inexperienced or not.

Against USC, Prothro would employ a single-wing attack, one last throwback to Red Sanders football. "We just didn't think we had a quarterback," Prothro said.

The Bruins relied on their defense. Despite the six setbacks, it was a confident group. "We're more sure of ourselves now," said linebacker Don Widmer. "We know what Simpson can do now. Anything he does isn't surprising to us."

The defense might have been too confident. A week before the game, Simpson met a few UCLA players at a party. "I had recorded a number of 200-yard games," Simpson recalled, "and they said to me, 'I bet you one thing, no matter what happens against us, you won't get 200 yards.'"

It was not a wise bet. Simpson got 205 yards in 40 carries, and USC won the 1968 battle, 28–16. But, typically, it was another struggle. "We almost lost," O.J. said. "We were supposedly the better team, and they weren't a great team. And we almost lost."

The game, played in smog and fog, hinged on a Bruin drive early in the fourth quarter. USC led 21–16, when UCLA started from its own

25. The Bruins, using an unbalanced line, had opened big holes for running backs Mickey Cureton and Greg Jones. Cureton, playing on a bad knee, scored two touchdowns and had a 68-yard punt return. Still, UCLA's chances of mounting a potential game-winning march against the top-ranked team in the country were as likely as Angela Davis serving in President-elect Richard Nixon's cabinet.

Yet, led by Nader, the Bruins slowly drove downfield. Nader repeatedly positioned the Bruin machine strong left and rolled right. With seven minutes to go, from the Trojan one-yard line, Nader rolled out one more time. The end zone—and a major upset—were in reach. But Nader slipped on the damp grass, and was smothered on the three. "I'm sure I could have made it," Nader said. "I got a chance to turn, but the turf gave out under my left foot."

USC linebacker Bob Jensen then knocked a fourth-down pass away from receiver Gwen Cooper. With Simpson carrying almost every play, USC marched down and put the game away with one more touchdown. "The thing about that year's defense," Simpson said, "was that they had some athletes, so that once they were in a single-dimension situation where all they had to do was penetrate, they were tough."

The defense, however, couldn't contain a powerhouse like Woody Hayes's Ohio State, losing the Rose Bowl 27–16, and the national championship.

O.J. won the Heisman, and could now stare at it every day. The poor kid from San Francisco who used to run with stolen pies was going to run with the best. He became the number one pick in the NFL draft, and starred with the Buffalo Bills.

From then on, every Trojan runner would be compared to O.J. Jon Arnett and Mike Garrett made running glamorous at USC. O.J. Simpson made it an institution.

In 1969, USC and UCLA had something to prove. The Trojans needed to demonstrate there was life after O.J. Simpson. The Bruins needed to demonstrate there was life at all.

It didn't take UCLA long. An opening-game 37–0 romp over Oregon State set the tone for the comeback season. Entering the USC contest, the Bruins were 8–0–1, the lone tie coming against Stanford, when UCLA kicker Zenon Andrusyshyn missed an extra point and a short field goal, leaving the score 20–20.

The biggest difference in the 1969 Bruins was at quarterback. Westwood could stop reminiscing about the Beban days. The new leader was a transfer from Long Beach Junior College who threw 30 touchdowns in two years. Stanford and Florida State wanted him, too. But Stanford had Plunkett, and Florida State talked about redshirting him for a year. Dennis Dummit wasn't going to way any longer for his initiation into big-time college football.

He instantly converted UCLA into a dangerous passing team. In 1969, before the USC contest, Dummit ranked second to Plunkett in both passing and total offense. His bombing attack opened the field up more for Jones and Cureton, who, behind USC's Clarence Davis, ranked second and third in the conference's rushing race. "I've never coached a game in which anyone could throw rhythmically better than Dennis Dummit," recalled former UCLA quarterback coach, Dick Vermeil.

Davis, meanwhile, tried all he could to make Trojan fans forget O.J. Like Simpson, he came from junior college. Like Simpson, he burst into the hole, and knew how to read his blockers. And he, too, wasn't afraid to run inside. He would finish the season with 1,351 yards on 297 carries. Moreover, he helped carry USC to another excellent season. Only a 14–14 tie with Notre Dame tarnished an 8–0–1 record.

Yet, this was still a team surviving on the brink. The Trojans came from behind in the fourth quarter to win or tie six of their nine games. How long could they keep flirting with defeat? They, too, possessed a new quarterback—Jimmy Jones. Jones would never be mistaken for Dummit. He was black, Dummit white. And Jones never met a receiver he couldn't overthrow.

The two teams showed up at the Coliseum on equal footing. At stake was the Pacific 8 Conference championship and a date with Michigan or Purdue in the Rose Bowl. USC was ranked fifth, UCLA sixth.

USC had the Wild Bunch defense, nicknamed after the gang in the slaughterhouse motion picture. The group included ends Charlie Weaver and Jimmy Gunn, tackles Al Cowlings and Tody Smith, and middle guard Bubba Scott. Gunn, Cowlings and Weaver became All-Americans.

"We went to see the film," said wide receiver Sam Dickerson, "and the next day, all the guys were talking like, 'let's do it like the Wild Bunch.' They just wanted to raise havoc."

The Bruins made the game's first statement. Halfback Greg Jones took a pitch from Dummit. It looked like the play UCLA had run so successfully all year. Suddenly, Jones stopped, and threw a 41-yard touchdown to George Farmer. The play shocked the Trojans, and even most of the Bruins.

"Prothro had only told myself, Jones and Farmer," Dummit recalled, "that the first time we run that play, Greg was going to pull up and throw it. We didn't want the linemen to tip it off. So when it was third down, I looked at Greg and George and we gave each other the nod."

The momentum didn't last long. Since a tie wouldn't qualify them for the Rose Bowl, the Bruins gambled for the two-point conversion, but failed. Near the end of the first half, Davis powered 13 yards for a touchdown, Ron Ayala's extra point giving USC a 7–6 lead.

Dummit was decked like never before by the Wild Bunch. Altogether, they sacked him ten times, and forced five interceptions. Dummit felt fortunate to be alive. In one drive, on successive plays, he was hurled for losses of nine, eight, and ten yards. One fierce hit by Weaver almost transported Dummit into another time zone. "After the game," he said, "I was in the car on the freeway and my whole body started to turn into a cramp. I was so exhausted."

Jimmy Jones, however, didn't fare much better. Jones was well known for horrendous starts, and this was no exception. He was 0 for 9 at one point, overthrowing everything but the peristyle end of the Coliseum.

At the same time, Dummit somehow summoned the energy for one last-ditch drive. With five minutes to go, he hit reserve wingback Brad Lyman for 57 yards, to the Trojan 10. Three plays later, from the seven, Dummit found Gwen Cooper in the end zone. Another two-point conversion attempt failed, but UCLA led 12–7 with three minutes to go.

Only another miracle from the Cardiac Kids could save USC from certain defeat. And Jones, despite his penchant for last-minute heroics, hardly looked like the guy to do it. He was 1 for 14 for one yard.

Jones didn't surrender, hitting for three quick first downs to take the ball to UCLA's 43. But, just a quickly, he became erratic again, and the Trojans faced a fourth down and ten.

The Bruins faced a trip to Pasadena. Prothro shouted instructions to his quarterback, anticipating that the Bruins were about to take possession. "Dummitt," Prothro said, "I just want you to call a quarterback sneak because they don't have any timeouts left."

Dummitt thought it was over. "Holy shit, we're going to the Rose Bowl," he thought. "We've got it."

On fourth down, Jones missed again, and UCLA had it. The ball and the conference title. Until a flag took it all away.

Officials called interference on Bruin defensive back Danny Graham, who had apparently hit Dickerson from behind as he tried to catch a short pass down the left sideline. The ball was probably uncatchable, and under today's rules, a penalty wouldn't have been called. But it was, and USC had another chance, first down on the Bruin 32. Prothro was furious, and would never get over the call.

"I thought I'd made a good play," Graham told The *Los Angeles Times*. "But I had slipped and didn't see Jones throw. I didn't know if the pass was thrown badly or not. It seemed like my whole life just went down the drain."

The Trojans capitalized immediately. Jones faked to Davis, and then settled behind right tackle, looking for Dickerson on a corner route. The play, 64-X Post Corner, had worked all season. Dickerson faked toward the center of the field, as if running a post pattern, fooling the Bruin defender near the sideline. He then darted back toward the corner. Jones, feeling a fierce UCLA rush, threw the ball.

"I thought it was one of the highest passes I'd ever seen," Dickerson said. "It seemed like a long time coming down." He was open, but there was another problem: He was running out of space. "I could see the flat out of the corner of my eye," Dickerson said, "and I knew I was close to being out of bounds. I dragged my feet and slid out of bounds all the way to the fence."

An official, seemingly in slow motion, moved his arms to make the call. "I was sure I had made it," Dickerson said. "But I didn't know if the refs were." Finally, the signal. Touchdown.

Some Bruins argued, and even McKay later admitted he wasn't

sure Dickerson had scored. "Of course they asked me after the game," McKay said, "and I said there was no question in my mind that he was in. If I could have told he was in, I would have been the smartest son-of-a-bitch in the world. I had the worst seat in the stadium."

The game wasn't over. USC may have scored too early. With the extra point, USC led 14–12 with 1:32 left. For Dummit, that was a lifetime. He knew he'd probably have to get six points because Prothro had lost all faith in Andrusyshyn.

After USC had regained the lead, according to Dummit, Prothro told his kicker to get ready for a possible game-winning field-goal attempt. Andrusyshyn had another idea. "Coach, how about a fake?" he said. Prothro knew his kicker's confidence was gone.

Taking possession on the UCLA 32, Dummit quickly marched the Bruins to the Trojan 39. Maybe he'd get them in the Rose Bowl, after all. But the Wild Bunch performed an encore. They rushed Dummit, who threw hurriedly into the left flat for split end Rick Wilkes. Ty Hudson intercepted. USC was headed to a fourth straight Rose Bowl, eventually defeating Michigan, 10–3.

UCLA, despite outgaining the Trojans, 325 to 229, had lost another heartbreaker. Emerging from the abyss of a 3–7 season, the Bruins were once again a worthy contender for football supremacy in Los Angeles. Yet, once again, the script favored the Trojans.

Prothro was devastated by the 1969 loss. He later called that team his greatest ever. Some contend the Graham interference call alienated him from college football forever, that he lost the will to match wits with other coaches. "Tommy was never the same after that game," a former UCLA assistant said. "We just flat-out stopped recruiting with any zest; we stopped doing a lot of things."

The turbulent 1960s passed into history, but 1970 didn't generate any immediate changes in America's political landscape. The U.S. was still in Vietnam, and the kids still didn't like it. On May 4, four students at Kent State University were killed by members of the Ohio National Guard at a campus demonstration. Americans were killing Americans. The next day, UCLA was declared in a state of emergency as 250 Los Angeles police clashed with hundreds of anti-war demonstrators after they went on a window-smashing march in Westwood. When police lined up for a charge, students gave Indian war whoops and sometimes clapped. They chanted "On strike, shut it down," and "Pigs on campus."

Six months later, John Sandbrook, sports editor of the UCLA Daily Bruin, pointed out that only 6,600 of the student's 26,000 students purchased tickets for the 1970 USC game, compared to 16,000 in 1967. "I think UCLA has discovered in the last two or three years a new value system," Sandbrook told the *Times*. "It's no longer just the Big Game, but the Big Draft, the Big Election, the Big Bomb."

Things, as usual, were a little quieter at Southern Cal. "It's still basically conservative here," a student said. "To be activist-oriented here is like beating your head against a stone wall. The Reagan-oriented trustees still have this campus in their grip. It's going to be a long, uphill road for the activists."

The week leading up to the 1970 version of the rivalry didn't carry its usual frenzied anticipation, and it wasn't just because of politics. Mediocre football had something to do with it. USC was 5–3–1; UCLA 5–4. Oregon and Oregon State would be extremely satisfied with these records, but not the two proud California institutions who frankly believed each year's conference title should be settled between them. Not this year. The only matter to be resolved would be the championship of Los Angeles.

The season hadn't started out that way. The Trojans looked impressive for the first four weeks of the season. They beat Alabama, Iowa and Oregon State, and tied perennial powerhouse Nebraska. Going back to the 1967 opener against Washington State, USC was 32–2–3 in its last 37 games.

The Trojans then visited Stanford, and Jim Plunkett. The night before the game, the team attended its Friday night ritual—the movies. From the days of John Wayne, the relationship between Hollywood and USC had always been strong. Many players used to work in the industry during the summer. On this night, the movie was "Soldier Blue," an old-fashioned western about the fight between the U.S. Cavalry and the Indians. In the film, the white man massacred the Indians.

This was a far cry from "The Wild Bunch." In an era of burgeoning race consciousness, the black players felt the film was a crude affront to minorities. In real, not reel, life the Negro had supplanted the Indian as the whipping boy of white society. Some white players laughed at the picture.

On the way back to the hotel, a fight almost broke out. A team, once united, once merely an innocent collection of teen-agers playing a game, suddenly reflected the sharp schisms in the racially divided America of 1970. "You've been playing with these guys for a year or two," said Dickerson, "and you've been a close friend, and now you find out you don't see things eye to eye, cause if we were out in life and we were down, this guy could be laughing at you."

And they still had a game to play the next day. Dickerson said the lingering tension contributed to the 24–14 loss. "It was always in the back of my mind," he said. "How can you be ready to fight someone one night, and work together the next day?"

UCLA also started well. Wins over Oregon State, Pittsburgh and Northwestern carried the Bruins to a key matchup with defending national champion Texas. Dummit went crazy. He passed for 340 yards. "It was like a dream," Dummit said. "Their linebackers and defensive backs took the exact same drop every time. So we just ran crossing and slant patterns and threw everything in the seams."

Defensively, the Bruins largely neutralized the feared wishbone attack. But a last-second bomb from Longhorn quarterback Eddie Phillips pulled it out for Texas, 20–17.

The Bruins, perhaps still reeling from the Texas game, blew a 19-point lead the following week at home against Oregon, and lost 41–40. Subsequent losses to Stanford (9–7) and Washington (61–20) officially closed down the road to Pasadena. But, Rose Bowl or not, UCLA desperately wanted revenge against the Trojans. They remembered Jones to Dickerson, the interference call, and the O.J. dashes of 1967 and 1968. McKay, meanwhile, was bidding to become the first coach in the history of the rivalry to score four straight victories.

Revenge came quickly. Once again, USC opened with trickery, sending flanker Reggie Echols on a reverse. The play gained 35 yards. Six plays later, Dummit hit Rick Wilkes for a TD. When Dummit hit Bob Christiansen later in the quarter for a 39-yard touchdown, UCLA lead 17–7. The senior quarterback completed eight of 11 passes for 148 yards—in the first quarter. What Wild Bunch? At halftime, it was UCLA 38, USC 14. And Dummit wanted more.

He approached Vermeil in the locker room. "Coach, I want to score 100," he begged Vermeil.

"Calm down, calm down," the coach responded.

"I wanted to beat them so bad," Dummit said. "I wanted payback. After the year before, it wasn't enough to win. I wanted to win big."

But UCLA didn't pour it on. For most of the second half, Marv Kendricks carried the ball, finishing with 182 yards in 28 attempts, then a UCLA single-game rushing record. Dummit completed 19 of 30 passes for 272 yards and three touchdowns, and broke some Beban records. Overall, UCLA outgained USC, 563 to 369.

"When we scored out last touchdown," Dummit said, "I was so happy. It wasn't enough to run off the field with my arms in the air. I started doing somersaults."

It was the most points the Bruins had ever scored in the crosstown rivalry. They hadn't beaten the Trojans so convincingly since the Red Sanders national championship team of 1954, which crushed USC, 34–0. Perhaps UCLA would own Los Angeles again.

If that were going to be true, the Bruins would have to seize the town without their field commander. Prothro quit to coach the Rams. He finished his Westwood career with a 41–18–3 record. He still denies the move to professional football was chartered months in advance, even though many claimed he became increasingly removed from the college game as 1970 wore on.

Rams owner Dan Reeves "called me three times to talk to him," Prothro said, "and I wouldn't even go back to him. Then, finally, I did talk to him and the contract he wrote up was very difficult to turn down."

To replace Prothro, UCLA once again appointed a former Bruin assistant, Pepper Rodgers. Rodgers, offensive coordinator under Prothro in 1965 and 1966, had turned Big Eight doormat Kansas into a midwest power. The Jayhawks even made it to an Orange Bowl.

Rodgers was much different than the imposing Prothro. He possessed a laid-back, down-to-earth demeanor, suggesting a Southern storeowner, not a head football coach. He'd play Kenny Rogers music in his office, and do somersaults in front of new recruits. "With Pepper," recalled quarterback John Sciarra, who played for him in 1973, "if you didn't know him, you'd say, 'He's the head football coach at UCLA?'"

Added Fred McNeil, a linebacker: "Pepper didn't come off as being real serious. I don't know if his style was the best to motivate the players."

Rodgers, known for his innovativeness on offense, didn't have the time or personnel to make any dramatic changes in his inaugural season. He stuck with a pro-style attack. Trouble is UCLA didn't have a pro-style quarterback. Dummit had graduated. Rodgers shifted between Mike Flores, Clay Gallagher and Scott Henderson. There wasn't a quarterback between the three of them.

Westwood missed Prothro. The Bruins lost their first four games of the Rodgers Era—their worst start since 1943. Michigan crushed them 38–0. Entering the USC contest, the Bruins (2–7) needed something new to salvage a season to forget. They found it in the wishbone.

Rodgers didn't invent it; he merely polished it. Throughout the season, he practiced it with his freshmen, preparing them for the years ahead. With an extra week of practice, he would unveil the wishbone against the Trojans. "We looked back and saw how Alabama had gone with it, and how Texas had gone with it," Rodgers said, "how both had gone to the top of the heap using it. And we studied people who had failed with it, and they failed because it's like studying religion. You believe or you don't believe. You can't just be half religious." Rodgers became one of its most devoted disciples.

"We ran the wishbone for two years at UCLA," he said, "and we never broke the formation once. That's because you don't have to. There's more pressure on the guy who doesn't know what you're going to do. You know what you're going to do."

Under the system, the quarterback has numerous options. He can keep it himself, or hand off to any of three running backs advancing toward the line with him. When run efficiently, the wishbone seems impossible to stop. Critics, however, point out it's extremely prone to turnovers, and it's almost useless when a team is trailing late in the game.

Rodgers never paid attention to its limitations. "I've never wanted an offense," he said, "where you had to come from behind. I always wanted one that got you ahead."

At Southern Cal, John McKay faced his own problems. After six weeks, USC stood an uncharacteristic 2–4. One mediocre season (1970) was plenty. The Trojan alumni were concerned about this new decade of losing. Forgotten were all of McKay's achievements in the 1960s. Because of injuries, the team had no true tailback. Sam "The Bam" Cummingham, 6'3", 218 pounds, had to do.

Jimmy Jones suffered the heaviest abuse. He was black, and the team was losing. "It was all part of the fact that SC people weren't used to having three or four losses," said Jones. "I was a black quarterback my sophomore year, (1969) too, and there wasn't that kind of criticism."

At first, McKay resisted the letters from fans asking him to start junior Mike Rae, who was white. He believed Jones was the better quarterback. But, as the troubled 1971 season dashed any hopes of a Rose Bowl bid, McKay turned toward the future. At South Bend, he began rotating Jones and Rae series by series. The experiment worked. USC won, 28–14, and started on a roll, beating Cal, 28–0, Washington State, 30–20, and Washington 13–12. Next up: UCLA.

Frequently, the USC-UCLA rivalry brings out the best in both teams, even when enduring lackluster seasons. They rise above their records to produce a classic. The 1971 game was not one of those times.

It ended in a 7–7 tie. Much of the normal hysteria was missing. Fewer cheers. Fewer boos. Mostly yawns. "That was the most boring game in the history of football," said Rae.

For USC, the tie symbolized the futility of two straight subpar seasons. McKay simply called the big game "the big nothing."

For UCLA, the tie symbolized new hope. "I really feel like we won," Rodgers said. "It was very important that we didn't lose this game. Obviously, they can't take the city championship away from us until they beat us."

More importantly, the Bruins tested the wishbone in a game situation. It only showed flashes of efficiency, as UCLA was outgained by USC, 295 go 158 yards. But there would be no turning back now.

The wishbone was the offense of the future for UCLA. It hardly mattered the Bruins didn't complete one pass all afternoon. They wouldn't need to pass under Pepper Rodgers.

For the troubled Trojans, the 1972 season actually started in the locker room after the 1971 Bruin game. Somebody had set off a stink bomb in the UCLA rooting section. John McKay wasn't happy.

"The only thing that smelled worse than that bomb was the way we played football," McKay admonished the troops in his post-game lecture. "When spring practice comes along, I'm going to reevaluate every single player. No consideration will be given to players who were starters. Nobody is secure."

When spring practice arrived, there was a new attitude at USC. McKay recognized immediately that this team might be special.

"I cut practice off after 14 days," McKay said.

He also hired a new assistant coach, John Robinson. Robinson had played for McKay in Oregon. He had an unbridled enthusiasm, which became contagious. Marv Goux fired up the defense, and now the offense had Robinson. He went over game films with players, perfectly balancing criticism with encouragement. He gave USC the spark it had lacked since 1969.

"He treated us like human beings," said All-American tackle Pete Adams. "You were gong to walk through a wall for this guy."

Adams recalled another incident that spring which invigorated the team. The players wanted to wear their hair long, but McKay had insisted on keeping it short, forbidding all facial hair. The players wanted to be hip; McKay still lived in the 1950s.

One day, the players came to McKay as a group and asked for the right at least to wear mustaches. McKay quickly realized he was coaching a different breed of athlete. He gave his permission.

"It was like he trusted us a little more," Adams said. "He wasn't treating us like kids anymore. He had seen us grow up, and he let us get a little looser. It really helped the team. We worked our trails off so hard that it was unbelievable."

The team was closer than it had been in years. No more racial divisions. No more quarterback controversies. At the end of training camp, the players had a party. They got up and imitated all the coaches.

Everyone laughed, even McKay. The following week, the coaches imitated the players. "We hadn't done those kinds of things before," said Rae. "We came out of there with real good feelings."

And real good talent. USC had been accused of stockpiling players for years, even recruiting all-state high school stars who would never see one down of college football. The idea was to keep them from helping other teams. In 1972, the talent meshed like perhaps never before, and maybe never again. The 1971 unbeaten freshmen team was now ready for the varsity.

There was Lynn Swann, the all-purpose receiver who would eventually help carry the Pittsburgh Steelers to four Super Bowls; Richard Wood, the All-American linebacker who, running the 40 in 4.5, kept opposing runners from ever finding daylight; Sam Cunningham, who moved back to his natural position of fullback, ran over dazed defensive linemen, and later starred with the New England Patriots; All-American tight-end Charles Young; and a sophomore running back from the San Fernando Valley, northwest of Los Angeles. His name was Anthony Davis. Everyone called him A.D.

McKay also planned a few new wrinkles for the offense. Believing the I-formation had become too predictable, he set up plays for the flankers to move in near the tailback and carry the ball on reverses or counter plays. Swann was the perfect pawn for that chess move.

UCLA, meanwhile, wasn't going to sit idly as its crosstown rival prepared for greatness. The Bruins found their own infusion of new ideas. Rodgers hired Homer Smith. Smith was known for his passing wizardry, but Rodgers was confident he was the man to fine-tune the still-raw wishbone attack. Rodgers was feeling the pressure. A 2–7–1 record wasn't the way to endear himself to the Westwood fans.

Both schools opened with stiff challenges. UCLA faced two-time defending national champion Nebraska, riding a 32-game winning streak. USC battled Arkansas, a team many expected to dethrone Nebraska. Both schools won, paving the way for memorable 1972 seasons.

Rodgers, who had defeated Nebraska twice when he coached Kansas, surprised the Cornhuskers with the wishbone. "We did a very good job of keeping it under wraps," he said. Emerging in the game as an outstanding practitioner of the formation was Mark Harmon, son of Michigan Hall of Famer Tom Harmon.

The Bruins enjoyed the advantage of playing Nebraska at home while the Trojans faced the Razorbacks in Arkansas. Neither team lacked incentive. Before the game, Arkansas quarterback Joe Ferguson practically dismissed USC as any threat. "He looked at our game as a stepping stone to a national championship," Wood recalled. "We went out and wanted to use them as a stepping stone to our national championship."

USC fumbled the opening kickoff, leading to an Arkansas field goal. But then the Trojans scored 24 straight points, and won, 31–10. Rae converted 18 of 24 passes, and Rod McNeil, returning from a year layoff for hip surgery, rushed for 117 yards. "We dominated that game," Robinson said, "and came out with a sense that we were talented."

McKay's team never looked back. The Trojans scored at least 50 points in three straight games—51–6 over Oregon State, 55–20 over Illinois, and 51–6 over Michigan State. They had only one close game, a 30–21 triumph against Stanford. The lopsided contests allowed McKay to insert sophomore quarterback Pat Haden, who gained valuable game experience.

Late in the season, McKay had to make another change. McNeil and backup tailback Allen Carter were hurting. McKay put in Davis. The temporary move became permanent.

A.D. was USC's most electrifying player since O.J. He may be the best Trojan never to win a Heisman. His six touchdowns against Notre Dame in 1972—he returned two kickoffs—will always stand as one of the sport's greatest moments. He was small, 5'9", 188 pounds, but dangerous. "He'd hit a hole so quick," Adams said, "that you didn't have to hold your blocks very long. He had that low center of gravity that it made him hard to bring down."

Davis made his first start against Washington State the week before UCLA. The Trojans won, 44–3. They entered the Bruin contest 9–0, ranked No. 1.

UCLA came in at 8–2, stumbling against Michigan, 26–9, and Washington, 30–21. The wishbone, however, rarely sputtered. With Harmon, and halfbacks James McAlister and Kermit Johnson, the

Bruins had the nation's number two rushing team, averaging 361 yards a game. UCLA needed only 190 yards to break the season record of 3,801 set by Howard Jones' Thundering Herd in 1929.

Game week arrived. America had just re-elected Richard Nixon, still believing Watergate was a third-rate bungled burglary. Four more years, everybody assumed. The UCLA-USC campuses remained as different as ever. "During the election campaign," said a USC coed, "there were as many kids working at Nixon's table as McGovern's. But I have friends who go to UCLA and say there's no way you'd find anybody at a Nixon table over there."

A president had been chosen, but a Rose Bowl representative was still undecided. The game would make the difference. UCLA (5–1 in the conference) needed a win; USC (6–0) could tie and go to Pasadena. But the Trojans were chasing history, and required perfection. The seniors, remembering 1970 and 1971, were rubbing their collective hands at this one final chance to beat the Bruins.

First, they had to stop the wishbone. With James Sims, Jeff Winans, Monte Doris, and Richard Wood, USC ranked number one nationally in rushing defense, yielding an average of only 75 yards a game. It would be strength against strength, but McKay had an edge. All season, preparing for UCLA, McKay and Robinson had simulated the wishbone in practice. Pat Haden was the guinea pig. "We never intended to use it," Robinson said. "McKay just wanted to make sure that he knew everything about it."

He knew enough. The Trojans stayed on course for another national title, defeating UCLA, 24–7. Using the quick outside pursuit of Wood and Sims, they held the Bruins to 198 rushing yards by forcing them into a conservative, up-the-middle game. When that's done, the wishbone is almost like any other offense. Rodgers couldn't rely on Harmon, a below-average passer, who completed only three of nine for 38 yards. Rodgers fell behind with the wishbone, and died with it.

"UCLA was racking up 300, 400 yards a game," said Wood. "We had the attitude of 'Not this game.' And we knew they had no passing game."

USC did have its chances. Down 10–7, the Bruins recovered a

fumble on the Trojan 27 but came away with nothing when Efren Herrera missed on a 33-yard field goal attempt. The Trojans then marched 80 yards for a touchdown to go up 17–7—Rod McNeil plunged in from the one—and tacked on a Rae seven-yard bootleg midway through the third quarter. The game was over.

In each drive, the key was Davis. He scored the game's first touchdown on a 23-yard run. He set up the last two scores with one sparkling move after another. He finished with 178 yards in 26 carries. In the last three games, A.D. dashed for 579 yards and six touchdowns. One week later, he made history against Notre Dame.

UCLA made remarkable progress in 1972, from 2–7–1 to 8–3. USC made the record books. The Trojans, in the Rose Bowl for the fifth time in seven years, knocked off Ohio State 42–17, in the Rose Bowl and won another national championship. Some still regard it as the greatest college football team ever.

By 1973, Watergate had become a serious threat to the Nixon presidency. And, as it turned out, there was a sizeable contingent from USC who helped bring him down. Among the Trojan graduates: Ron Ziegler, Nixon's press secretary; Dwight Chapin, the presidential appointments secretary; Donald Segretti, the all-purpose dirty tricks operator; Bart Porter, a former White House advance man who had received money from the famous slush fund, and Gordon Strachan, a political aide to H.R. Haldeman. The university was embarrassed. It couldn't understand how some of its finest could break a nation's trust.

But UCLA had produced Haldeman, who became president of the alumni association.

Watergate became part of the rivalry. Why not? Everything else was. "One of the concerns," said Robert Mannes, former Dean of Student Life at USC, "was that the people from SC who were involved were on the second echelon, while the people form UCLA were on the first echelon. There was a certain amount of competition."

America lost faith in its politicians, not its athletes. As the 1973 season approached, there were many questions: What could USC do for an encore? Could UCLA's wishbone operate at will again? Was A.D. on the way to a Heisman?

Long before he broke the color barrier in major league baseball,
Jackie Robinson was a star at UCLA.

Bob Waterfield is best remembered as L.A.'s first big pro football star with the Rams. But at UCLA, they remember him as the quarterback of the 1942 team, the first to beat the Trojans.

Burr Baldwin was on the other end of Waterfield's 42-yard touchdown pass in UCLA's 14-7 victory over USC in 1942.

It was famous sportswriter Grantland Rice who suggested UCLA hire Red Sanders, and it was the best idea the school ever had. Under Sanders, the Bruins dominated the rivalry in the 1950s. Next to Sanders is his disciple, future Bruin coach, Tommy Prothro.

Jack Ellena was one of the leaders of the 1954 squad, the only UCLA team ever to go undefeated (9-0).

Donn Moomaw became a much-heralded linebacker for Red Sanders. After football, he became the minister of the Bel-Air Presbyterian Church in Los Angeles, and delivered the invocation at President Reagan's inauguration.

After George Dickerson quit early in the 1958 season, another assistant, Bill Barnes, took over. Barnes, however, was replaced in 1964 after three straight losing seasons.

Mel Farr was a spectacular runner, and the perfect complement to Gary Beban in the UCLA backfield of the mid 1960s.

Bruin players carry Tommy Prothro and his briefcase off the field. Prothro brought his briefcase to every game (inside were plays and other information in case he ever forgot anything), but he claims he never opened it.

Gary Beban was the only Heisman Trophy winner UCLA produced. Although a great passer, Beban was also often utilized on the sweep.

His professional career never took off, but Beban will always be idolized for his Bruin exploits, and his classic confrontation with O.J. Simpson.

Soon after becoming head coach in Westwood, Pepper Rodgers installed the wishbone, turning UCLA into an unstoppable offensive machine. He left, however, after three years to coach his alma mater, Georgia Tech.

The fiery and devoted Dick Vermeil replaced Rodgers, and led UCLA to a major upset over Ohio State in the 1976 Rose Bowl. But he too left quickly, to become coach of the Philadelphia Eagles.

Running back Wendell Tyler made many spectacular plays for UCLA, but also earned a reputation for fumbling. He turned the ball over four times in the 1975 USC game, but the Bruins still prevailed, 25-22.

Safety Kenny Easley hit as hard as any player in the history of the rivalry. He was finally rewarded with a victory against USC, 20-17, in 1980.

Wide receiver Cormac Carney was an outstanding target for UCLA quarterback Tom Ramsey as the Bruins revamped their offense in the early 1980s.

Only 31 when he took over for Vermeil in 1976, Terry Donahue is still coaching the Bruins. He rebounded from a crushing loss in 1979 to win the series against the Trojans in the 1980s.

James Owens may not have had the marquee name of the other great tailbacks, but he was always a valuable asset for UCLA.

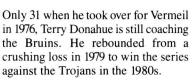

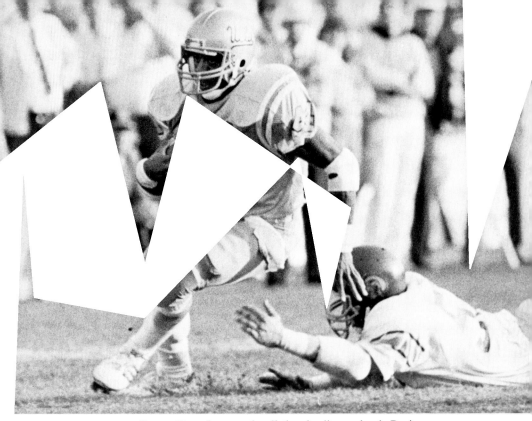

Gaston Green became the all-time leading rusher in Bruin history with 3,731 yards. He had several great games against USC.

Troy Aikman didn't fit in Barry Switzer's plans at Oklahoma, so the quarterback transferred to UCLA. Aikman guided the Bruins to magnificent seasons in 1987 and 1988, but lost to Rodney Peete and USC both years.

USC, to be sure, retained plenty of talent. First-round draft choices Young, Adams and Cunningham were gone, but Davis, McNeill and Swann remained on offense, while Wood, Sims and Doris still anchored the defense. Plus the graduation of Rae handed the job to Haden, perhaps the most promising quarterback ever to attend a tailback school.

Haden was at home with McKay—literally. After his parents moved to San Francisco, Haden lived with the McKays during his senior year in high school. He and the coach's son, Jake, were inseparable. At Bishop Amat High School, they formed a deadly passing-receiving combination. They attended USC games in the lean years of 1970 and 1971, and dreamed about the future.

"We're better than these guys," they said. It might have been true.

The best friends always knew they'd enroll at the same university. They considered Notre Dame and Nebraska before choosing USC. As freshmen, they aimed high. "We wanted to win every game for four years," Haden said.

By 1973, they were halfway there; the 1971 freshman went 4–0; the 1972 team finished 12–0. Haden, 5'11" and 175 pounds, wasn't a mere bystander, either. Rae started, but Haden chipped in with seven touchdown passes and was instrumental in the Oregon win. He had a great arm—he could throw 50-yard bombs on the run—and a great mind; he became a Rhodes Scholar after college.

UCLA also had a new quarterback. He was sophomore John Sciarra. In 1973, Sciarra and Harmon split time. Harmon was the better runner, Sciarra the better thrower. The Bruins stuck to the wishbone. "It's wishbone time, wishbone time," players yelled before practice.

Against Nebraska in the 1973 opener, it was whitewash time. The Cornhuskers, anxious for revenge, buried UCLA, 40–13. The Bruins weren't discouraged. They proceeded to win nine straight, rolling up unprecedented scores and yardage totals. In five of their games, they scored 55 or more points. In 10 games, entering the USC matchup, the wishbone had produced a total of 457 points, averaging 415 rushing yards. John Wooden didn't work the only wizardry in Westwood.

No wonder they came into the Trojan game more confident than any Bruin outfit ever, and that includes the Sanders years. No wonder they donned white shoes, expecting the first UCLA Rose Bowl appearance since 1966. No wonder they started a war of words. Said

McAlister: "I was afraid against USC last year, and so were a lot of other guys on this team. But we're not afraid anymore. They're (USC) in trouble. They're going to get theirs."

No wonder they lost.

The final was USC 23, UCLA 13. The Trojans had lost their unbeaten streak—23 straight since losing to Stanford, 33–18, in 1971—when Notre Dame defeated them, 23–14, in South Bend, McKay's first lost to the Irish since the humiliating 51–0 game in 1966. They had lost that aura of invincibility. The Haden class wouldn't go undefeated in four years.

But the Trojans hadn't lost their quickness on defense, the balanced attack of Haden, Davis and Swann, and the dedication to return to Pasadena. The Bruin arrogance only made USC want it more. "They must have thought they were playing the University of Pacific or one of those Division II schools," Wood said. "They were forgetting who they were playing."

Once again, USC neutralized the wishbone, holding UCLA to 331 total yards—only 249 on the ground. The Bruins, fearful of Sims' lateral pursuit, rarely went outside. That left middle guard Monte Doris as the defensive hero; he made 18 tackles, 11 unassisted. Robinson said the Trojans always knew which way the Bruins were going, and just slanted Doris in that direction.

Anthony Davis also had another outstanding game—145 yards on 27 carries, blunting some of the nagging criticism he'd received that season. After such a remarkable sophomore year, Trojan fans expected A.D. to be all-world in 1973. Somehow, 893 yards, his total entering the UCLA game, wasn't enough.

The Bruins were also plagued by six turnovers. USC didn't turn the ball over once. Two of the miscues came late in the game when UCLA still had a chance to win. Once, Sciarra was blindsided by Sims and lost the ball to Trojan linebacker Dale Mitchell. Then, a minute later, Sciarra, pressured by Mitchell, was intercepted by Ted Roberson. Game, set and match.

UCLA got the conference record for most total yards in one season, 5,177, but didn't get the roses. Again.

One month later, the Bruins suffered another loss. This time, it was their coach. Pepper Rodgers, after 17 wins in his last two years, after amassing an offensive machine never seen in Westwood, went South. He returned to coach his alma mater, Georgia Tech. At the time, Rodgers claimed he was moved by nostalgia, the chance to give something back to the university where he started his football career. Two decades later, another story emerges.

"I wish I hadn't gone," said Rodgers, who never beat USC in his three-year tenure. "It was money. It was a lot of money. It wouldn't have sounded good back then to tell your alma mater you're going back because of money."

Whatever his reasons, UCLA was again stuck with a coaching vacancy. This would be their fourth coach since John McKay started for USC in 1960. And coaching turnovers usually don't do wonders for recruitment and continuity. So the Bruins didn't waste much time. And once again, they dipped into the extensive pool of former UCLA assistants. They hired Dick Vermeil.

He had served as offensive coordinator in 1970, and is credited with helping Dennis Dummit mature into one of the nation's best quarterbacks. Vermeil jumped with Prothro to the Rams in 1971, and stayed on when Chuck Knox assumed command.

Vermeil was the total opposite of Pepper Rodgers. Rodgers was ingratiating; Vermeil intimidating. Rodgers walked the practice field; Vermeil stalked it. "There were certain things you could say to Pepper you wouldn't dare say to Vermeil," Sciarra said.

Practices got tougher. Vermeil was an organizational fanatic. Years later, his work ethic cut short his coaching career when he burned out with the Philadelphia Eagles. "I'm watching everyone of you," Vermeil yelled in practice, and the players knew it.

The challenge wasn't easy. First, he decided to scrap the wishbone in hopes of eventually implementing a more pro-style offense. But in order to make a smooth transition, Vermeil settled on a veer attack. That's where halfbacks split left and right and operate like they do in the wishbone, except there's no fullback. Two receivers, meanwhile, line up on the outside. The system carries the best of both styles—the options of the wishbone, the threat of the pass.

The Bruins didn't take long to adapt. With Sciarra at the controls, they were 3–1–2, still a threat to win the conference. But injuries kept cropping up, the most severe when Sciarra broke his ankle in the Cal game. He was gone for the season. Jeff Dankworth, his backup, then hurt his ankle, and couldn't start the next game against Washington. With freshman Steve Bukich, the Bruins went down, 31–9. They rallied to beat Oregon and Oregon State, and were fired up for another chance at the Trojans.

USC was having another USC season—7–1–1. Only an opening loss to Arkansas (22–7) and a 15–15 tie with Cal marred another run at the national championship.

Before the season, McKay said the 1974 version could be better than the 1972 team. They still had Haden and Wood, and A.D. Haden slumped early in the season, forcing McKay to resort to more of a running game. But the quarterback returned to form as the season progressed.

The pre-game hype didn't come close to matching the anticipation in 1972 and 1973. Everyone expected the Trojans to massacre the Bruins. The Southern Cal campus wasn't filled with "Beat UCLA" signs. Tommy Trojan only received precautionary protection.

UCLA players must have known the game would be no contest. They didn't say anything that might end up on USC's locker room bulletin board. And they certainly didn't make much of a statement during the game. Final: USC 34, UCLA 9.

The Trojans' margin of victory was their largest in the rivalry since 1944, when they downed the Bruins, 40–13. They also extended their unbeaten conference winning streak to 25 games, breaking the mark of 24 shared with California (1947–51). USC would play in its seventh Rose Bowl in nine years, beating Ohio State, 18–17, and go on to win another national championship. It was the fifth straight time USC had won the crosstown rivalry when the Rose Bowl was on the line for both teams.

Once again, UCLA was doomed by turnovers; five this time. And, for the third straight year, Davis was the offensive star—195 yards on 31 carries, the second best rushing day of his career. He also surpassed O.J. Simpson's rushing total. Haden didn't have to do much. He threw only eight passes, including a 17-yard scoring toss to McKay to make it 17–3 in the second quarter. McKay had to reach behind on the 3-yard line to grab the ball with his left hand, not gaining control until he reached the end zone. The two childhood buddies had beaten UCLA three straight years.

"The seniors got together before the game," Wood recalled, "and we said, 'let's give them one more whooping.' As freshmen, we had a goal that we would never lose to them. And we never did."

In 1974, UCLA finished 6–3–2, tied for third in the conference. It was a respectable showing, especially for a first-year coach who had to revamp the offense and develop the team's trust. But Vermeil felt the team underachieved. "I don't think I did a great job my first year," he said. "I don't think we could've beaten USC, but we shouldn't have lost to any other team. I think people felt I should leave after the first year."

There was no grass-roots campaign to dump him in 1975, but the pressure in Westwood was building. No wins against USC since 1970. No Rose Bowls since 1966. With Sciarra healthy again, and junior running back Wendell Tyler gaining confidence, it seemed the drought might end. Vermeil, to take advantage of Sciarra's passing skills, loosened the veer. UCLA opened with wins against Iowa State and Tennessee, before tying Air Force. Next up was Ohio State, and Heisman Trophy winner Archie Griffin. Were the Bruins capable of playing the big boys?

No and yes. For two and half quarters at the Coliseum, the Buckeyes dominated, leading 38–7.

A game was lost. But a season was saved. The Bruins battled back to lose 41–20, proving they could score against the nation's elite. Vermeil, in the midst of a blowout, saw enough encouraging signs to make an outrageous prediction.

"We're going to play these guys again in the Rose Bowl," he told his team.

Meanwhile, at Southern Cal, the games became secondary to the rumors: Was he or wasn't he?

The he was John McKay, and the word since May was that he planned to become the first head coach of the new Tampa Bay

Buccaneers franchise in the NFL. The reports intensified, especially after McKay made a rare congratulatory speech to his players after they beat Notre Dame, 24–17. There had been reports of offers in past years from other professional teams, including the Rams, but this one wouldn't go away. Instead of focusing on such an important triumph in South Bend, the writers wanted to know about the rumors. Finally, on Oct. 31, McKay, 52, confirmed it. After 16 years and four national championships, "Johnny Who" was jumping to the pros.

"I finally said, 'listen, I might as well tell them yes now, as wait till the end of the season because the rest of the season is going to be this way," McKay said.

Once the news was official, everyone focused on the cast of characters likely to replace the wise-cracking legend. Would it be the fiery Marv Goux, the long-time McKay assistant? Goux, according to some players, was crazy. One remembered him yelling to the Washington players in the tunnel before the game: "This is going to be a great game, isn't it?" The Huskies stared in disbelief. Another time, he told a team meeting: "I was born a Trojan and I'll die a Trojan. You've got to beat the Bruins for yourselves because it isn't possible to go through life without beating UCLA."

Would it be Dave Levy, who joined McKay in 1960, and became his top assistant? Or would it be Craig Fertig, the former quarterback turned assistant coach?

None of the above. The job went to John Robinson. Robinson, uncertain of McKay's future intentions, had left USC in 1975 to work for his friend, John Madden, head coach of the Oakland Raiders, as backfield coach. But when the USC job opened up, Robinson jumped at it.

At the news conference introducing Robinson, there was a notable no-show: John McKay. That fueled speculation that he favored one of the other candidates. Two decades later, he doesn't do much to change that perception.

"I knew who should be the head coach," said McKay, who was also athletic director, "but week after week, I realized that somebody else was going to decide this, and then I accepted that. . . . They made their decision. Johnny won pretty good, so it was a good decision."

The timing didn't seem too good. McKay's announcement altered the team's chemistry. Ranked fourth and undefeated—they had out-scored opponents, 174 to 66—the Trojans immediately disintegrated. They lost three in a row, to Cal, Stanford, and Washington. Players insist the change isn't responsible for the sudden losing streak. McKay knew better. "When you start thinking of those things rather than winning," he said, "I don't think you're as well prepared as you should be."

USC, however, didn't lose anything at tailback. Replacing A.D. was Ricky Bell, the junior from Fremont High. They couldn't have been more different. Davis was small and ran around tacklers. Bell was big—6'2", 215 pounds—and punished tacklers. Davis was flamboyant and cocky; Bell, low-key and modest. Facing the Bruins in 1975, Bell, in nine games, had logged 1,739 yards, 318 more than Davis amassed in 12 games a year earlier.

UCLA had its own running threat in Tyler. Five-foot-ten, 185 pounds, Tyler was closing in on Kermit Johnson's single-season Bruin rushing record.

But the battle between runners would be overshadowed by the bigger subplot of the 1975 USC-UCLA matchup: The farewell of John McKay.

It was not a pleasant goodbye. The Trojans lost 25–22, extending McKay's losing streak to four games for the first time since he took over in 1960.

The Bruins tried to give the game to USC, fumbling eight times. Perhaps they really didn't want to be invited to the Rose Bowl, after all. In the past three games against the Trojans, UCLA had committed 19 turnovers.

"I tried every back I had," Vermeil said, "but they all fumbled. Tyler I could anticipate fumbling, but not the other guys. I'd be grabbing guys by the throat, and they'd still fumble. So I put Tyler back in there. Might as well have the guy in there who could make a long run."

Tyler, who fumbled four times, finished with 130 yards on 17 carries. Bell got 136 yards on 36 carries. Perhaps the most revealing statistic of the game, beside turnovers, was the abysmal performance of Trojan quarterback Vince Evans. In one stretch, Evans threw 14 straight times without a completion. Quipped *Sports Illustrated:* "Vince Evans couldn't throw a football into the bottom of the Grand Canyon if he was standing on the edge."

The next test for Evans was the Liberty Bowl and highly ranked Texas A & M. The Trojans won 20–0, finally giving McKay a worthy send-off. "I would have voted against going," McKay said. "I don't think SC should go to the Liberty Bowl."

UCLA, meanwhile, in the Rose Bowl for the first time in ten years, faced top-ranked Ohio State in a rematch. Nobody gave the Bruins much of a chance, and the strain on Dick Vermeil and his team didn't take long to show. Vermeil made his players go through two practices a day. The conference champions, proud of their accomplishment, assumed they had earned the right to cruise through the rest of the season.

The team's executive committee went to Vermeil to request an easier practice schedule. It never had a chance. "If I don't have enough players, I'll go out on Bruin Walk and recruit students," Vermeil shouted back at the insurgents. "You guys can go home, but there's no way I'm going to embarrass myself on national television with putting out an inferior team."

The only people embarrassed in Pasadena on New Year's Day 1976 were the folks from Ohio State. Down 3–0 at half, UCLA stormed back to upset the Buckeyes, 23–10. Unable to execute the option effectively in the first half, the Bruins came out throwing after intermission. When Ohio State adjusted to shut down the passing attack, UCLA went back to the option.

In two years, Vermeil had risen from an unknown to a genius. And UCLA had arisen from a decade of failure. It had been a long drought, even by the standards of water-scarce Southern California.

8

Games of Sudden Death
1976–1982

The Vermeil Era lasted as long as leisure suits.

So impressive was this upstart's upset of a living legend—Woody Hayes—that Vermeil immediately became a hot commodity to NFL owners. Especially Leonard Tose, owner of the Philadelphia Eagles. Shortly after the 1976 Rose Bowl, Tose contacted Vermeil. Vermeil, only 39, told Tose he wasn't interested in abandoning the university which gave him his first head coaching opportunity. The stubborn Tose tried again. This time, Vermeil listened.

After Tose formally offered him the job, Vermeil brought it to a family vote. The Vermeils loved Los Angeles, and voted against Philadelphia. So much for democracy in the household. "It was hard to turn that down," said Vermeil, who would earn significantly more than the $30,000 salary he was making at UCLA.

Nobody will ever know how the Bruin football program would have developed if Vermeil had stayed. He says many highly-rated recruits who eventually made it to the NFL—Arizona State quarterback Mark Malone (Steelers, Chargers) and USC tackle Anthony Muñoz (Bengals), among others—told him they would have gone there if he hadn't bolted. Vermeil quit just a week before high school players could sign letters of intent.

To keep as many recruits as possible committed to UCLA, Athletic Director J.D. Morgan had to move fast. He also had to hire someone he trusted would stay a long time. Looking at the rate of Bruin head coaches, one might have guessed George Steinbrenner was running the show. Rodgers stayed three years, Vermeil two. Maybe the next coach would quit during spring practice.

Almost immediately after hearing about the vacancy, one eager Bruin assistant tossed his name into the pool of candidates. He was only 31, and possessed no head coaching experience. But Terry Donahue never paid attention to the odds.

He was never supposed to play college football. Recruiters weren't interested in a 170-pound linebacker. He played one year at San Jose State as a walk-on. When told he wasn't big enough to stay, he landed at tiny Valley College, north of Los Angeles. He was just another small kid with big dreams.

He never gave up. He gained twenty pounds and became an amateur fighter, winning his only bout by decision. A year later, Donahue earned the only title he cared about—UCLA football player. He joined the Bruins without a scholarship, and became a regular defensive tackle for two seasons and a star of the 14–12 upset of Michigan State in the 1966 Rose Bowl. After graduation, he joined Pepper Rodgers' staff at Kansas, accompanying his former coach to Westwood in 1971.

The choice reportedly came down to Donahue and Lynn Stiles, Vermeil's defensive coordinator. The kid won another fight. "I told J.D. Morgan that if he hired me, although I was inexperienced, I would grow," Donahue said, "and I'd stay a long time." He's still there.

Morgan also might have suspected Donahue was likely to take a pro assistant's job with either Vermeil, or Tommy Prothro in San Diego. He certainly stood to receive a head coaching job in college, having apparently came close earlier in the year with Oregon State.

Donahue's first task was to keep the recruits from enrolling elsewhere. He managed to hang on to many of them. Of the 56 players on the North and South teams for the state's annual Shrine high school all-star game, Donahue signed ten. But Vermeil's assistants weren't so amenable. Stiles, Jerry Long, Jim Criner, Rod Dowhower, and Carl Peterson found different jobs. Only Dick Tomey, Bill McPherson and Billie Mathews remained.

Once he assembled a new staff, Donahue began concentrating on the season ahead. Like Vermeil, he realized he didn't have the time or the mix of players to install new offensive strategies. He stuck with the veer, and was fortunate to have an experienced quarterback in Jeff Dankworth, and a high-caliber runner in Wendell Tyler.

At Southern Cal, Robinson also inherited top-notch talent. Bell was back, and geared for a run at the Heisman. On defense, USC returned future pros Dennis Thurman, Marvin Powell, and Gary Jeter. And there was a freshman running back from San Fernando High, the same school that delivered Anthony Davis. His name was Charles White, and he would be something special.

Robinson still faced a challenge far tougher than Donahue's. Donahue followed a Rose Bowl win. Robinson followed a legend.

Right away, Robinson sought to carve his own identity. "The thing that I felt I had to do," he said, "was make sure to sell the fact that the job was a series of people who bore the flag, and that John McKay was not SC. SC was SC. John McKay carried the flag for 16 years, and now it was my turn."

When Robinson took over, he quickly discovered the unique pressure encountered by any coach of USC. On his desk were hundreds of letters from fans who professed greater knowledge than his staff. "The first thing you got to do," the letters stated, "is get rid of this quarterback."

Fans still had not forgiven Evans for his sub-par performance in the 1975 UCLA game. The fact he was black didn't help either. "I'd get letters from people saying, 'Nigger, if you go out there, we're going to blow your brains out,'" Evans said. Robinson, perhaps sensing the need to establish his authority and separate himself, once and for all, from McKay, came back with an immediate response: USC's quarterback is Vince Evans.

Evans spent the summer with quarterback coach Paul Hackett, fine-tuning his mechanics. He probably studied enough film to take over for Siskel or Ebert. "Vince had problems," Robinson said, "in that he would make two good plays, and then two bad plays."

Finally, the 1976 season arrived. America had just celebrated its 200th birthday. President Gerald Ford and peanut farmer Jimmy Carter were criss-crossing the counter in search of votes. Donahue and Robinson had to satisfy more narrow constituencies, and the first primaries weren't going to be easy.

For UCLA, it was Frank Kush's Arizona State team. Coming off an Orange Bowl triumph over Nebraska, the Sun Devils were expected to be tough again. And Kush, coach of the year in 1975, certainly enjoyed the edge over the rookie from Westwood. Because of his age, Donahue knew he'd be watched with even more scrutiny.

For USC, a loser of four of its last five in 1975, it was the University of Missouri, recognized for a string of upsets in the 1970s.

Before the Arizona State game, Donahue received some advice from Rodgers. "I remember being so nervous," he said, "and Rodgers said to me, 'You know, Frank Kush doesn't play this game. His players do.' Sometimes you look at a coach and you say he's had so many victories, how am I going to get my team to play him?"

Donahue found a way. The Bruins upset Arizona State, 28–10, on the road. Working the veer to perfection, Dankworth rushed for two touchdowns.

Robinson wasn't so fortunate. Missouri humiliated the Trojans at the Coliseum, 46–25. The team was in shock. "I'm thinking to myself, 'Wait a minute, this isn't supposed to happen. This isn't why I came here. This isn't what USC is all about,'" said quarterback Paul McDonald, who would start for the Trojans in 1978 and 1979. "We were loaded with talent, but just to see that happen, the doubt creeped in for everybody."

Robinson remembers walking off the field with Evans. It was not the same Coliseum. "We both had a sense, looking up at the crowd," Robinson said, "that they were all booing both of us."

After the press interviews, Robinson faced another unenviable task. he had to address an alumni get-together. This, too, was not going to be an appreciative audience. "Here's their loved program, and their coach for 16 years is gone, and here's this guy who has destroyed their program, and now I'm going to talk to them," Robinson said. "I told them we weren't going to lose again, that I had screwed up, and I will correct it."

He proved quite a prophet. The Trojans won eight in a row. Robinson blamed himself for the Missouri debacle. "I probably had them overprepared. I think I had them ready for the Super Bowl," he said. "I think we had them worried and jittery, as opposed to free and relaxed and aggressive."

While continuing to work hard, Robinson made sure his players enjoyed themselves, from then on. He had brought that kind of enthusiasm to USC when he arrived as an assistant coach in 1972, and perhaps he had become a little too hardened in his early days as head man. And if he ever saw them get too cocky, he'd remind them of Missouri. He became a master motivator, adopting the right psychology at the right time.

"There were a couple of time I remember," McDonald said, "in which he would just kick us off the practice field. 'You guys are terrible, worthless,' he'd say. So we'd walk off with our tail between our legs, so we'd have a team meeting and get focused. It would work."

The players, in any case, usually didn't have much trouble motivating themselves. "It was really an intense week," said White, of the week between the Missouri opener and the second game at Oregon. "I remember looking around the guys in the Oregon game, and thinking, 'Somebody's going to get the hell kicked out of them, and it's not us.'" It was Oregon. USC won 53–0.

In Westwood, the Bruins were rolling along. Except for a 10–10 tie with Ohio State in their third meeting in two years, UCLA carried an unblemished record (9–0–1) into the Trojan game.

Donahue had opted not to gamble for a first down late in the Buckeye game. Critics said he was too conservative. Critics said that a lot during Donahue's coaching career. But the kid was learning. He combined Prothro's grasp of fundamentals, Rodgers' offensive innovativeness, and Vermeil's organizational skills. On the practice field, he walked from group to group with a clipboard in his hand. He took notes, sometimes said a few words, and moved on.

Students at both schools couldn't wait for the 1976 game. At stake was the Rose Bowl, the conference championship, and a possible national championship. UCLA was ranked second, USC third. In other words, things were back to normal.

"There is no big cause now that Vietnam is over," UCLA sophomore Beverly Verna told the *Los Angeles Times*. "We can get back to being students. There is nothing pushing us. We're growing up awfully slow."

The pranksters were back at it, too. The new UCLA student store was attacked by mysterious invaders who left the letters USC in bright red paint on it. Who could have done such a thing? Hard to say, but, by a strange coincidence, the USC Activities Building was subsequently vandalized by invaders bearing bright blue paint.

The coaches were new, but the outcome the same. With the Rose Bowl on the line for both teams, USC won for the sixth straight time. The final: USC 24, UCLA 14.

It wasn't that close. USC jumped out to a 24–0 lead; the farthest Bruin possession in the first three and one half quarters being the Trojan 34. Only two late touchdowns made the score respectable. Bell, playing on an injured ankle, rushed for 167 yards, but the game belonged to the USC defense, and to Vince Evans. His numbers weren't dominating—seven of 13 for 79 yards—but Evans controlled the game. His 36-yard touchdown run on a quarterback draw, which put the game away, was, according to Robinson, "one of the most deserving things I've seen in sports." *Sports Illustrated* certainly wouldn't make any more Grand Canyon cracks.

Just as they did after the Missouri opener, Robinson and Evans walked off the field together. But this time, they were greeted with a more familiar Coliseum reaction. "We kind of hugged each other," Robinson said, "and I remember flashing back to the earlier time (against Missouri) and realizing the crowd felt a little differently now."

For UCLA, Tyler, suffering from a shoulder injury, gained only 52 yards in 13 carries. Dankworth completed just eight of 16 for 90 yards. All day, USC forced the Bruins outside, right into the fast pursuit of the Trojan linebackers.

UCLA moved on to the Liberty Bowl, losing to Alabama 36–6. The Trojans defeated Michigan in the Rose Bowl, 14–6. There was life after John McKay.

There was also life after Ricky Bell. Like the Red Sox, who went from Ted Williams to Carl Yastrzemski to Jim Rice without interruption, the USC tailback assembly line kept making new models.

The 1977 model was Charles White. He was built tougher than the rest. At San Fernando, just north of Los Angeles, White rushed for 2,315 yards to become one of the nation's top high school stars. His hero, Anthony Davis, was dispatched to recruit him. "Anthony lived right next door to my best friend," White said, "so that when we'd hear he was coming home, there would be 20 kids hanging out there pretending to be at my friend's house just to get a glimpse of Anthony."

Like Davis, White never suffered from modesty. "I'm going to win two Heismans," he said during freshman year when he strode into Heritage Hall and saw the statues earned by Garrett and Simpson. His teammates laughed in disbelief. Just another naive freshman who thinks he's going to conquer the world.

Before he could run to a Heisman, White had to learn to run sprints. In one drill, he went about ten yards and was very proud of himself. He walked back to the huddle, and immediately learned the difference between San Fernando High School and the University of Southern California.

"Sixty yards down the field," backfield coach John Johnson yelled. The message was clear. Anthony Davis ran 60-yard sprints in practice, and so did Ricky Bell. That's just what USC tailbacks do. From then on, nobody ever questioned Charles White's work ethic.

And nobody ever questioned his talent. He was the one positive to emerge from the Missouri embarrassment. Six carries, 93 yards. Suddenly, his Heisman prediction sounded prophetic. "I remember looking at the papers the next day," White said, "and seeing my name there, and it was like, 'Yeah, I can do it.'"

The statistics only got better. Against Oregon State, three touchdowns. Against Cal, 91 yards on 14 carries. Against Stanford, 136 yards on 23 carries. Against UCLA, however, freshman White only gained three yards on one carry, as senior Bell was still the main man.

In 1977, the title was passed to White. He was different than Simpson and Davis and Bell. He had explosive speed *and* power. Defenses didn't attack him; *he* attached defenses. At 6'0", 185 pounds,

White ran straight into frightening collisions, and got right back up for the next one. He learned this aggressiveness by necessity in high school. He played fullback in a wishbone offense, and took more pounding than Joe Frazier. "I learned how to say, 'I'm going to absorb this blow.' I learned how to attack and protect myself," White said. It was either that or the bench.

Besides USC, White considered attending Washington and Ohio State. He didn't like the rain in Seattle, and the reign in Columbus. Hayes told him "we're going to win with you, we're going to win without you." Ohio State was going to have to win without him.

In Robinson, White found a coach who loved the running game. Often in his career, with both USC and the Rams, Robinson was criticized for his reliance on ball-control football. Like Howard Jones, Robinson realized the passing game carried too many risks. He always felt that "physical dominance is how you win this game, and quarterbacks don't understand that."

After a remarkable debut in 1976 (11–1), Robinson set out a year later to prove it was no fluke. The Trojans first exacted revenge from Missouri, 27–10, and then defeated Oregon State, Texas Christian University, and Washington State. But three defeats in four weeks— 21–20 to Alabama, 49–19 to Notre Dame, and 17–14 to Cal—quickly made it a lost season.

White says the team suffered from a lack of leadership. "We had some imitation leaders who would yell but there was no action," he said. "When I came in my freshman year, we had guys to take you by the throat, people like Vince Evans and Marvin Powell."

Quarterback Rob Hertel, a fifth-year senior, says the play-calling in 1977 was another problem. Robinson admitted he lost faith in the passing game—Hertel had 16 interceptions through 10 games—and began to resort to even more of a controlled attack, with passes to backs and tight ends. Then there were the turnovers, 34 in all, often positioning opponents for easy scoring drives.

Whatever the case, USC was 6–4 entering the Bruin matchup. UCLA was 7–3. The Bruins had their own star runner, freshman Freeman McNeil, and one of the fiercest defensive players in their history, safety Kenny Easley. But a rash of injuries and the lack of an identity on offense had caused some inconsistency.

After the 1976 loss to USC, Donahue had decided to scrap the veer in favor of a more pro-style offense. Critics said the veer was too conservative, and Donahue listened. "It became apparent to me that in order to have long-term success in a town as competitive as Los Angeles," he said, "we needed to make sure our offense was entertaining."

But like Vermeil, Donahue couldn't implement a new system overnight. Vermeil had specifically recruited players to execute the veer. These players were still around. It wouldn't be until 1980 that UCLA's complete offensive transformation could take effect.

Still, for the second time in his two years, Donahue had a chance to carry the Bruins to a Rose Bowl. The only obstacle, as usual, was USC. For the Trojans, a victory meant an appearance in the Bluebonnet Bowl. And a rare chance to play the role of spoiler.

USC played its role perfectly. Frank Jordan's 38-yard field goal with two seconds left lifted the Trojans to a 29–27 triumph, spoiling a courageous comeback by the Bruins and knocking them out of the Rose Bowl.

It was 1969 all over again. Again, the Trojans marched downfield to pull the game out. Again, a pass interference call played a pivotal role in the last-ditch drive. And again, it was the Bruins who were the victims.

Danny Graham, the culprit eight years earlier, now had a colleague in the annals of Bruin frustration—Johnny Lynn. On third and ten from the 50-yard line, with just under a minute left in the game, Hertel threw a down and out to flanker Kevin Williams. Defensive back Lynn reached for the ball and touched it, but the head linesman ruled he touched Williams before the ball. Like Graham, Lynn will probably always plead innocence. But, as NFL referees usually say after the instant replay officials take another look, the play stands. Forever.

Donahue still hasn't forgotten it. "A very bad call," he said. "We were down and came storming back and fought like crazy, and to have that thing decided in the final seconds on that kind of call . . ." His voice trailed off, the memory too painful for words.

USC led 26–10 midway through the third quarter and seemed headed to an easy win. "But then we became too conservative," Hertel recalled, "because Robinson felt we could hold them defensively."

They couldn't, thanks to UCLA sophomore quarterback Rick Bashore, who directed touchdown drives of 63, 48, and 80 yards. Bashore wasn't supposed to play. Because of a fractured rib and a collapsed lung, he had been medically cleared for the game only a few days earlier. His last pass, a one-yard touchdown to tight end Don Pederson, put UCLA on top, 27–26, with 2:51 to go.

This time, it was Hertel, not Jimmy Jones, who played last-minute hero. One short pass after another, plus the interference call, set up Jordan for the winning kick. Hertel, like Evans two years earlier, found vindication. He completed 15 of 24 for 254 yards.

In some ways, trying to salvage a disappointing season placed even more pressure on USC than trying to earn an invitation to Pasadena. "If we had lost that game," Hertel said, "we would have really been under fire as a team that wasn't successful."

Once again, in 1978, the battle for the roses came down to UCLA and USC. Guided by Bashore, the Bruins still had an offense in transition. But in Easley and inside linebacker Jerry Robinson, UCLA had some superior athletes on defense.

They would need them. The Trojans, perhaps for the first time since Haden, found a quarterback who could throw with consistency— southpaw Paul McDonald. Teaming with White, he helped give USC its most balanced offensive machine in years. Entering the Bruin contest in 1978, McDonald had completed 87 of 155 passes for 1,289 yards and 14 touchdowns. McDonald believed throwing lefthanded was actually an advantage. "It made it more difficult for the defense," McDonald said. "Most teams put their best pass rusher on the defensive right end, and the guy came from the blind side. Except I'd see him."

UCLA started Bashore, who was far more effective as a runner than a passer. Against Oregon State, Bashore had a Vince Evans-like stretch: 0 for 10.

It came down to UCLA's quick defense trying to contain USC's power and balance. UCLA came up short. The final: USC 17, UCLA 10.

The Trojans jumped out to a 17–0 lead in the first half, and then hung on as the fast-charging Bruins simply ran out of opportunities. With just over a minute left, and USC leading by seven, White broke loose for 11 years on a third-and-six play, clinching the game by denying the Bruins one final possession.

By gaining 145 yards on 33 carries, White, in the same game, broke the school and conference career rushing records of Bell and Davis. McDonald also made a significant contribution, completing a 36-yard touchdown pass to split end Calvin Sweeney.

The pressure began to build on Donahue. Even though his overall record—24–9–2—was commendable, it contained one huge flaw. Against USC, Donahue was 0–3. That's how coaches in this rivalry lose their job. Just ask Jess Hill and Bill Barnes. A wire service report even suggested Donahue's job was gone if he lost the 1978 game.

For Robinson and USC, the best part of the 1978 season was yet to come: A 27–25 win over Notre Dame capped by another last-second Jordan field goal; a 21–5 win over Hawaii, and a 17–10 Rose Bowl triumph over Michigan.

In the Rose Bowl, White was credited with a touchdown run that according to replays, clearly showed the ball popping out two yards before he crossed the goal line. It became known as the phantom touchdown. "What was I going to do?" White joked years later. "Hey, Mr. Referee, it was a fumble."

At 12–1, the Trojans were again national champions, and Robinson was well on his way to becoming one of the school's all-time coaching greats.

The 1979 season was a forgettable one for the Bruins. They won only five games. They gave up 256 points, the most in their 61-year history. And they were absolutely disgraced by USC.

The year began in tragedy. Mike Mikolayunas, a new assistant coach who had arrived just a few months earlier, died of a heart attack. He was only 30.

Tom Ramsey, the freshman quarterback who took over midway through the season, blames a lack of leadership for the team's decline. "We had a bad element on the team that year," Ramsey said. "It was a real mishmash team."

It was also the last Terry Donahue team in transition. The seniors wee recruited by Dick Vermeil. Donahue had begun implementing the I formation, but still lacked the explosive personnel at the skill positions to make that system effective. The old days of veer football were still haunting the Bruins. Still, the team had its moments. It upset Purdue 31–21, and scared highly-ranked Ohio State for 58 minutes before Art Schlichter rallied the Buckeyes to a 17–13 escape. It also shocked Oregon 35–0 at Eugene. Junior running back Freeman McNeil was among the nation's rushing leaders all year. But there were also dark moments, like an upset loss to Washington State, and a 34–14 humiliation by the Huskies.

USC, meanwhile, was on top again. And, in terms of offensive balance, the 1979 team might have been even more formidable than the undefeated 1972 squad. This was not just a tailback school anymore.

With White and McDonald, the Trojans seemed, at times, unstoppable on offense. After ten games, White was the nation's leading rusher, McDonald the third-ranked passer. McDonald had completed 63 percent of his passes for 16 touchdowns, and hadn't thrown an interception in his last 126 attempts. Against Notre Dame, the balance was never more evident. White ran for 261 yards, McDonald passed for 311. The Trojans won, 42–23—at South Bend. Notre Dame Coach Dan Devine called the USC offense the best he had ever seen. It averaged 459 yards a game in total offense.

But even one of the best is not always good enough. Against Stanford, the Trojans stumbled to a 21–21 tie after leading 21–0. They ran the ball so effectively in the first half that they forgot to throw it in the second. "We just fell asleep in the second half," McDonald said.

As usual, Trojans' offensive line dominated the line of scrimmage. Guard Brad Budde, tackle Keith Van Horne, guard Roy Foster and tackle Don Mosebar opened huge holes for White and gave McDonald forever to pass. Perhaps the best lineman of all, Anthony Muñoz, was out for most of the season.

Still, the Trojans needed to beat the Bruins to earn another Rose Bowl trip. The conference title they apparently had earned weeks earlier was stripped away when league officials ruled Arizona State must forfeit its wins because it used ineligible players. One of those wins was against Washington, who now stood to take the title if USC fell to UCLA.

The 1979 Trojan-Bruin game didn't figure to be close. UCLA (5–5) almost couldn't match fourth-ranked USC (9–0–1) at any position. Southern Cal was favored by two touchdowns.

The Bruins were trying to avoid their first losing season since 1971. The Trojans were looking for their sixth Rose Bowl appearance in eight years.

The game wasn't close. USC opened up a 35–0 halftime lead, and coasted to a 49–14 triumph. The balance was there again. McDonald completed 17 of 23 passes for 199 yards. White gained 194 yards on 35 carries. He also scored four touchdowns. The Trojan defense was equally impressive, neutralizing McNeil and completely shutting down Ramsey. Ronnie Lott, the future great NFLer, had two interceptions.

For Donahue, the loss was devastating. Standing helpless on the sidelines, he had to watch as the Trojan players and fans wildly celebrated another win over UCLA, and another trip to Pasadena. Donahue was still looking for his first win over USC and first trip to the Rose Bowl. "We were just overwhelmed in that game," Donahue said, "and in addition to getting our brains kicked in, we had to endure the additional humiliation of them parading their players off the field."

This loss, like none before, created a new Donahue. A Donahue who would work harder than ever. A Donahue who would make certain USC never humiliated his team again. A Donahue determined to win in the 1980s.

He was right about one thing. USC would never humiliate UCLA again. At least not in the 1980s.

Before he could find ways to avoid humiliation, Terry Donahue had to do something fast about the exodus of UCLA assistant coaches finding other jobs in college or the pros. This had been a problem since he took over, and was only getting worse—12 had left in four years, five after the 1979 season. The coaches were too talented to stay put, and Donahue hurt his own cause by always giving them his recommendation or approval. By 1980, only defensive coordinator Jed Hughes and offensive line coach Don Riley remained from Donahue's original staff. Another reason for the attrition was economics. It was expensive to live in Los Angeles, and assistant coaches in college football didn't make that much money.

The turnover wasn't good for the players. Just as they became accustomed to an assistant who favored one style, he was gone. The team had no continuity; 1979 was no accident. Donahue acted fast. He hired replacements with California backgrounds, believing they would be more reluctant to bolt in a hurry. It took valuable time away from planning spring practice and other responsibilities, but he knew too much was at stake to do otherwise. How much longer would Bruin alumni tolerate a coach who couldn't beat USC? More importantly, though, Donahue rehired the man credited by many with revitalizing the Bruins a decade earlier. Homer Smith was back.

This time, Smith came to reintroduce UCLA to the forward pass. He had performed magic with the wishbone, so hopes were high he would have the same results with a new passing attack. After an unsuccessful run as head coach at Army, and a brief time away from the sport, Smith was ready for the new challenge. Donahue made him his first offensive coordinator. UCLA, however, would have to win without three starters—Billy Don Jackson, Mark Tuinei, and Danny Lei—who quit the program in the spring.

USC, meanwhile, had to deal with its own departure—the graduation of Charles White. He left behind many records and memories, and he got his Heisman. The freshman wasn't kidding. But, once again, the factory sent in a worthy replacement. His name: Marcus Allen.

Allen, 6' 2", 202 pounds, from Lincoln High in San Diego, was never supposed to play tailback. He was recruited as a defensive back. USC told him they had plenty of offensive backs. "The first time I saw Marcus," said *San Diego Tribune* writer Nick Canepa, "I was convinced he was going to be an All-Pro defensive back. I quit counting that day after he'd made 30 tackles."

In 1978, Robinson, however, moved Allen to tailback because there wasn't much depth behind White. A year later, Allen was moved again, this time to fullback. The team had a pressing need, and Allen filled it. He became admired for his versatility at USC, and later with the Los Angeles Raiders.

In 1979, Allen was a great supporting player behind White, the leading man. But, in 1980, Marcus Allen assumed his place alongside the great tailbacks of the past. He had speed and power, and much more. "He could move his body like a contortionist to get into certain kinds of holes that nobody else could get into," recalled Robinson. "He was a great finisher who had that extra thrust for the last two or three yards. You got the feeling he saw a game others couldn't see."

UCLA and McNeil. USC and Allen. One team fighting for its respectability. Another fighting for its reputation. It promised to be a fitting way to usher in the new decade.

It wasn't. Because of numerous academic violations, the conference declared several teams ineligible for postseason play, including both USC and UCLA. They would have to fight for pride.

For UCLA, that seemed to be enough. On the first day of spring practice, Easley and a couple of teammates invaded the weight room and affixed a sign to the mirrors that would inspire them all year. "49–14." Enough said.

The 1980 Bruins posted early wins against Colorado, Purdue and Wisconsin. But there were still plenty of skeptics who expected them to slip against second-ranked Ohio State in Columbus. Even Donahue acknowledged the team hadn't been tested yet. "We haven't beaten anybody worth a darn," Donahue said.

The Ohio State game changed all that. The Bruins shut out quarterback Art Schlichter, the Heisman Trophy candidate, and his Buckeyes, 17–0. McNeil, UCLA's own Heisman hopeful, returned from a week layoff to gain 130 yards.

McNeil could have been a Trojan. USC heavily recruited him, but he was no dummy. The Trojans already had a crowded backfield. "I didn't know how well I'd do right away, coming in behind Charles White," McNeil said. "But, if I came to UCLA, I'd have at least two years as a starter."

In the Ohio State game, McNeil was still nursing a hyper-extended knee. Just imagine if he were healthy? A week later against Stanford, he was. And it made the Indians sick. Playing at the Coliseum, Stanford opened a 21–7 lead. Stanford had John Elway, and UCLA was without Kenny Easley. And without much chance, it appeared, of remaining undefeated.

But the second half reminded fans of another Coliseum comeback, when Anthony Davis and USC overcame a 24–0 deficit to beat Notre Dame in 1974. The hero, this time, was McNeil. After intermission, he scored four touchdowns, gained 220 yards, and kept UCLA on track. The Bruins won 35–21.

Donahue made a move in that game that astounded the critics who had labeled him conservative. Astounded even Donahue himself. He took a gamble midway through the final period that even John McKay might not have tried. UCLA was ahead 28–21. Fourth and one from its own 14. The book dictated a punt. Sanity dictated a punt.

Donahue dictated a run. Ramsey kept the ball, grinding out the single yard that allowed the Bruins to maintain possession and continue a drive that eventually culminated in an insurance touchdown. "After I ordered it, though," Donahue said, "I thought I would have a nervous breakdown. I was thinking, I can't believe I'm doing this."

No amount of gambling would help a few weeks later. The Bruins lost two straight, to Arizona and Oregon. UCLA surrendered 43 points in two games after giving up just 58 in the previous six. The team's early-season euphoria evaporated in a hurry. The Arizona loss came on the same day top-ranked Alabama had been upset. At halftime, the news spread quickly in the locker room of the No. 2-ranked Bruins. UCLA was No. 1. For all of two hours.

"You would have expected that news to shoot us up," Donahue said. "But it didn't."

USC was strong again. With Allen leading the nation in rushing and quarterback Gordan Adams playing well, the second-ranked Trojans moved up to No. 2 in the rankings and were chasing the national championship when they hosted Washington at the Coliseum, the week before the UCLA game.

The Trojans were wonderful hosts. The Huskies won, 20–10, spoiling any USC championship illusions, and handing the Trojans their first loss in 28 games, since early in the 1978 season. It was also their first conference defeat at home since 1975.

Moreover, Adams injured his knee and was lost for the season. Some suggested inserting Allen as quarterback in a shotgun formation. He had played the position in high school. But Robinson stuck with sophomore backup, Scott Tinsley. In the loss to Washington, Tinsley was intercepted three times and completed only four of 10 for 62 yards. Just imagine if the Trojans had someone like John Elway waiting for his chance. Just imagine a backfield of Elway and Allen.

It almost happened. USC heavily recruited Elway, and it looked like he might become a Trojan. But Robinson made one big mistake. He told the truth.

"John, you'll play in a national championship game and a Rose Bowl, if you come here," Robinson said.

"Yeah, but I'll only throw 20 times a game," Elway responded, fully aware of Robinson's reputation for running the football.

"You're right, you will only throw it 20 times."

Elway chose Stanford.

The 1980 USC-UCLA matchup was jokingly referred to as "The Probation Bowl." With no Rose Bowl or national title at stake, something had to spice things up. Something did. The game.

UCLA won 20–17 on a deflected pass. The Trojans called it fortune. The Bruins called it fate. With just over two minutes to go, UCLA, trailing 17–14, had possession on its own 42. Jay Schroeder, who had replaced season-long starter Ramsey in the first quarter, threw long to McNeil. Trojan cornerback Jeff Fisher settled under the ball, ready to make the interception and clinch USC's fifth straight win against the Bruins. Even the overcautious John Robinson started to celebrate.

"It happened 15 feet from me," Robinson recalled. "It was one of the first times in a game that while the ball was in the air, I was saying, 'It's over. Jeff will intercept and we'll win.' I can still close my eyes and see it."

Jeff did not intercept, and USC did not win. He deflected the ball right into the hands of McNeil who kept going for a 58-yard touchdown. USC got the ball back, and marched to UCLA's 29, but that was it. McNeil's catch, "the act of God," as Donahue called it, had spared the Bruins another winter of shame.

Moreover, it spared Terry Donahue. Five losses to USC in five years might have been too much for any coach to survive. Asked if his first win in the city series had taken the monkey off his back, he responded: "It wasn't a spider monkey; it was a gorilla."

But Jeff Fisher wasn't so fortunate. He never got a chance for redemption against the Bruins. Instead, the deflection will remain forever as his contribution to the rivalry. "Do you remember a defensive back who played for USC?" a write asked Fisher shortly after the game.

"No," Fisher said.

"He played here about 10 or 15 years ago and was called for pass interference toward the end of the game and cost the team the game," the writer said.

"What's your point?" said an annoyed Fisher.

"Well, I just want you to know that he's married, has a nice family, a good job, and everything is going well."

Fisher nodded. He understood.

Today, Fisher is the defensive coordinator for the Los Angeles Rams. His boss, John Robinson, must have forgiven him.

"The sun did come up the next day," Fisher said.

In any case, the 1980 loss can't be blamed on one play. UCLA had an edge throughout the game. On defense, using an eight-man front for the first time all season, gambling that Tinsley wouldn't beat them with the bomb, the Bruins stopped Marcus Allen. Allen, averaging 165 yards a game, logged only 72 yards on 37 carries. His longest gain was 11 yards.

Offensively, Schroeder gave UCLA the boost it needed after Ramsey faltered. Schroeder completed nine of 11 for 165 yards and two touchdowns, even though his most important pass, the touchdown to McNeil, was probably his worst. "It was a horrible pass. I bet Jay would've taken it back," Ramsey said.

The game ended the careers of McNeil and Easley. Against USC, McNeil finished with 111 yards on 24 carries. For his career, he gained 3,195 yards and became the school's all-time leading rusher. He proved USC wasn't the only tailback school in Los Angeles.

Easley shouldn't even have played the second half against the Trojans. After injuring his shoulder in the first quarter, he was told to go to the hospital. Instead, he went to the huddle. He deflected three passes in the game including one that helped contain USC's last-ditch drive.

Easley brought a tradition of fierce, enthusiastic defensive play to Westwood that was later copied by Don Rogers and others. Next to Kenny Washington and Jackie Robinson, he may be the greatest athlete to ever play UCLA football.

McNeil and Easley arrived near the start of the Donahue reign. They survived Frank Jordan's field goal and The Crash of '79. And, now, finally, they had stayed long enough to see a victory against the Trojans, and the blooming of hope again in Westwood.

Yes, it was a new decade.

During the off-season, Ramsey went to see Donahue. Ramsey was still upset over his benching in the USC game. "I will not play at this school again," Ramsey said, "if I ever have to play looking over my shoulder."

Donahue assured him it wouldn't happen again. It didn't. In 1981, Schroeder left to concentrate on baseball though he returned to football professionally and played for the Redskins and Raiders. Ramsey stayed to concentrate on taking the Bruins to Pasadena.

Once again, in 1981, the Bruins started well with wins against Arizona and Wisconsin. The Badgers had just upset top-ranked Michigan the week before. But the collapse came earlier this season. UCLA stumbled at Iowa, 20–7, and at Stanford, 26–23. Yet, entering the USC game, the Bruins (7–2–1) had a chance for the Rose Bowl with a victory.

The Trojans (8–2) didn't. It was a strange season. USC beat the marquee names—Tennessee, Oklahoma, Notre Dame—while falling to Arizona and Washington. Perhaps the school had taken the tailback tradition one step too far. No question Allen was having a superb senior season, leading the nation in rushing while going over 2,000 yards. But Allen was almost the entire USC offense. Quarterback John Mazur averaged 15 passes a game. He was no Paul McDonald.

"I'm thinking that if we keep giving the ball to this guy wearing number 33 (Allen), he'll run until the sun goes down and we'll win," Robinson said. "The negative side is that if you don't pass pretty soon, you can't pass."

In his last two games, against California and Washington, Mazur threw only six passes on first down, completing two. And critics thought Donahue was conservative.

For the second year in a row, the Big Game came down to the Big Play. With four seconds to go, the Bruins had possession on the Trojan 29. Ramsey had just driven the team 51 yards, and this time it was UCLA benefiting from a pass interference call that kept a drive going.

Norm Johnson came on the field to kick UCLA into the Rose Bowl. The Bruins would be conference champions with a win. And they would get USC back for Frank Jordan's last-second kick four years earlier.

Johnson knew what was supposed to be done. But so did George Achica. Achica, USC's 6' 5", 260-pound nose guard, was told to squeeze somehow through the gap between UCLA's right guard and center, and block the kick. The opening had been noticed on film by USC defensive line coach Marv Goux.

"The only thing I was worried about," Goux said, "was whether I could get all our guys in there because their rears are so big." Achica certainly got in there. He stopped the ball with both hands, the first blocked kick of his career.

UCLA simply goofed. Normally, the right guard is supposed to take one step to his left and close the gap. If a defender gets through, he should have to come from the outside rather than the inside. That should give the kicker enough time. But UCLA's regular right guard, Mike Mason, had been injured during the game, and was replaced by Steve Williams. "Obviously, nobody closed it off," said Bruin assistant coach Jim Colleto.

For Robinson, it would be his last win against the Bruins. It's a victory he still savors. The Fisher play, Robinson said, referring to the 1980 deflection, "was bad luck. This play (Achica's block) was justice."

Achica's play also overshadowed the Jeckyll-Hyde performance of Marcus Allen. Allen, playing his last game at the Coliseum, fumbled three times, but gained 219 yards on 40 carries, and scored two touchdowns. He established more NCAA records: more 200-yard games in a season (11); best per-game rushing average for a season (212.9), and best per-carry rushing average for a season (5.8). And he became the fourth USC tailback to win the Heisman.

From 1963 to 1981, the Trojans almost always found one great runner to replace another: Garrett, O.J., A.D., Bell, White, Allen. But in the last decade, nobody has replaced Marcus Allen.

In 1982, Terry Donahue finally accomplished his long-sought goal. He took his team to the Rose Bowl. But he did it in September.

Because of conflicts with the commission running the Coliseum, it was time to move on. No longer would the Bruins feel as if they were second-class tenants at somebody else's stadium. Fifty-three years after building its own campus, UCLA had its own place to play football, relocating in the Rose Bowl Stadium in Pasadena. It would make quite a difference.

"It gave UCLA an identity," Ramsey said. "We were determined not to lose on our home field."

And they didn't. At the Rose Bowl, the Bruins beat Long Beach State, Washington State, Oregon, and Stanford. The Stanford contest featured a memorable duel between Tom Ramsey and John Elway, which UCLA won, 38–35.

Only a tie with Arizona and a 10–7 loss to Washington tarnished UCLA's record heading into the Trojan game. Ramsey, now a senior, had blossomed into one of the nation's finest quarterbacks, ranking first in passing efficiency. With receivers like Cormac Carney and Jojo Townsell, the Bruin offensive attack had completed its personality transformation from the old days of veer football. The players finally understood the Smith system.

The most explosive demonstration of the new UCLA offense came in the den of conservative football—Ann Arbor, Michigan. Pepper Rodgers never would have believed it.

Trailing, 21–0, late in the first half, the Bruins stormed back for a shocking 31–27 victory. Ramsey and the offense deserve a lot of credit, and so does Donahue. He became Knute Rockne for a day.

At the end of the opening half, Michigan coach Bo Schembechler apparently taunted Donahue as they headed toward the locker rooms. Donahue was no rookie anymore. He had dealt with Kush, and Hayes, and he wasn't going to be bullied by Bo. "He was screaming and yelling and throwing things in the locker room," Ramsey said. "He gave one of the most inspiring halftime speeches ever. It rattled our cages."

UCLA then dominated the second half. This was the Donahue Ramsey had wanted to see.

"What used to drive me nuts," Ramsey said, "was that we had a great team in 1982, and Donahue goes, 'We have a nice team.' A lot of players used to talk among ourselves and say, 'we have a *nice* team?' What the hell is this? We were a bunch of mean, crazy guys. That used to drive guys up a wall."

Entering the USC game, the Bruins (8–1–1) had only an outside chance at the Rose Bowl game. They would need two conference upsets to make it. USC, because of NCAA sanctions, had no chance.

But John Robinson had more than the 1982 season and the UCLA game on his mind. Like resignation, for example.

Robinson, after six years, had lost his passion for the job. Perhaps more than any other coach in the history of the crosstown rivalry, John Robinson relied on passion to fire up his team and himself. "I kind of got to the point where I just wasn't enjoying it as much," said Robinson. "Someone told me that if I stayed there and coached for many years, I'd wind up with some of the legends who had coached here. I didn't care about that."

Robinson only cared about finding passing somewhere else. First, he thought he discovered it as the school's senior vice-president for university relations. He was wrong, and miserable.

John Robinson is a football coach. He was fortunate the Los Angeles Rams offered him a job just a few months after he joined USC's administration. That's where he remains today.

But there was still one last season to coach. And one final duel with Terry Donahue and the UCLA Bruins.

No longer blessed with a Heisman-caliber tailback, the Trojans relied on defense. That was usually enough. In nine games, USC (7–2) had allowed only 110 points, including shutouts of Oregon State, California, and powerful Oklahoma. Players like linebacker Jack Del Rio, linebacker Keith Browner, and cornerback Troy West helped form a defense quick enough to stop the pass and strong enough to contain the run. For USC, the UCLA game was its Rose Bowl. Robinson's resignation hadn't been announced yet, so that wasn't going to be a factor.

For UCLA, the game was about revenge. And not just for George Achica's block. The seniors still remembered 1979. Winning on Fisher's deflection in 1980 wasn't enough to erase the humiliation of 1979's 49–14 blowout.

During pre-game stretching exercises, Ramsey and UCLA nose guard Karl Morgan brought it up again. "49–14," Morgan said softly to Ramsey.

Ramsey looked at Morgan knowingly. "You got it buddy," Ramsey replied.

First, in the 1980s, there was Jeff Fisher, and then George Achica. Who would decide this year's tussle? Once again, it came down to one play.

USC had just scored a touchdown with no time left, but still trailed, 20–19. The Trojans were going for the two-point conversion and the win. A tie would mean nothing to John Robinson.

Trojan quarterback Scott Tinsley dropped back. Tinsley, the senior, looked for a receiver, and redemption. He was the starting sophomore quarterback in USC's 1980 loss to the Bruins, and had lost his job in successive seasons to John Mazur and Sean Salisbury. But Salisbury was hurt, and Tinsley was granted one final opportunity to make a difference. He had already completed 14 of 23 for 137 yards, including the fourth-down one-yard pass to tight end Mark Boyer that got the Trojans within one point.

On the conversion play, Tinsley had the option of throwing to split end Jeff Simmons in the flat, flanker Timmy White in the corner, or Boyer in the middle. He quickly looked to see who was open.

On the other side, the Bruin defense tightened. Morgan was just happy the game wasn't over. "I didn't realize what the score was at the time," Morgan said. "So when they scored, I thought we'd lost the game. But then I saw the look in everybody's else's eyes, and they were still saying we've gotta hold them."

UCLA lined up in a 5–3 defense, and blitzed linebacker Neal

Dellocono. Morgan burst up the middle. Tinsley got ready to throw. The pass was . . .

Never thrown. Morgan sacked Tinsley.

"I had enough time," Tinsley said. "I should've gotten rid of the ball."

But he didn't, and the Bruins won. And because of help from Washington State and Arizona, UCLA went home to its first Rose Bowl in seven years—only second in 17 years—and defeated Michigan, 24–14.

John Robinson lost his last Bruin encounter, but won his last game when the Trojans defeated Notre Dame, 17–13. In seven years, Robinson compiled a 67–14–2 record, three Rose Bowls victories, and a national title. In the annals of Trojan football, John Robinson didn't stay long enough to deserve a seat alongside the legends of Howard Jones and John McKay.

But he'd certainly be in the next row.

9

Games of Measles and Mediocrity
1983–1989

Ted who? That's what Trojan fans wondered after Ted Tollner, USC's offensive coordinator, was named to replace John Robinson. Yet the selection of a relative unknown to assume one of the most highly-coveted coaching jobs in sports fit in consistently with the Trojan pattern.

Few outside the football program had heard of an Oregon assistant named John McKay, or an Oakland Raider backfield coach named John Robinson. Neither possessed head coaching experience, and yet both excelled. Why shouldn't Tollner?

Robinson hired Tollner in 1982 to diversify a one-dimensional offense that, even with Heisman Trophy winner Marcus Allen, couldn't put enough points on the board. Tollner coached at two schools with high-powered passing machines: San Diego State and Brigham Young University. Under Tollner, BYU quarterback Jim McMahon led the nation in passing and set 70 NCAA records.

Robinson realized it was time for USC to finally enter the modern age of college football. Only he decided the Trojans would go without him. It would be up to Tollner, and it wouldn't be easy.

USC still faced NCAA sanctions for recruiting violations and improper sales of athletes' tickets to benefit players. That was bound to hinder recruiting. And it did, as Tollner found himself with uncustomary—for USC—second-rate talent. Without the necessary skill players for a balanced offensive attack, Tollner had to rely on ball-control football and solid defense. "We really didn't have the ingredients," Tollner said. "The best thing for us was to play that style until we could get the people we wanted, like the Rodney Peetes."

But, in 1983, Rodney Peete, the future star quarterback, was still playing high school ball. And the Trojans were in trouble.

Struggling from the start—three loses and a tie in its first six games—USC couldn't do much with the likes of Sean Salisbury, Fred Crutcher, Michael Harper, and Todd Spencer. Against Arizona State at the Coliseum, the Trojans trailed, 27–0, at the half. The players were booed off the field. It may have been the lowest moment in Trojan football since Robinson's debut against Missouri. Against Washington, things got so desperate that Tollner, trailing 24–0, called for a 44-yard field-goal attempt with 1:32 to play merely to avoid a shutout.

The kick was no good.

It was the first time USC had been blanked since 1967. The Trojans had scored in an NCAA record 186 straight games.

Tollner called for patience. The alumni called for his job. USC president James H. Zumberge had to rescue Tollner. "I have no hesitation in reflecting my own confidence," Zumberge said, "that this isn't the beginning of the demise of football at USC. It is one of those years no one likes to see but is inevitable in the program of any great school."

It was the kind of year the Trojans hadn't had since 1961—a losing one. John McKay's team went 4–5–1 that year. Entering the UCLA game, the Trojans were also 4–5–1. They couldn't block, tackle or hold on to the ball. Other than that, they weren't bad.

Not that the Bruins were that great, either. Not at the start.

Their first win came in their *fifth* game, 39–21 over Stanford. Until then, they had lost to Georgia, Nebraska, and BYU, and tied Arizona State. But UCLA quarterback Rick Neuheisel suddenly couldn't miss. The Bruins won five in a row, and even a loss to Arizona the week before the USC game didn't stop UCLA from thinking about the Rose Bowl. A win against the Trojans, coupled with a Washington State victory over Washington, would send them to Pasadena for the second year in a row.

At halftime, the Bruins looked like they were going to eliminate themselves. They trailed, 10–6, to a Trojan team they should have dominated.

Fortunately, Terry Donahue had found a new psychological weapon to motivate his team. "As I was walking out of the locker room at halftime," said fifth-year tight end Paul Bergmann, "Coach Donahue looked me in the eye and said, 'Washington State is beating Washington.' He didn't have to say anything else."

The Bruins quickly assumed command, scoring three touchdowns in the first 11 minutes of the third quarter to go ahead, 27–10. Like the Trojan squads of the late 1960s, these Bruins knew how to come from behind. "The tempo of the game changed," said Donahue. "Something clicked."

The Trojans scored again, but never threatened to get back in the game. Final: UCLA 27, USC 17.

After losing his first four encounters with the Trojans, Terry Donahue was now a respectable 3–5. The Bruins had captured the Big Game two years in a row for the first time since Prothro's 1966 squad. UCLA was headed to another Rose Bowl. Once there, it crushed Illinois, 45–9.

USC was headed nowhere, and some feared the program would stay there for years to come.

Ted Tollner knew he'd better produce in 1984, or else George Orwell's Big Brother would seem benevolent compared to the wrath of Trojan diehards. Perhaps he could pass off 1983 as a rookie's difficult initiation into big-time college football. Or he could attribute the losing record to players and a system he inherited. Or he could blame the school's probation for robbing the players of the motivation of the Rose Bowl. But he would have no excuses for 1984. He would have to find a way of improving a defense which had yielded a school-record 238 points, and revamping an offense which rarely produced.

Somehow, Tollner did it. The losses turned into wins, the boos into cheers, and the antagonism into adulation. USC won nine of its first ten games, stumbling only to LSU, 23–3. The patient was alive, after all.

Tollner credited the improved play to the mix of stubborn seniors who had felt ashamed of the 1983 team's performance. "We still weren't a highly gifted team," Tollner admitted. "We won because the players played over their heads."

Crutcher, a 190-pound junior who pounded his way to a 1,000-yard season, sensed a renewed enthusiasm. "People are flying around now and everybody wants a piece of somebody," he said.

Moreover, the Tollner system was finally in effect. Against Washington, USC quarterback Tim Green threw 28 passes, a season high. This is why Tollner came to USC in the first place, to put the ball in the air.

On defense, the Trojans were also a different team. Anchored by its linebackers—Jack Del Rio, Duane Bickett, and Neil Hope—USC ranked sixth nationally in scoring defense, allowing just 12 points a game. The Trojans were back.

UCLA was going the other way. After two successive conference championships and Rose Bowl victories, the Bruins were expected to win again. *Sports Illustrated* made them the preseason No. 1.

UCLA had experience in fifth-year starting quarterback Steve Bono, and potential in freshman running back Gaston Green. Plus there was John Lee, perhaps the preeminent collegiate field goal kicker in the country.

None of that mattered. Bono was hurt early in the season, and that cost the team a few games. Green was still raw. And Lee couldn't do it all himself. The Bruins came into the USC game at 7–3, out of Rose Bowl competition for the first time since the probation year of 1980. The *Sports Illustrated* jinx was working again.

But, if the Bruins ever needed incentive against their crosstown rival, it came wrapped in a package delivered by outspoken Trojan quarterback Tim Green. Green was a cocky youngster who had to be restrained by his coaches. Tollner even put him off-limits to reporters, except for postgame interviews.

He probably should have muzzled him altogether. Because after USC beat Washington to clinch a Rose Bowl berth, Green committed the same mistake that James McAlister and Kermit Johnson made in

1973. He talked trash. He said UCLA was going to get a whipping. It became instant bulletin board material.

There was a whipping, all right. The Bruins, showing little respect for the conference representative to the Rose Bowl, buried the Trojans 29–10, in Pasadena. UCLA intercepted three Green passes, sacked him twice, and roughed him up numerous other times.

The only Green who did anything was Gaston. The freshman sensation, replacing injured starter Danny Andrews in the second quarter, rushed for 134 yards, becoming the only back to rush for over 100 yards against the Trojans all season. He would soon make such games a habit. UCLA went to the Fiesta Bowl, while USC went to regroup for Pasadena.

Tollner said the UCLA loss showed a letdown from a team which had already achieved its primary goal of winning the conference. Critics said the Trojans weren't that talented in the first place. And after Notre Dame beat USC a week later at the Coliseum, 19–7, the once-promising return to glory now looked like it had been a mirage all along.

Tollner always handled trouble well. Perhaps that's because he had already survived his biggest threat 24 years earlier. On October 29, 1960, a plane crash killed 22, including 16 members of the Cal Poly San Luis Obispo football team. Shortly after takeoff, the plane lost power in the left engine. It lurched downward and to the left, crashed, cart-wheeled, broke into two and burst into flames.

Tollner was sitting by the wing. The front half of the plane didn't make it. The back half did. He was right at the cutoff point. He suffered multiple lacerations and severe leg damage. His leg had to be wired together. "I draw strength from it in some rough times," admitted Tollner, who played quarterback. "I reflect on that and it makes me put things in perspective."

Once again, in 1985, Tollner would have to draw strength from somewhere. Rough times were back to USC. The upset win over Ohio State in the Rose Bowl didn't carry into the season. Tollner faced the likely but highly unpleasant prospect of two losing seasons in three years. Until USC traveled to Seattle to play the Huskies the week before the UCLA game. Washington won the game, but the Trojans won the future.

They learned they had a quarterback in freshman Rodney Peete.

Of the many schools that recruited him, USC didn't seem a logical destination. Peete grew up around the University of Arizona, where his dad was an assistant to Wildcat coach Larry Smith. As a water boy in 1980, Peete remembers a game with the Trojans. "They brought the bank, I swear, 500 people, and it was so exciting and intimidating," Peete said. "There was a feeling the game was over before it started . . . I hated it."

Besides, USC was a tailback school. Why would a quarterback like Peete go there and give up an opportunity to establish better statistics at more passing-oriented programs. Like, for example, Stanford? Because he wanted to win national championships. And they didn't do that at Stanford. Just ask John Elway.

Peete had always trusted his judgment. When friends in high school suggested he consider moving to fullback because black players were always shifted to defensive back or another position, he wouldn't hear of it. "I guess I was greedy," he said. "I wanted the ball in my hand all the time."

Ted Tollner gave him the ball for the Washington game. And why not? Tollner had tried everything else. Salisbury was struggling. The team needed a spark.

With Peete, it was more like a jolt. Against the Huskies, he completed 12 of 17 passes for 175 yards. He also rushed for 50 yards. The game was a sample of what Trojan fans would watch for the next three years: A 195-pound quarterback who could both run and throw, and who was always exciting.

"He had all of it," Tollner said. "He had intelligence, charisma, the touch, plus he could make plays with his athletic ability. He was the future, no question."

For USC, Peete was now the present. And the days of tailback domination were in the past. From 1972 to 1981, the Trojans averaged 275 yards a game on the ground. From 1982 through 1985, the average plummeted to 173. Gone were stars like Anthony Davis, Charles White, and Marcus Allen. The new names were Ryan Knight, Aaron Emanuel and Steve Webster. It was truly a different era.

UCLA was the new tailback school in town. The Bruins had Gaston Green, and a talented supporting cast including James Primus and Eric Ball. Despite missing four games with a knee injury, Green led the team in rushing. "He just goes by you—Shoooh," said Bruin offensive coordinator Homer Smith.

The Bruins could throw, too. Quarterback David Norrie was the conference's passing efficiency leader.

Such offensive balance, coupled with the nation's best rushing defense, threatened to make the annual rivalry another annual mismatch. UCLA, riding a six-game winning streak, seemed destined for Pasadena again. Plus there was the Tollner Factor.

Tollner stood 0–5 against USC's fiercest rivals—UCLA and Notre Dame. He was on the verge of becoming the first Trojan coach to lose three straight years to both schools.

Anti-Tollner letters began appearing regularly in The Los Angeles Times: "What was once a proud declaration of 'We Are SC' has been Tollnerized into an embarrassed whimper of 'We Were SC,'" wrote one disgruntled fan from San Bernardino.

"I can no longer tolerate Ted Tollner as head coach," epistlized a fan from North Hollywood. "He appears to be a fine man, but so was Jimmy Carter. Results are what count."

In 1985, after three years of shame, Trojan fans finally got the only result that counts against UCLA. Victory.

The final was 17–13, and the star was Peete. UCLA was used to Salisburys, and Mazurs, and Tinsleys—quarterbacks, not *athletes*.

Peete beat the Bruins with a quarterback draw designed specifically for this game, and he beat them with poise. With just under four minutes to go, trailing, 13–10, USC had a fourth and two on UCLA's six-yard line. Like Robinson who went for the two point-conversion at the end of the 1982 game, Tollner had no choice. He needed a victory to salvage the season—and, perhaps, his job.

So he let the freshman try to win it. Peete rolled out, and made the first down. A few plays later, he scored the winning touchdown. Some freshman. "There wasn't any doubt I'd lead the team to a touchdown on that last drive," said Peete after the game. "For an encore, I want to end up with a winning season, and I plan on going to the Rose Bowl several times in my career."

The encore would have to wait; the main act was wrenching enough for Terry Donahue. Gone was a chance to be the first Bruin coach in the rivalry's then 55-year history to win four straight times. Not even Red Sanders accomplished that. Perhaps Donahue would have joined Sanders if tailback Eric Ball hadn't fumbled. UCLA was leading, 13–10, early in the fourth quarter, and had reached the Trojan one-yard line when Ball lost the ball.

Donahue still got the Rose Bowl bid when Arizona upset Arizona State, and it did heal the wounds more quickly. (The Bruins rebounded to beat Iowa, 45–28. Ball redeemed himself by scoring four touchdowns.)

But the critics took a break from Tollner and descended again on Donahue. The charge was familiar: Too conservative. Donahue elected to go for a field goal when UCLA had fourth down and a foot on USC's six-yard line early in the second quarter. Later in that quarter, he called for safe running plays to set up another field goal attempt. By playing not to lose, the critics complained, Donahue had done just that. By gambling, Tollner had won. And the greedy kid who wanted to play quarterback, who opted for titles over stats, secured his first win as a Trojan starter. The band played on, and this time, Rodney Peete loved it.

It only got better for USC in 1986. The Trojans won their first four games, including upsets of highly ranked Baylor and Washington.

Tollner felt vindicated. Finally, the players he, not John Robinson, had recruited were assuming key positions as juniors and seniors. And with Peete still only a sophomore, the Trojans clearly seemed headed back to championship form. Even losses against Washington State and eventual Rose Bowl representative Arizona State couldn't dampen Tollner's optimism. The passing attack he had envisioned when Robinson hired him as offensive coordinator was now in place, and he wasn't about to let go.

But Gaston Green was only a junior, and UCLA was still dangerous. And cocky. "We're just going to beat USC so bad," said Bruin linebacker Ken Norton Jr., son of the famous boxer. He must have learned some psychology from his dad's nemesis, Muhammad Ali.

Norton didn't study the rivalry's history, or he would have known how the words of James McAlister, Kermit Johnson, and Tim Green came back to haunt them.

This time, the only person haunted was Ted Tollner. The 1986 season, which had started in a blaze, went down in flames. Final: UCLA 45, USC 25. Ouch.

Inflicting the most punishment was Gaston Green, who finished with 224 yards rushing, the most ever gained in one game by a runner against USC.

For Donahue, the victory was revenge, and not for 1985. As the Bruins began to dictate every phase of the game, Donahue flashed back to the 1979 USC contest, the 49–14 rout which made him swear his team would never be humiliated by the Trojans again. He recalled how USC slowly paraded its stars off the field, only prolonging his misery. He was even tempted to return the favor, but didn't.

"The 1986 game was a payback for 1979," Donahue said. "Winning in 1980 was sweet, but it wasn't the same as thrashing them in 1986. We really could've scored more points."

By beating the Trojans for the fourth time in five years, Donahue had catapulted the UCLA program to its greatest heights since Sanders. He was becoming another wizard in Westwood.

The 1986 massacre also meant the end of the Tollner era. A loss the following week to Notre Dame only made it official. Four years was enough.

Nobody was surprised, especially Tollner. He always knew his tenure was tenuous, and saw the end coming after losing again to UCLA and Notre Dame. In retrospect, Tollner believes he should have played smarter politics by establishing better relationships with the alumni and the school administration. He thinks that could have bought him more time.

But the only thing that could have saved his job was victories. In four years, Tollner finished at 26–20–1. That might be good enough for other conference schools, but not at USC. "Some people said I never had the chance," Tollner said, "but I had a chance. I just didn't get it done."

Ted Tollner lost games. But, equally important, he lost the special sense of history that made USC one of the sport's elite.

"He didn't become the spokesman for USC," said Foster Andersen, an assistant coach under McKay, Robinson, and Tollner. "He didn't become the living image of our past. He said things like, 'We're not playing for other people, we're playing for ourselves.' "

So USC, in 1987, began searching for a coach who would embody the rich Trojan heritage. This time, it wouldn't be an unproven assistant like the three previous selections. It would be Larry Smith, head coach at the University of Arizona.

Smith was familiar with the special responsibilities of coaching in arch rivalries—Arizona vs. Arizona State was a hard-fought battle for state supremacy. Smith, in fact, beat the Sun Devils five straight years before taking the USC job.

He also recognized the mistakes of the Tollner regime, and made certain to avoid repeating them. Unlike Tollner, Smith embraced the past. Ex-Trojan superstars like Lynn Swann and Mike Garrett became regular guests at practice, and sometimes rode the team bus on game day.

For many, the past is what brought them to USC. And Smith sensed that reinforcing this connection would inspire the current crop of Trojans to play with even more intensity. "It was great to see the alums come around," Peete said. "It's a big deal to see O.J. on the sideline in a USC jacket."

Smith didn't stop with player visits. He initiated a new Friday night ritual—Trojan Trivia. The players had to answer five questions about the school's football history. Winners received an extra candy bar. And, on game days, key highlights from the past were shown on a big screen when the players were warming up.

"The tradition is just as important as blocking and tackling," Smith said. "I think that's what sets USC apart." But Smith had to teach more than history to revitalize the once-glamorous program. He had longer practices, tougher drills, and a mental toughness Tollner never displayed.

"He didn't let guys get away with anything," Peete said, "and he didn't care who you were. It was just a different attitude."

But it wasn't enough in Smith's first game. The Trojans lost to Michigan State, 27–13. Smith blamed the defeat on poor execution, and, like Robinson who also lost his debut game, he vowed to turn things around immediately.

And, reacquainted with his ex-Wildcat waterboy, Peete, Smith did just that. USC entered its appointment with the Bruins at a respectable 7–3, and with another chance for the Rose Bowl.

In Westwood, there was also a new stranger in town. He came from Oklahoma, and it was the first time Bruin fans ever fell in love with Troy.

Troy Aikman was supposed to star for Barry Switzer's Sooners. Aikman, at 6'3", 217 pounds, looked like the prototypical professional quarterback. As a sophomore, he led Oklahoma to three victories. But he broke his leg in the fourth game, giving Jamelle Holieway a chance to play. Holieway ran the wishbone brilliantly, effectively running Aikman out of town.

Some wondered why, if he wanted to impress pro scouts with his passing ability, Aikman ever attended Oklahoma in the first place "I'd been in Oklahoma since I was 12," he said. "In the state of Oklahoma, OU football is everything. Everybody wants to go to OU."

Realizing he had no room for Aikman, a pure passer lost in the wishbone system, Switzer recommended him to Donahue. It was the best present Donahue ever received.

Aikman was forced to sit out the 1986 season because of the transfer, but made an immediate impact in 1987. Through 10 games, he completed 148 of 217 passes for 2,183 yards and 16 touchdowns, with only three interceptions. He was leading the nation in passing efficiency.

More importantly, UCLA now had a star quarterback to complement Gaston Green. Except for a loss to top-ranked Nebraska, 42–33, the Bruins (9–1) couldn't be contained, especially in the second half when they outscored opponents, 181–46. It was UCLA's best team since 1982.

Furthermore, Donahue believed he had finally made the Trojans view their annual showdown with UCLA as the biggest game on the schedule. "USC would always say their big game was Notre Dame in kind of a slap toward UCLA," Donahue said. "They would act like UCLA was a stepchild."

Not anymore. For the first time since 1978, the Rose Bowl was at stake for both teams. No more chatter about playing for the city's bragging rights, or to salvage subpar seasons. This is what the rivalry was supposed to be about.

And the game certainly played along. Especially one play.

UCLA led, 10–0, with only 14 seconds left in the first half. USC faced a first and goal on the Bruin five-yard line. The Trojans seemed about to score a touchdown and seize the momentum for the second half.

Peete faded back to pass, and fired toward the left corner of the end zone for split end Ken Henry, but the ball was deflected by UCLA linebacker Marcus Patton into the hands of defensive back Eric Turner. Turner, a high school track star, took off the other way. A touchdown would probably seal another Donahue victory over the Trojans.

"I saw the end zone," said Turner. "I saw daylight. I thought I was gone."

On the outside, though, came Peete, the *quarterback*. He was gaining. But he was also running out of territory. "The only thing I thought about," Peete said, "was that they couldn't get that touchdown."

They didn't. Peete knocked Turner out of bounds at the Trojan 11-yard line, grabbing him first by the shoulders and then the face mask. The officials were too far behind the play to see it.

UCLA still led by 10 points at intermission, but USC, without scoring, had turned the game around.

An energized Larry Smith charged into the lockerroom. He couldn't stop pacing. "We're going to win this game, we're going to win this game," he kept shouting. "We've done everything wrong the first half, and we're down just 10–0."

Early in the third period, after an 18-yard USC punt gave the

Bruins excellent field position, it was 13–0, thanks to a Alfredo Velasco field goal. Some speech.

But the Trojans finally did begin to rally. A Quin Rodriguez field goal got them on the board, and a Peete six-yard touchdown pass to flanker Randy Tanner early in the fourth quarter made it 13–10. Nevertheless, with eight minutes to go, USC, with the ball on the Bruin 33, still trailed by three.

On first down, when UCLA might be expecting a run, Smith called for a bomb to split end Erik Affholter. Affholter, normally used on short routes, faked inside. UCLA cornerback Marcus Turner went for it. Affholter turned outside. Peete lofted the ball into the corner of the end zone. Touchdown, USC.

Or was it? Affholter bobbled the ball, finally gaining possession before tumbling out of bounds. The Bruins argued he was out *before* he got possession.

The replays were inconclusive. The ruling was not. USC led, 17–13.

UCLA still had plenty of time. But free safety Mark Carrier made his second interception of the day just over a minute left, and the game was over.

Once again, with the Rose Bowl on the line for both teams, USC won. It owned the rivalry—13–5–1 in those situations.

The turnovers, like it did in the early 1970s, buried the Bruins again. This time, they commited four in the second half, including a key fumble by Green in the third quarter. Green gained 138 yards, but only 41 after intermission.

The duel of glamour quarterbacks went to Rodney Peete—23 of 35 for 304 yards and two touchdowns—while his counterpart, Aikman, completed 11 of 26 for 171 yards and three interceptions. Still, Aikman wasn't overly impressed with the opponent. "I still feel we are a better team than they are," he said.

Better or not, UCLA went to the Aloha Bowl, beating Florida, 20–16, while USC, went to the Rose Bowl, losing to Michigan State 20–17.

Larry Smith had made his team study Trojan history. And now they were making some of their own.

In the fall of 1988, as George Bush and Michael Dukakis staged a sometimes vicious battle for the presidency, the city of Los Angeles was the scene of another two-man confrontation: Troy Aikman vs. Rodney Peete.

The encore of their 1987 meeting promised to be even better. Never before had the Bruins and Trojans offered such a classic matchup at quarterback. Usually, when one school showcased a pro prospect, the other was committed to a running game.

At stake for both players, besides the standard spoils of the conference championship and a Rose Bowl bid, was perhaps the Heisman Trophy. Both USC and UCLA promoted their star quarterbacks with the skill and persistence of Madison Avenue ad agencies. Neither suffered from lack of publicity.

Aikman took the early lead. But, as their Rose Bowl rendezvous grew near, Peete narrowed the gap. The USC quarterback threw three touchdowns in each of the three games leading to the UCLA matchup. Meanwhile, Aikman, who had thrown 19 touchdowns in the first seven games, converted only two in his three prior games. Overall, Aikman ranked fourth nationally in passing efficiency; Peete was seventh.

Their Heisman competition became reminiscent of the 1967 race between O.J. Simpson and Gary Beban. Only this was even better because they played the same position. Many assumed the more spectacular player in their battle would gain the edge with New York's Downtown Athletic Club.

Both teams seemed destined to enter their showdown with unbeaten Pac-10 records. But Washington State showed little regard for destiny. At the Rose Bowl, the Cougars rebounded from a 21-point deficit to shock the Bruins, 34–30, who were the nation's top-ranked team for the first time in many years. UCLA had an excellent chance to win in the final minute with first-and-goal from Washington State's six-yard line. Four plays later, the top-ranked Bruins had moved nowhere. Except off the unbeaten ranks.

No such stumbling blocks for USC. In fact, only Stanford and Washington gave the Trojans any trouble at all. Entering the Big Game, USC was 9–0. The Bruins, despite losing Green to graduation, were 9–1, and hungry for revenge.

In 1987, "we went in there with a résumé," said UCLA cornerback Darryl Henley. "We could have gotten a job with IBM or Xerox. I mean, we had the credentials—greatest quarterback, best running back, great wide receivers, great defense."

Those credentials turned out to be only good enough for the Aloha Bowl.

Five days before the 1988 UCLA-USC game, or Aikman vs. Peete II, something threatened to deflate one of the most highly-anticipated matchups in the rivalry's history. Rodney Peete got the flu.

At first, when he started feeling weak, Peete naturally assumed it was just the normal post-game pains. But by Tuesday, when the pain had not subsided, he was admitted to the hospital. "I couldn't eat anything," Peete said. "I couldn't sleep. My whole body ached from head to toe. I lost 15 pounds. I didn't feel like seeing anybody." The next day, it got worse. Peete had the measles. He might miss the UCLA game.

Trojan fans went into mourning. It just wouldn't be the same with backup quarterback Pat O'Hara at the helm. O'Hara had appeared in only three games, completing five of seven for 61 yards.

Everything suddenly seemed lost—the Rose Bowl, the national championship, the chance for another Trojan to win the Heisman.

Peete's measles became the story of the week. He even had to change hospital rooms three times to avoid reporters. He registered under the name Willie Jackson, his father's first name and his mother's maiden name.

Yet, in some way, his uncertain status in the game might actually have benefited USC. "We told our guys we can't worry whether he would play or not," Larry Smith said, "But UCLA couldn't know for sure, and psychologically, that was to our advantage. They wouldn't know who to prepare for." Furthermore, Donahue admitted, his team was distracted by having to have measles shots that week.

USC also had some history on its side. Twice before in the Trojan-Bruin rivalry, in 1949 and 1966, backup quarterbacks had emerged from nowhere to carry their teams to victory. In 1949, it was Dean Schneider, in 1966, Norman Dow.

On Thursday night, USC was running its routine drills when a car drove around to the edge of the practice field. Out came a man walking ever so gingerly, carefully measuring each step. It was Rodney Peete.

He walked down the field. Later, he watched some film and threw a football around for 25 minutes. "Seeing him there was a huge inspiration," Smith recalled. "You could see it in everybody."

The next day, Peete, feeling much better, went out in his sweats and selected which footballs the team would use the next day. The message was clear. He was going to play.

And play he did. Not like the Rodney Peete he had been all season, but good enough to carry his team to another Rose Bowl, 31–22, before 100,741, the largest crowd for a USC-UCLA game since 1954.

Aikman won the battle of statistics, completing 32 of 48 for 317 yards and two touchdowns. But Peete won the battle on the scoreboard.

After missing four of his first five attempts, he came back to finish with 16 of 28 for 189 yards and a touchdown. From the hospital to the huddle in just two days, Peete capped off an amazing week.

He was so exhausted that after every series, he had to get oxygen. USC also received a big game from running back Aaron Emanuel, who gained 100 yards in the second half.

"It was superhuman," said Smith, referring to Peete's effort. "If that wasn't a Heisman performance, I don't know what is."

Peete didn't win the Heisman, and neither did Aikman. The award went to Oklahoma State's Barry Sanders.

Peete's health problems weren't over. He got laryngitis a few days later, and the timing again posed a problem. USC, second-ranked and now positioned for its first national championship since 1978, was to play top-ranked Notre Dame in the Coliseum. It would be a battle for No. 1, but even with such a lofty prize, Peete said it wasn't easy to get motivated for the Fighting Irish.

"It's difficult to build all season to get ready for UCLA," Peete said, "and then you win that game, and right back the next week, you have to play Notre Dame. It's tough to get up for two big games right in a row."

Apparently, it was very tough. Notre Dame beat the Trojans, 27–10, to knock USC out of the national title picture. But Peete was going back to Pasadena. Again, he lost to a school from the state of

Michigan. This time, it was Bo Schembechler's Wolverines who won, 22–14.

At least he made it there. That's something Troy Aikman never did. Aikman, however, did help carry UCLA to a 17–3 Cotton Bowl win over Arkansas, giving Donahue his seventh straight Bowl win, an NCAA record. And he was still only 43 years old.

Both Aikman and Peete graduated to pro careers. Aikman was made the top choice of the NFL draft by the Dallas Cowboys. Peete didn't get selected until the sixth round by the Detroit Lions. Yet, as the 1990s progress, both seem destined for long and profitable careers. That wouldn't mean much to Larry Smith and Terry Donahue. All they knew was that, in 1989, they had huge holes to plug.

In high school, Marinovich staged epic battles with another Orange County quarterback, Bret Johnson. As so often happens in the Trojan-Bruin rivalry, Johnson enrolled at UCLA and Marinovich at USC, and their duel started all over again.

Marinovich set the records in high school, but some insisted Johnson was the better player. In the 1989 collegiate season, however, Marinovich got the accolades. Johnson got only abuse.

USC won eight out of nine after an opening loss to Illinois, and Marinovich was touted as a future Heisman Trophy candidate. Meanwhile, UCLA struggled with Johnson and Jim Bonds at quarterback. Entering the Trojan game, the Bruins (3–7) had lost five straight for the first time since 1943, and Donahue was assured of his first losing season since 1979. His vow that year to never be humiliated again by USC was in serious jeopardy.

UCLA was certainly not humiliated in the 1989 Trojan game.

After a USC fumble late in the fourth quarter, UCLA took over on its 12-yard line, with the score tied, 10–10. Johnson hit Scott Miller with a 52-yard pass for a first down on the Trojan 36. UCLA, the 17-point underdog, was in position to pull off a major upset.

But instead of trying for the end zone or throwing short passes to get better field position for a closer field-goal attempt, the Bruins stayed on the ground. "We were just trying to get it to the 32 because we thought he (kicker Alfredo Velasco) could kick a 49-yard field goal," Donahue said.

Shawn Wills took a pitchout to the 35. Fifty-three seconds to play. On second down, Johnson kept the ball and picked up a yard to the 34. Rather than call time out and, perhaps, give USC a chance to strike back, Donahue elected to let the clock run.

On third down, however, Wills, who was supposed to cut inside, went outside and was knocked down at the 37. Loss of three. And suddenly, the 49-yard field goal attempt was a 54-yarder.

The ball hit the crossbar, bounced up, and then fell short into the end zone. The game ended in a tie.

UCLA got its moral victory. Nobody expected the game to be close, so a tie was almost like a win. This time, it was USC who commited the turnovers, six in all.

"I felt that USC was looking to blow us out that game," Donahue said, "and that really hurt them. It was going to be a '79 game to pay us back for '86. Their play-calling, particularly in the early part of the game, indicated they were trying to kill us, and the longer it went and the less they could kill us, the more our players started to get confidence." Smith, however, is still puzzled by the tie. He admits the senior class, even after two victories in a row against the Bruins, hadn't forgotten the 1986 massacre they witnessed as freshmen. It makes the 1989 final even more shocking. "We had excellent practices that week," Smith said. "And it was one of the best Friday nights we ever had."

But the way the game ended revived the perception among critics that Donahue plays not to lose instead of to win. But he has won plenty. He is in fact the winningest coach in UCLA history, surpassing the accomplishments of even the revered Red Sanders. He is also the first coach in college football history to win bowl games in seven consecutive seasons.

But even that hasn't been enough to alter his image with some Trojan critics. "After a while," said a former USC coach who prefers to remain anonymous, "I think he (Donahue) just to started to accept the fact in some subconscious way UCLA isn't supposed to win these games. If I was coaching there, the first thing I would do is get rid of that 'gutty little Bruin' shit. You use that line and you start to believe you're the little guy."

Added Peete: "I think their attitude is, 'God, I *hope* we win this game.' Whereas our attitude is, 'We're *going* to win this game. We expect to win this game.'"

UCLA finished the 1989 season at 3–7–1, its worst record since 1971. USC, meanwhile, came back from its disappointing tie with the Bruins to give Larry Smith his first Rose Bowl win, 17–10 over Michigan.

In his first three seasons, Smith was 27–8–1. Even without a Heisman-caliber runner, he came to rescue USC just when UCLA had begun to dominate the crosstown rivalry and was threatening to install a permanent shift of power.

Donahue made good on his vow and won the 80s, going 5–4–1 against USC. He also captured three Rose Bowls. But a new decade was about to begin, and the pressure to beat the Trojans would be just as intense.

From Howard Jones against Bill Spaulding, to Jess Hill against Red Sanders, from John McKay against Tommy Prothro, to Larry Smith against Terry Donahue, everything changed and nothing changed.

It was some rivalry.

10

The Game that Would Not Die
1990

It had taken three agonizing years to get to this point. Now, he was just 10 days away. Just a routine scrimmage. Just a few practices. And then, the season opener.

Pat O'Hara had waited and watched while Rodney Peete quarterbacked the Trojans. He had waited and sweated while Coach Larry Smith decided between him and Todd Marinovich for the role of Peete's successor. And finally, O'Hara, after throwing just seven passes in three seasons, had gotten the tap on the shoulder. The starting job was his.

It was a warm, sunny afternoon at UC Irvine, late in the summer of 1989, in the last full USC scrimmage of the preseason. O'Hara was fading to his left to pass when he was hit by an onrushing defender. O'Hara went down screaming, his tibia broken, ligaments in his right knee torn. His Trojan career was over before it had started.

One man's dream ends. Another man's dream begins.

Todd Marinovich began preparing to be a quarterback early in life. *Real* early.

His father, Marv, was a USC lineman in 1959, '61 and '62. The older Marinovich went on to play in the NFL with the Raiders, became a coach and scout, and eventually got into the sports fitness business. So it wasn't surprising that he got his son involved in fitness. It's *when* he got him involved that raised a few eyebrows.

Would you believe at the age of one month?

It began with stretching and strengthening exercises in the crib. Todd had a medicine ball in his hands before he could walk.

But he never had a Coke or a Big Mac. His diet was monitored so strictly, he was given his own food to bring to friends' birthday parties. No cake and ice cream for Todd.

His father brought in 13 specialists to work with Todd, everybody from an eye specialist to a biochemist. "It was done," Marv said, "for fitness. . . . If he had been a musician, that would have been fine."

But he wasn't. Todd was exposed to athletics as soon as possible and he thrived at it. "I've done everything so-called normal kids have done," he said. "I don't really know what normal is."

Those words would become all too real later on.

Naturally, the younger Marinovich was recruited by USC where another relative, his uncle Craig Fertig, had been a star quarterback. But being a quarterback himself, Marinovich was also thinking about Stanford where John Elway had filled the air with footballs. USC was hardly a quarterback factory.

But school officials knew a thing or two about recruiting. They took Marinovich to the empty Coliseum and brought him out through the famous tunnel his father and uncle had run through so many times. Emerging onto the floor of the Coliseum, Marinovich was greeted with a full-fledged production. The Trojan fight song was playing, a recording of fans cheering was mixed in and the scoreboard flashed, "Welcome, Todd Marinovich."

The message got through. "I got the chills," Marinovich admitted. And USC got a quarterback.

Marinovich was given the starting job as a redshirt freshman after O'Hara went down. But there weren't a lot of fans cheering him in his first game. And that was Larry Smith's fault. Determined to bring the inexperienced Marinovich along slowly, Smith shackled him for the 1989 season opener against the University of Illinois. Smith decided to cut the long passing game out of his playbook, run a lot and hope that his strong defense could hold Illinois.

It couldn't. The Trojans lost, 14–13. Only on the last two desperation plays of the game was Marinovich allowed to go deep and both passes missed their mark.

But Marinovich was determined not to miss his opportunity. His moment of truth came in USC's third game. Playing Ohio State at the Coliseum, Marinovich threw an early interception, fell behind 3–0 and was then injured early in the second quarter when Buckeye defender Tom Lease landed on his wrist.

Junior Shane Foley, Marinovich's backup, came in and threw a short touchdown pass to give the Trojans a 7–3 lead. The fickle crowd cheered excitedly for the hero of the moment.

Had Marinovich lost his job already? After years of preparation, was this all he was destined for? Smith never indicated that was the case, but Marinovich knew it was important to reestablish himself quickly. When USC regained possession of the ball, Smith asked Marinovich how the wrist felt. He said fine.

He lied. But Marinovich felt he had too much at stake to do otherwise. So he sucked up the pain in his throbbing wrist, trotted back on the field and, on his first pass, let it be known he wasn't about to fade away so quickly. He threw 87 yards to John Jackson, the longest touchdown pass in Trojan history.

Before the afternoon was over, Marinovich had thrown four touchdown passes in all, USC had a 42–3 victory and any thoughts of a quarterback controversy were over.

It just got better from there for Marinovich. He engineered a 91-yard, 18-play, game-winning drive against Washington State in the final minutes, earning a congratulatory call from former President Ronald Reagan.

He led the Trojans to a 9–2–1 record, including a 17–10 victory over Michigan in the 1990 Rose Bowl, breaking a string of four straight bowl losses for USC. The Trojans had lost two straight Rose Bowls, their last victory there coming on New Year's Day, 1985.

Along with his poise, awareness of the field and pinpoint passing, Marinovich showed a toughness rare for a first-year player. After throwing a touchdown pass against Notre Dame in South Bend, Marinovich deliberately ran into menacing defensive end Scott Kowalkowski from behind. "I just gave him a little nudge," Marinovich said, "to let him know I was there."

Everybody knew. Marinovich was on the cover of *Sports Illustrated* at the start of the 1990 season. He was rapidly moving up on the all-time USC passing list. And there were stories that he was already flirting with the idea of turning pro.

Then, like a shooting star, Marinovich seemed to flame out as quickly and as dramatically as he had appeared. He was suspended for a week by Smith for not attending classes. He was yanked from a game against Oregon State for being ineffective. There were constant rumors of drug use. His performances were up and down.

By the time, the Trojans headed into their 60th showdown with UCLA at 7–2–1, Washington had already clinched the Rose Bowl berth. But beating the Bruins would still, as always, mean a lot to USC. Especially to Marinovich, who needed a big game to regain his tenuous grip on the starting job and restore his once-sparkling credentials.

That was fine with Marinovich. The bigger the game, the better he seemed to play.

Terry Donahue had his own quarterback problems at UCLA. And they had begun before the season had. Bret Johnson had stormed out of school in August, furious at the announcement that Jim Bonds would start in the season opener. Donahue and his staff denied it, but Johnson insisted the decision to demote him had been made in spring ball. So off he went to Michigan State.

Bonds may have held off Johnson, But he couldn't do the same with redshirt freshman Tommy Maddox. Although the Bruins came into the USC game at just 5–5, Maddox took the field as the newest UCLA sensation. He was the Pac 10's total offense leader, averaging 238.5 yards per game. He had completed 54.4 percent of his passes for 2,273 yards and 14 touchdowns with 11 interceptions.

In a year's time, Maddox had replaced Marinovich as the new kid on the block. But would he, at 19, have the poise to produce in a game that had broken more experienced stars?

Not at first. USC opened the scoring by picking off a Maddox pass. Stephon Pace grabbed a Maddox lob and raced 27 yards for a touchdown 52 seconds into the game, the quickest TD in the history of the series. Tough start for a freshman.

But Maddox never blinked, getting it back before the quarter was over. He put UCLA in front on a nine-yard run. Maddox added a 47-yard touchdown pass in the second quarter, but USC took a 24–21 lead into the final quarter.

In this fourth quarter, however, there wasn't much security to be found in any lead. Pace was at it again early in the quarter, tipping a Maddox pass that also went off the fingertips of a Bruin before landing in the grasp of Trojan cornerback Jason Oliver, who took the ball into the end zone 34 yards away to give USC a 31–21 advantage.

Back came Maddox. To Scott Miller for 29 yards and a touchdown. USC 31, UCLA 28.

To Scott Miller for 38 yards and a touchdown. UCLA 35, USC 31.

Now it was Marinovich's turn. He hit Johnnie Morton on a 21-yard touchdown pass with 3:19 to play. USC 38, UCLA 35.

Maddox's move. And, sure enough, he responded with a brilliant 75-yard drive with Kevin Smith going over from the one-yard line with 1:19 remaining. UCLA 42, USC 38.

It appeared only the clock was capable of stopping this offensive orgy, played out before a frantic Rose Bowl crowd of 98,088. It was the epitome of UCLA-USC football, husbands and wives, business partners and best friends divided by their loyalty to one school or the other. One team would score and half the fans would explode with joy. Then the other team would respond and so would the remainder of the crowd.

The ball went back to Marinovich and Bruin fans went back to biting their nails. Starting from his own 23, Marinovich hit his favorite receiver, Gary Wellman, with two big passes, for 27 and 22 yards.

USC was on the UCLA 23-yard line with 26 seconds to play. As Marinovich hunched over center, he looked at Morton, his primary receiver on the play. Then he looked at Bruin cornerback Dion Lambert who was shaking his head. No way, Lambert was telling the Trojan quarterback.

Marinovich faded back. His target remained Morton. Tough target to hit with double coverage. But Lambert fell, leaving only single coverage, Morton and free safety Michael Williams, game on the line.

Morton was well covered. Marinovich needed a perfect pass and that's exactly what he threw. The ball spiraled into the left corner of the end zone. No way Williams, on Morton's right side, could get to the ball. It was either Morton or nobody.

It was Morton. He leaped and his straining fingers closed around the ball. Touchdown. USC 45, UCLA 42.

Marinovich, on the ground, was about the only person in the Rose Bowl who didn't see the catch. No matter. The roar of the crowd and the mob of Trojans attacking him in celebration told him something good had happened.

With 16 seconds to play in a game like this, Smith had to caution his players not to celebrate just yet. The ball was going into Maddox's hands.

Only 11 seconds remained after the kickoff with Maddox and his Bruins 61 yards away. This time, it was too much. Two final bombs proved futile.

But Maddox certainly had nothing to be ashamed of. He had completed 26 of 40 passes for a school record 409 yards and three touchdowns. Did someone say this team was conservative?

Marinovich had been equal to the challenge, competing 16 of 25 for 215 yards and two touchdowns, including the clutch game-winner. His vindication was short-lived, however. At the John Hancock Bowl on New Year's Eve, Marinovich got into a shouting match with Smith after being pulled from the game. That seemed to seal Marinovich's fate.

In January of 1991, he was arrested for possession of cocaine and marijuana and wound up leaving USC, but not L.A. Continuing to follow his father's lead, he was drafted by the Raiders.

What Marinovich left behind was the memory of another classic Trojan-Bruin confrontation. The '67 game, still considered by many the best in the series, had far more at stake, but even it could not match this one, thrill for thrill, in the fourth quarter.

Marinovich would soon be replaced by another worthy opponent for Maddox. It's been that way for over 60 years.

USC leads the series 34–19 with seven ties. But both sides have had their memories and their moments. With the backdrop of a once tiny pueblo growing into one of the great cities of the world, with the support of two mighty universities, the UCLA-USC rivalry has prospered, serving as a rite of passage for generations of football players, a rallying point for six decades of students and a never-ending source of entertainment for football fans.

The Bruins and the Trojans.

The Thundering Herd and the gutty, little Bruins.

Howard Jones and Bill Spaulding.

Don Paul and John Ferraro.

Bob Waterfield and Jim Hardy.

Red Sanders and Jess Hill.

O.J. Simpson and Gary Beban.

Tommy Prothro and John McKay.

John Robinson and Terry Donahue.

Todd Marinovich and Tommy Maddox.

The names change, but never the intensity over six decades and 60 games.

They play for 60 minutes every November.

And replay it in their minds for the rest of their lives.

Where Are They Now?

Pete Adams, 40, (USC tackle 1970–72), works in the restaurant business. Adams lives in Lucadia, California.

Jon Arnett, 55, (USC tailback 1954–56), is an investment banker. Arnett lives in Palos Verdes Estates, California.

Gary Beban, 45, (UCLA quarterback 1965–67), is president of CB Commercial, a Los Angeles based brokerage and property management company. Beban lives in Northbrook, Illinois.

Tay Brown, 79, (USC defensive end 1930–32), coached football and basketball at the University of Cincinnati. Brown lives in Los Angeles, California.

Paul Cameron, 58, (UCLA tailback 1951–53), is a film producer. Cameron lives in Long Beach, California.

Al Carmichael, 57, (USC tailback 1950–52), is a real estate broker. Carmichael lives in Palm Desert, California.

Cormac Carney, 31, (UCLA receiver 1980–82), is an attorney. Carney lives in Laguna Hills, California.

Sam Cunningham, 40, (USC running back 1970–72), owns a landscape construction business. Cunningham lives in Long Beach, California.

Anthony Davis, 38, (USC running back 1972–74), works in the real estate business. Davis lives in Santa Monica, California.

Terry Debay, 58, (UCLA blocking back, 1951–54), is a real-estate broker, and raises money for Christian ministries. He lives in Newport Beach, California.

Norman Dow, 45, (UCLA quarterback 1965–66), is football coach at Live Oak High School in Morgan Hill, California.

Dennis Dummit, 42, (UCLA quarterback, 1969–70), is an investment advisor and stockbroker for the investment firm of Bateman, Eichler, Hill, Richards, Inc. Dummit lives in Long Beach, California.

Mike Garrett, 47, (USC running back 1963–65), is an assistant athletic director at USC. Garrett lives in Pasadena, California.

Jimmy Jones, 41, (USC quarterback 1969–71), is a minister who does youth counseling. Jones lives in Harrisburg, Pennsylvania.

Paul McDonald, 33, (USC quarterback 1977–79), is a senior vice-president in marketing for the investment management group of Wells Fargo Bank. McDonald lives in Newport Beach, California.

John McKay, 68, (USC coach 1960–75), plays golf much of the time. McKay lives in Tampa, Florida.

Tommy Prothro, 71, (UCLA coach 1964–70), has retired from football, and plays a lot of bridge. Prothro lives in Memphis, Tennessee.

Mike Rae, 40, (USC quarterback, 1970–72), is a physical education teacher at Long Beach City College. Rae lives in Irvine, California.

Tom Ramsey, 29, (UCLA quarterback 1979–82), does commentary on UCLA football games for a local cable station. Ramsey lives in Palos Verdes, California.

Pepper Rodgers, 58, (UCLA coach 1971–73), is trying to acquire an NFL franchise for the city of Memphis. Rodgers lives in Memphis, Tennessee.

Ambrose Schindler, 74, (USC tailback, 1936–39), coached football and track, and taught physical education at El Camino College in Torrance for 43 years until his retirement in 1989. He lives in Torrance, California.

John Sciarra, 37, (UCLA quarterback, 1973–75), is the senior vice-president and head of marketing and sales for National Associates. Sciarra does pension consulting and actuarial services. Sciarra lives in La Canada, California.

Jim Sears, 60, (USC tailback 1950–52), is general manager of a car dealership. Sears lives in Las Vegas, Nevada.

Woodrow Strode, 77, (UCLA receiver 1937–39), had a brief professional football career, and then went into motion pictures. He appeared in "Spartacus." Strode lives in Glendora, California.

Ted Tollner, 51, (USC coach 1983–86), is the offensive coordinator of the San Diego Chargers. Tollner lives in La Mesa, California.

Charles White, 33, (USC running back 1976–79), is a special assistant to the athletic director at USC. He played nine years in the NFL. White lives in Los Angeles, California.

Gwynn Wilson, 94, (USC graduate manager in 1920s), was executive vice-president of the Santa Anita Race Track until his retirement in 1960. Wilson lives in Rancho Palos Verdes, California.

Line Scores

1929

UCLA	0	0	0	0	—	0
USC	7	25	24	20	—	76

1930

UCLA	0	0	0	0	—	0
USC	13	13	20	6	—	52

1936

UCLA	0	7	0	0	—	7
USC	0	0	7	0	—	7

1937

UCLA	0	0	0	13	—	13
USC	7	0	6	6	—	19

1938

UCLA	7	0	0	0	—	7
USC	0	13	9	20	—	42

1939

UCLA	0	0	0	0	—	0
USC	0	0	0	0	—	0

1940

UCLA	6	0	0	6	—	12
USC	7	0	7	14	—	28

1941

UCLA	0	0	7	0	—	7
USC	0	0	7	0	—	7

1942

UCLA	0	7	7	0	—	14
USC	0	0	0	7	—	7

1943 (first game)

UCLA	0	0	0	0	—	0
USC	0	13	7	0	—	20

1943 (second game)

UCLA	0	13	0	0	—	13
USC	6	0	7	13	—	26

1944 (first game)

UCLA	0	0	0	13	—	13
USC	0	13	0	0	—	13

1944 (second game)

UCLA	0	0	0	13	—	13
USC	7	13	14	6	—	40

1945 (first game)

UCLA	0	6	0	0	—	6
USC	0	7	0	6	—	13

1945 (second game)

UCLA	0	0	7	8	—	15
USC	6	13	7	0	—	26

1946

UCLA	6	0	0	7	—	13
USC	0	6	0	0	—	6

1947

UCLA	0	0	0	0	—	0
USC	0	6	0	0	—	6

1948

UCLA	0	6	7	0	—	13
USC	0	14	6	0	—	20

1949

UCLA	0	0	7	0	—	7
USC	0	7	0	14	—	21

1950

UCLA	7	12	7	13	—	39
USC	0	0	0	0	—	0

1951

UCLA	7	0	7	7	—	21
USC	0	0	0	7	—	7

1952

UCLA	3	9	0	0	—	12
USC	0	7	7	0	—	14

1953

UCLA	0	7	0	6	—	13
USC	0	0	0	0	—	0

1954

UCLA	7	0	0	27	—	34
USC	0	0	0	0	—	0

1955

UCLA	7	3	0	7	—	17
USC	0	0	0	7	—	7

1956

UCLA	0	0	0	7	—	7
USC	0	0	7	3	—	10

1957

UCLA	6	0	7	7	—	20
USC	2	0	0	7	—	9

1958

UCLA	0	0	8	7	—	15
USC	0	0	7	8	—	15

1959

UCLA	0	0	0	10	—	10
USC	3	0	0	0	—	3

1960

UCLA	0	0	0	6	—	6
USC	7	7	0	3	—	17

1961

UCLA	0	3	7	0	—	10
USC	0	7	0	0	—	7

1962

UCLA	0	3	0	0	—	3
USC	0	0	0	14	—	14

1963

UCLA	0	0	6	0	—	6
USC	7	6	7	6	—	26

1964

UCLA	0	0	7	6	—	13
USC	7	7	7	13	—	34

1965

UCLA	6	0	0	14	—	20
USC	0	7	0	9	—	16

1966

UCLA	0	0	7	7	—	14
USC	0	0	7	0	—	7

1967

UCLA	7	0	7	6	—	20
USC	7	7	0	7	—	21

1968

UCLA	3	7	0	6	—	16
USC	0	14	7	7	—	28

1969

UCLA	6	0	0	6	—	12
USC	0	7	0	7	—	14

1970

UCLA	24	14	0	7	—	45
USC	14	0	6	0	—	20

1971

UCLA	0	0	7	0	—	7
USC	0	7	0	0	—	7

1972

UCLA	7	0	0	0	—	7
USC	10	7	7	0	—	24

1973

UCLA	3	7	0	3	—	13
USC	7	10	3	3	—	23

1974

UCLA	0	9	0	0	—	9
USC	7	10	10	7	—	34

1975

UCLA	6	12	7	0	—	25
USC	7	7	0	8	—	22

1976

UCLA	0	0	0	14	—	14
USC	0	7	3	14	—	24

1977

UCLA	10	0	7	10	—	27
USC	0	17	9	3	—	29

1978

UCLA	0	0	3	7	—	10
USC	3	14	0	0	—	17

1979

UCLA	0	0	7	7	—	14
USC	14	21	7	7	—	49

1980

UCLA	0	7	7	6	—	20
USC	3	0	7	7	—	17

1981

UCLA	7	11	3	0	—	21
USC	3	9	0	10	—	22

1982

UCLA	14	3	3	0	—	20
USC	3	7	0	9	—	19

1983

UCLA	3	3	21	0	—	27
USC	0	10	0	7	—	17

1984

UCLA	3	16	7	3	—	29
USC	0	3	7	0	—	10

1985

UCLA	7	6	0	0	—	13
USC	7	0	3	7	—	17

1986

UCLA	14	17	14	0	—	45
USC	0	0	7	18	—	25

1987

UCLA	7	3	3	0	—	13
USC	0	0	3	14	—	17

1988

UCLA	3	13	0	6	—	22
USC	7	14	7	3	—	31

1989

UCLA	0	7	0	3	—	10
USC	7	3	0	0	—	10

1990

UCLA	7	7	7	21	—	42
USC	14	7	3	21	—	45